TRUE WEST

Authentic Development Patterns for Small Towns and Rural Areas

Christopher J. Duerksen
James van Hemert

AMERICAN PLANNING ASSOCIATION

True West

Authentic Development Patterns
for Small Towns and Rural Areas

True West

*Authentic Development Patterns
for Small Towns and Rural Areas*

Christopher J. Duerksen

James van Hemert

PLANNERS PRESS
AMERICAN PLANNING ASSOCIATION
Chicago, Illinois
Washington, D.C.

Copyright 2003 by the American Planning Association
122 S. Michigan Ave., Suite 1600, Chicago, IL 60603

ISBN (paperback edition): 1-884829-80-5
ISBN (hardbound edition): 1-884829-81-3
Library of Congress Control Number: 2002114223
Printed in the United States of America
All rights reserved

Interior composition and copyediting by Joanne Shwed, Backspace Ink (www.backspaceink.com)
Art scans by Charles Eaton
Cover design by Susan Deegan

COVER PHOTO

A family farm in Gallatin County, Montana.
Source: James van Hemert

To Benjamin and Matthew
in hopes that their children will have a True West landscape
to enjoy, cherish, and protect.

—CJD

To Shannon, Trevor, and Taran:
may your tending of the western garden be the envy of the angels.

—JVH

Contents

Acknowledgements

We offer this work to our fellow citizens and local governments throughout the West with optimism and the hope that it will truly shape development worthy of our mountains, our landscape, and our people.

We learned much in writing this book and were continually struck by how much historic growth patterns teach us about shaping better development today—development that is authentically western and fits with our unique western landscape and environment. It is right there in front of us if we will only look, measure, and read.

We are convinced that now is the time to act aggressively and with resolve to manage and shape growth in a positive way. The West has boomed over the last decade, and there are few who would say that development could not have been done better, with more care, and with more authenticity. We should ask if our children and their children will think of us as good ancestors when it comes to our land, our environment, and our communities. We hope the verdict on our performance is still out, and that we can build a record and evidence of our wisdom.

The great Supreme Court Justice William O. Douglas wrote a moving epitaph for himself. For all of his landmark legal decisions and learned legal writing, he wanted most to be remembered as a man who made the earth a little more beautiful. That is how we feel about this book, and offer it in that spirit.

Many people and institutions made this work possible. We would like to thank the Henry M. Jackson Foundation of Seattle, the Rocky Mountain Land Use Institute, and the American Planning Association for their generous support of this publication. Special thanks to Nancy Friedman, executive director of the Rocky Mountain Land Use Institute, for hectoring us and keeping the project on track over its extended life.

Numerous other people were very generous with their time and thoughts, including our advisory committee of leading planners and designers from throughout the West. Leslie Bethel, Ben Herman, Ralph Becker, Sherry Dorward, and Vern Swaback helped to shape our thinking and research in the early stages of the project. Lee Nellis of the Sonoran Institute, drawing on his extensive local experience throughout the West, was a font of ideas when it came to identifying worthy case studies. In addition, we would like to thank Joy Polis, Ben Duerksen, and Nicole Bowles for research assistance, and tip our hats to Joyce Algaier, Brad Mueller, and Arlo Braun who provided insightful comments on the draft manuscript. Importantly, Darcie White created a series of illustrative maps to help readers keep their bearings.

Anyone who has written a book full of photos and citations knows what a herculean task it is to get to the finish line. We could not have made it without the help of Amy Fisher and Matt McCoy in producing the manuscript, tracking down photos, and nailing down those pesky citations. The essential project scout master/den mother role was filled admirably by Cara Snyder, who not only rode herd on the whole enterprise but performed research, tracked down reference materials, and did anything else that needed doing. We are deeply indebted to her and absolve her of any blame.

Finally, we recognize the invaluable assistance we received from planners, local officials, and developers from throughout the West in putting together the case studies in Chapters 3 and 4. One of our main sources of optimism about the future is knowing that these smart and dedicated people are in the trenches, carrying the *True West* banner:

Boulder County (Colorado)
- Glen Segrue

City of Claremont (California)
- Ginger Elliott
- Anthony Witt

City of Moab (Utah)
- McKay Edwards

City of Walla Walla (Washington)
- Linda Kastning
- Bob Martin

DC Ranch (Scottsdale, Arizona)
- Dale Gordon

Deschutes County (Oregon)
- George Read

Douglas County (Colorado)
- Betty Allen
- Stan Brown
- Cheryl Matthews

Fremont County (Idaho)
- Karen Lords
- Lee Nellis
- Connie Rowedder

Gallatin County (Montana)
- Randall Johnson

Jefferson County (Colorado)
- Heather Scott

Larimer County (Colorado)
- Brenda Gimeson
- Ken Ludwick
- Jim Reidhead
- Ted Yelek

Lewis & Clark County (Montana)
- Lane Coulston

Rio Arriba County (New Mexico)
- Patricio Garcia

Routt County (Colorado)
- Allison Willets

Salt Lake County (Utah)
- Tina Axelrad

Santa Cruz County (Arizona)
- Cynthia Lunine
- Lee Nellis

Santa Fe County (New Mexico)
- Jack Kolkmeyer
- Faith Okuma
- Joe Porter
- Bob Taunton

Summit County (Utah)
- Kerwin Jenson

Teton County (Wyoming)
- Teresa de Groh
- David Quinn

—CHRIS DUERKSEN
AND JAMES VAN HEMERT

List of Acronyms

FHWA   Federal Highway Administration

GIS   Geographic Information System

IDSA   International Dark-Sky Association

LPS   Land Preservation Subdivision [Exemption]

LRV   Light Reflectance Value

NRO   Natural Resources Overlay [District]

PDR   purchase of development rights

RLUP   Rural Land Use Plan

RSP   Rural Site Plan

SPR   Site Plan Review

SRO   Scenic Resources Overlay [District]

TDR   transfer of development rights

Introduction

I-1 Mountain Vista (Grand Tetons, Wyoming).

Source: James van Hemert

In the beginning God created the heavens and the earth.
God saw all that he had made, and it was very good.[1]
—GENESIS 1:1, 31

We are remodeling the Alhambra with a steam shovel,
and we are proud of our yardage.[2]
—ALDO LEOPOLD, *A SAND COUNTY ALMANAC:*
WITH ESSAYS ON CONSERVATION

1

For nearly everyone, the term "The American West" conjures up images of amazing landscapes; wide, open spaces; a wild epochal history; cowboys and Indians; and romance. Everything is somehow larger than life; a land of unimaginable distances and infinite horizons. Yet it is not infinite, and it is not changeless. The Old West is rapidly giving way to a new West that bears little resemblance to the past. In the past decade, Colorado has grown by 30%, mushrooming from 2.9 to 4.3 million people; Utah from 1.7 to 2.2 million, also a 30% increase; Arizona, by 40%, increasing from 3.7 to 5.1 million. Nevada stands in a league by itself with a whopping 66% increase during the 1990s from 1.2 to 2 million people[3] (Figure I-2).

Even more telling is how these states have moved over the past two decades in their respective national population rankings: Colorado has moved from 28th to 24th place; Arizona from 29th to 20th; Nevada from 43rd to 35th. After a slowdown in the late 1980s, California is growing again, continuing to outdistance other large states such as New York and Texas. The population of the mountainous western states[4] grew from 51 million to over 61 million between 1990 and 2000, an increase of 20%. California alone tops 33.8 million.[5] This population growth is having a signifi-

cant impact on the once seemingly endless open landscape.

What is driving this boom? Many westerners say they live there for the landscape before career or family. The wide, open spaces, the outdoor recreational opportunities, and the awesome scenery are attracting a new breed of immigrant. Technology and wealth allow people to work and live almost anywhere today. Add to this a second home boom fueled by an affluent Baby Boom generation who are building second homes in anticipation of retirement. The complexion of this growth is very different from that of the energy boom of the late 1970s. Rather than the compact apartment buildings and trailer parks of the 1970s, the current boom features sprawling "cookie-cutter" subdivisions and second home "McMansions" spread across the landscape.[6] In Colorado, cattle ranches are giving way to subdivisions at the rate of 1 million acres per year[7] (Figure I-3).

Indeed, the very landscape that attracts so many is seriously threatened by their arrival. The ensuing development is reshaping the western landscape. Small towns are surrounded by subdivisions that seem to have been transplanted from the East, ridgeline development mars scenic vistas, and rural subdivisions sprout in meadows that only

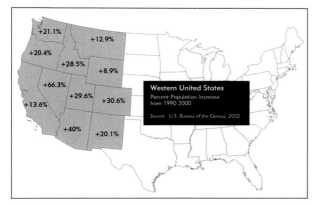

I-2 Population growth map.

Source: U.S. Bureau of the Census (data); map by Darcie White

I-3 During the 1990s, cities and towns throughout the West sprawled into the countryside.

Source: Edward Ziegler

recently were grazed by cattle or elk. The growth is having serious adverse impacts on transportation systems, housing costs, the environment, and wildlife (Figures I-4 and I-5). We seem to have embraced the philosophy of a recent pop song: "Wide open spaces, room to make the big mistake."[8] Aldo Leopold's thoughts about development in a different era ring true for many westerners today: "We are remodeling the Alhambra with a steam shovel, and we are proud of our yardage."[9]

Where have we gone wrong? Our technology, ambitions, "can do" attitude, greed, and love of the land are taking us collectively where we don't want to go: destroying the place that we love and that attracted us here in the beginning. There was a time when our ambitions were limited by our technology, economy, culture, and political realities—and there were a lot fewer of us.

Without zoning regulations, planning departments, architectural review boards, and professional staff, many pioneers built settlements that accommodated the land and climate in a natural, organic manner. Places of beauty and harmony were created that respected the natural environment and functioned effectively in their social and cultural contexts. Of course, we recognize that

even then there were abuses. The scars around mining towns such as Leadville and Fairplay, Colorado, are a stark reminder of the excesses of the gold and silver rushes.

Today, we know better. Despite all of our knowledge, wealth, and resources, we are developing ugly places that destroy the natural beauty and do irreparable harm to the natural environment. Somewhere we lost the common DNA of appropriate development. Apparently, we have lost, or simply don't care about, an intimate relationship and understanding of the land and climate. Our mentality is seemingly one in which technology triumphs over nature. We have been hell-bent to conquer nature; and our population, affluence, and technological resources have become so great that they make it easier to brush aside natural resources and constraints. It would seem that if we can build the road high enough into the mountains, drill the well deep enough, carry electricity far enough to the remotest corners, and pack enough insulation into a building, we can live wherever we want—regardless of the environmental or social consequences (Figure I-6).

Recent legislative developments in several western states (such as Arizona, where state legislation stripped significant growth management

I-4 Where the houses are: among the wild things, Estes Park, Colorado.

Source: Chris Duerksen

I-5 Rural post boxes signal sprawl in them thar hills, Park County, Colorado.

Source: Chris Duerksen

I-6 "King of the Cuts," western Colorado. In sharp contrast to the old barn at the edge of the meadow, this home's location demonstrates that with enough will, money, and technology, a home can be placed anywhere, regardless of environmental constraints and visual consequences.

Source: Chris Duerksen

THE ROCKY MOUNTAIN WEST: A UNIQUE AMERICAN PLACE

- Much of the West remains a "blank space" with most westerners jammed into a few cities and their suburbs: 86% of westerners live in cities, while only a few counties outside the metropolitan areas contain population densities of even 25 souls per square mile.
- Almost half of the Rocky Mountain West is federally owned land—over 80% of Nevada is publicly owned.
- The West has thousands of homes occupied only a few weeks a year. Two-thirds of the homes in ski towns such as Vail and Park City are owned by out-of-towners who drop in for occasional stays.
- Despite the apparent vast, empty, inaccessible places, a large portion of the Rocky Mountain West is within 60 miles of scheduled airline service. The high-end western air traveler flies private jets, headed for landing fields near world-class trout streams or ritzy resorts.
- Much of the West is accessible by paved road, including some areas of very high elevation:
    - Trail Ridge, Colorado (summer only)   12,183 feet
    - Loveland Pass, Colorado   11,992 feet
    - Hoosier Pass, Colorado   11,541 feet
    - Monarch Pass, Colorado   11,312 feet
    - Bear Tooth Pass, Montana (summer only)   10,947 feet
    - Snowy Range Pass, Wyoming (summer only)   10,800 feet
- All the major western rivers sport dams. In 1936, the four biggest dams in the world were under construction in the American West: Hoover, Shasta, Bonneville, and Grand Coulee. Between 1930 and 1980, the federal government built over 1,000 large dams in the United States.

Source: Riebsame, William E. *Atlas of the New West: Portrait of a Changing Region.* New York: W.W. Norton & Company, 1997.

and land use planning authority from counties) are disturbing, emphasizing the immediacy and importance of clearly establishing models and precedents for appropriate development patterns for the West. The irony of inappropriate development is that, by all accounts, it is often less economical or profitable for all concerned. The case studies presented here demonstrate that good development sells well and can generate greater profits for developers.

While an increasing number of citizens of the West are worried about this development boom, many local governments responsible for controlling growth do not have adequate resources to plan for this development, or experience to ensure that it fits in well with their unique western surroundings. Indeed, many rural jurisdictions and small towns in the West do not even have professional planning staffs. While it is unrealistic to think this growth can or should be stopped completely, much can be done to ensure that the landscapes and communities that we pass on to the next generation will retain their distinctive western character—be it in mountain communities, rural agricultural valleys, the foothills, or the desert.

The primary goal of this book is to illustrate and establish a systematic approach that can be used by rural and small-town local governments in reviewing development proposals and expansion plans—one that identifies and applies historic, traditional western development patterns drawn from their communities and region that fit better in the western landscape. We offer a rational methodology by which western towns and rural areas can take control of their futures, building on the best of the past. The book also examines examples of appropriate modern developments that can serve as models as the West continues to grow.

More specifically, we:

- explore historical western development patterns that may serve as models for new projects around small towns and in rural venues: architectural styles, site layout, landscaping and vegetation, accessory structures such as outbuildings and fences, and roads

- examine and critique recent developments in rural areas and small towns to learn what works and what does not

- identify key elements of projects that appear to respect the character of the areas in which they are located

- learn from local officials and developers the role of development review processes, design standards, and market economics in shaping projects

- discuss examples of regulations, incentives, and implementation tools that are working

To meet these objectives, we undertook seven major case studies in significant detail, and examined over a dozen smaller cases that further augment and complement this review. We distill key lessons from the case studies and present them in a format that provides a western rural pattern language for development, as well as specific methods of achieving appropriate development that is consistent with local character.

The use of patterns is an effective method of creating new things while respecting "tried and true" principles. We have reviewed historical western development patterns and contemporary development with an eye to distilling appropriate patterns, in a manner not unlike that of Christopher Alexander in his seminal work, *A Pattern Language*.[10] We organize these patterns throughout the book in a general scheme with seven major categories:

Western Rural Development Pattern Language

- **Regional Development Patterns**
- **Town**
  - public places
  - streets/access
  - public realm

— community

— environmental

• **Dispersed Rural Settlement**

— environmental

— cultural

— visual

• **Architecture/Design**

— form

— color and materials

• **CultureCommunity**

• **Site Design**

• **Other Elements**

Not every community or development—historical or contemporary—will involve or illustrate every pattern; however, taken together, the patterns from various examples begin to build a dictionary of patterns that can help us in shaping future growth.

The guiding theme of this book is that we must understand intimately the unique character of the natural and cultural landscapes in which we find ourselves and build accordingly. This will differ from place to place within the West. Most work and thinking on rural design has focused on "eastern" or "midwestern" landscapes. The frequent solution—hiding development behind trees or building narrow roadways or streets—may not be feasible or even appropriate in the West. Indeed, it may be the antithesis of true western development patterns (witness the wide main streets of many small western towns). The unique characteristics of the western natural and cultural landscapes are significant:

• *A very dry climate:* Everything beyond the 100th meridian is the dry line; nearly all terrain receives less than 20 inches of precipitation per year. Thus, many areas have relatively sparse vegetation and limited water availability. Wildfires are a constant threat in large swatches of the West.

• *Wide, open spaces:* Human settlement and agricultural activities are concentrated in

areas with water availability, thus leaving vast areas with little or no settlement.

• *Majestic and unique scenery:* Few places on earth have such a concentration of beautiful, almost surreal, scenery.

• *Geographical extremes:* The landscape ranges from rugged mountain terrain to broad, sweeping valleys and wide, open spaces.

• *High altitude and high sun exposure:* These factors lead to both weather and temperature extremes.

• *Federal government land ownership:* Nearly half of all the land in the intermountain West is owned by the federal government.

• *Native American cultural influences:* The Native Americans have left a physical imprint on some towns in the West, particularly in New Mexico and Arizona, not seen elsewhere in the U.S.

These factors, combined, create a very different and unique environment in which planning for small town and rural development occurs in the West.

This book comprises five major sections:

1. an overview of historic development patterns in the West, both in towns and rural areas

2. seven major case studies exploring positive western development examples

3. 16 focused case studies that further identify key rural western patterns

4. a discussion of development standards and incentives that can be utilized by local governments to achieve true western development patterns

5. a summary of the historical and contemporary rural development patterns that we present to help guide and shape western development in the 21st century

We offer what we hope will be a thoughtful but simple and systematic approach to managing community growth and evaluating development proposals. It will need to be applied carefully so that creativity is not stifled, and the landscape and built environment are not ossified by romantic notions of the past.[11] Rather, if applied successfully, our approach will draw on the wisdom of historical precedent mixed judiciously with the best thinking of today based on our growing knowledge of the environment and technology.

NOTES

1. *The Bible, New International Version* (Grand Rapids, MI: Zondervan, 1978).
2. Aldo Leopold, *A Sand County Almanac: With Essays on Conservation* (New York: Oxford University Press, 1949), p. 190.
3. U.S. Census. quickfacts.census.gov/qfd/states/00000.htm.
4. The states that we include in our definition of the American West are Arizona, California, Colorado, Idaho, Montana, New Mexico, Nevada, Oregon, Utah, Washington, and Wyoming.
5. U.S. Census. quickfacts.census.gov/qfd/states/00000.htm.
6. William E. Riebsame, *Atlas of the New West: Portrait of a Changing Region* (New York: W.W. Norton & Company, 1997), p. 57.
7. Kit Miniclier, "Home on Range Getting Crowded," *Denver Post* (December 26, 1999), p. 1B.
8. Dixie Chicks, *Wide Open Spaces* (Sony), 1998.
9. Aldo Leopold, *A Sand County Almanac: With Essays on Conservation* (New York: Oxford University Press, 1949), p. 190.
10. Christopher Alexander, *A Pattern Language* (New York: Oxford University Press, 1977).
11. In this regard, witness the debate in Santa Fe, New Mexico over what is true "Santa Fe" style, as discussed by Chris Wilson in *The Myth of Santa Fe* (Albuquerque: University of New Mexico Press, 1997).

1

Lessons from the Past: Historical Western Development Patterns

. . . two hundred years ago almost everywhere human beings were comparatively few, poor, and at the mercy of the forces of nature, and 200 years from now, we expect, almost everywhere they will be numerous, rich, and in control of the forces of nature.[1]

—HERMAN KAHN, *THE NEXT 200 YEARS: A SCENARIO FOR AMERICA AND THE WORLD*

The Native Americans, Spanish colonial settlement, and American westward expansion have played the most significant historical roles in establishing the character of development in the American West. A critical understanding of the nature of these human settlement patterns and how they influenced each other provides a solid framework for the evolution of a unique western rural design language. Each of these settlement patterns provides us with lessons about what we should pursue in our efforts to design thoughtfully and appropriately in the western context.

1. NATIVE AMERICAN COMMUNITIES

For thousands of years, Native American tribes have lived in the West, many of whom were nomadic and left little or no evidence of settlement patterns. The Anasazi, Navajo, Hopi, Pueblo, and Zuni Indians, however, provide us with the most significant and enduring historical legacy of permanent settlements.

Geographically centered in what is today known as the "four corners" region (Colorado, New Mexico, Arizona, and Utah), these peoples have constructed permanent settlements for over 1,000 years. Some of the best known examples are found in Mesa Verde National Park. Built between 1200 AD and 1300 AD by the Anasazi Indians, these communities or "houses" reflect the religious and social culture in terms of their architecture and spatial arrangements. Experts believe that modern-day Navajo, Hopi, and Pueblo Indians share a common ancestral relationship with the Anasazi. The Anasazi's built environment is a product of a particular spiritual view of the universe: they viewed themselves as being one with nature.[2]

The graceful and natural integration of the cliff dwellings into the landscape is particularly striking. The Spruce Tree House (Figures 1-1 and 1-2) is representative of a "great house"—a planned multistory structure with large rooms and enclosed "kivas" (ceremonial centers, either for individual family groups or entire communities).[3] This particular cliff dwelling contained about 114 rooms and eight kivas. These dwellings were constructed primarily of sandstone, and held together with mortar and tiny "chinking" stones to create very straight walls and sharp corners. Over the stone, the Anasazi placed a thin coating of plaster. As many as 250 people lived within a great house.[4]

1-1 Spruce Tree House, Mesa Verde National Park. Constructed of sandstone, mortar, and plaster, this sheltered settlement integrates gracefully into the natural environment.

Source: Denver Public Library, Western History Collection, Harry M. Rhoads, RH-267

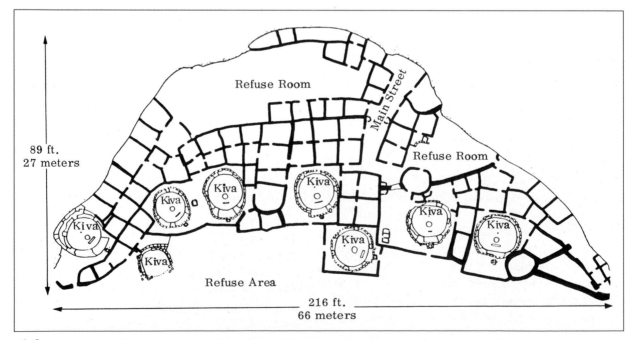

1-2 Spruce Tree House plan view. Approximately 114 rooms are organized in a manner that creates common areas centered on ceremonial "kivas."

Source: Mesa Verde Museum Association

More commonly, the Native Americans of the intermountain West constructed "pueblos" consisting of numerous rooms arranged in single or multiple stories, which were used primarily for living and storage. Pueblos were compact, fortified, and geometrically organized around large, open ceremonial town courts, and were often characterized by complex, multistoried residences that reached up to four stories.[5]

The height never exceeded four stories due to the structural strength of the building material and practical limitations for stair or ladder climbing. Consequently, the building complex maintains a human scale that is always subservient to the natural landscape. Pueblos accommodated as many as 500 people (Figure 1-3). They were constructed of durable materials such as stone, compacted earth, and adobe. "Adobe" is a Spanish word that refers to (1) sun-dried bricks composed of a mix of clay and straw, (2) the buildings made from those bricks, or (3) the clay soil used in the making of those bricks. Most adobe clay is very plastic and can easily be molded into almost any shape. Once it has dried, however, it is virtually indestructible.[6]

Pueblos were built by individual families and thus were not subject to any preplanning. New rooms were joined to rooms built by other families.[8] Despite the lack of formal planning and their incremental development, the entire pueblo was of one piece: a communal form of architecture of modest character. Pueblos were often located at the edge of a mountain slope with an orientation to the most prominent mountain.[9]

Many Native American settlements have an apparent regularity likely due to traditional manipulation of solar heating. Since this region is sparsely wooded, with forests often at great dis-

1-3 Taos Pueblo. Buildings of adobe rise to a height of four stories, blending well into the arid, mountainous landscape without ornamentation or extraneous landscaping. Father Dominguez in the 16th century described Taos Pueblo as "resembling that of those walled cities with bastions and towers described to us in the Bible."[7]

Source: Denver Public Library, Western History Collection, H.S. Poley, P-1193

1-4 In this typical pueblo, orderly spacing of rows of houses maximizes exposure to the winter sun. Adequate spacing provides sunlight penetration to all structures.

Source: Ralph L. Knowles, *Energy and Form* (Cambridge, MA: MIT Press, 1978, p. 26).

tance from inhabited pueblos, the greatest conservation of human energy and of wood for fires is essential. The orderly spacing of rows of houses maximized exposure to the winter sun (Figure 1-4).

The architecture, spatial structure, and location of settlements reveal an effective adaptation to the hot, dry climate; the efficient use of readily available, durable natural materials; the accommodation of the communal nature of society; and easy proximity to water and agricultural lands. The Spanish colonizers, who were to appear toward the end of the 16th century, built towns that were complementary to the Native American settlements; correspondingly, nearly all the major elements of the ideal Spanish town plan were already evident in the Native American settlements.[10]

Historical Western Patterns

Adaptable lessons that we can derive and characterize as patterns for the rural West today include the following:

Regional Development Patterns

- *Encourage the growth of new, self-contained towns in a dispersed manner across the countryside, allowing ample open space between them. Concentrate development in a compact manner within the towns (Figures 1-5 and 1-6).*

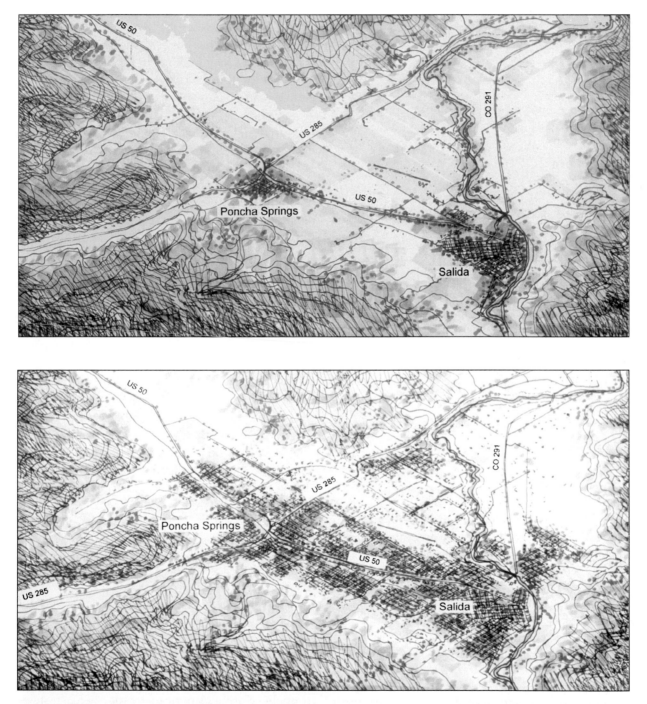

1-5 and 1-6 Many western small towns are facing choices between compact development and sprawling into their neighbors. Top image shows current development patterns in Chaffee County, Colorado; bottom image shows projected development patterns without growth management.

Source: Prepared by Jim Leggitt, RNL Design, for the Chaffee County, Colorado, Comprehensive Plan

- *Protect sacred sites, to preserve people's spiritual roots and their connection to the past.*

Town

Public Places

- *Provide and incorporate common areas within clusters of homes.*

Architecture/Design

Form

- *Limit the majority of buildings to four stories high. Taller buildings in small towns and rural areas should be exceptional and reserved for cultural or civic purposes.*

Color and Materials

- *Use natural materials in a manner that reflects an organic integrity and harmony with the natural surroundings.*
- *Use relatively thick, well-insulated exterior walls.*

Site Design

- *Orient space, buildings, and groups of buildings in such a manner so as to take full advantage of the sun for winter warmth.*

2. SPANISH COLONIZATION

The Spanish colonization of what is today known as the American Southwest was accomplished primarily under the aegis of the "Laws of the Indies," of which a substantial portion was devoted to town planning.

> *Don Felipe, by the Grace of God, King of Castille . . . let it be known: That in order that the discoveries and new settlements and pacification of the land and provinces that are to be discovered, settled, and pacified in the Indies be done with greater facility and in accordance with the service to God Our Lord, and for the welfare of the natives, among other things, we have prepared the following ordinances.*[11]

So begins the city planning ordinances, ultimately codified within the "Laws of the Indies," a document that has left a significant physical imprint and social heritage in all areas of Spanish influence in the Americas. In what is now the United States, Spanish colonial influence extended as far north as modern-day southern Colorado and coastal California. Expanding on previous decrees by Ferdinand and Charles V, on July 13, 1573, Philip II issued this comprehensive compilation of 148 ordinances that deals with every aspect of site selection, city planning, and political organization.[12] (See Appendix A—Spanish Laws of the Indies for a selection of relevant ordinances.)

Some argue that in fact these ordinances were the most complete such set of instructions ever issued to serve as a guideline for the founding and building of towns in the Americas. Furthermore, in terms of their widespread application and persistence, they are probably the most effective planning documents in the history of mankind.[13]

New Mexico contains the richest trove of Spanish ordinance influences in the United States that are readily apparent today.[14] Spanish ordinances also influenced early town development in what is now Arizona and California, including Tucson[15] and San Diego.[16] The town of San Juan Bautista claims to have the only Spanish plaza remaining in California.[17] Santa Fe, New Mexico, with its plaza and Spanish street layout significantly intact, provides the bulk of the illustrations and is considered the best expression of the city planning ordinances of the "Laws of the Indies" on the soil of the United States.[18]

Size and Location

An important aspect of Spanish subjugation was the planned and deliberate "urbanization" of native peoples for the purpose of securing colonial frontiers. Native American towns were strategically used by the Spanish for demarcating their territories and defending against hostile natives.[19] Native American converts were required to erect a church and a convent, and to ultimately physically relocate to centralized villages, or "villas." Once a villa became established enough and met the necessary requirements of a township, it was eligible to become formally recognized by the Spanish Crown as a pueblo, and thus enjoy a higher degree of rights and privileges.[20] Ordinance 39 directs neighboring Indian towns and properties to be demolished in order to build an Iberian-style town:

> *The site and position of the towns should be selected in places where water is nearby and where it would be possible to demolish neighboring towns and properties in order to take advantage of the materials that are essential for building; and, [these sites and positions should be suitable] also for farming, cultivation, and pasturation, so as to avoid excessive work and cost, since any of the above would be costly if they were far.*

Present-day Santa Fe (Spanish for "Holy Faith") was established as the colonial capital in 1609 and constructed on the ruins of the Pueblo village, Analco.[21] Ironically, many of the Native American vernacular pueblos were superior with respect to the quality of building materials and defensive capabilities.[22] Taos pueblo (Figure 1-3), described by Father Dominguez as ". . . resembling that of those walled cities with bastions and towers that described to us in the Bible . . ."[23] served as a far more effective refuge than did the Spanish communities.

Santa Fe, located at the foot of what is now called the Sangre de Cristo Mountains and bifurcated by a small river, lies in an elevated and healthy location with access to fresh, navigable water as directed by Ordinance 111:

> *. . . the town is to be . . . in an elevated and healthy location; . . . [have] fresh water . . . ease of transport, access and exist; [and be] open to the north wind; . . . and if possible not near lagoons or marshes in which poisonous animals and polluted air and water breed.*

Ordinance 123 expands on public health by suggesting that buildings causing filth be placed on the side of the river below town.

The minimum size of a settlement was to be 30 individuals and their domestic animals (Ordinance 89). Settlements were to be established within a hierarchical framework of city [cabecera], town [municipal], or village [pueblo] (Ordinance 43).

Streets and Open Space Pattern

While no precise street layout is specified, most towns developed with a modified gridiron pattern, which in the American Southwest rarely produced perfectly perpendicular or parallel streets, as can be seen in the 1893 map of Socorro, New Mexico (Figure 1-7). The influence of the Native American pueblo form further "softened" the overall street pattern, although it is necessary to recognize that pueblos were often constructed in a linear, grid-like pattern in order to take advantage of the sun.[24] Ordinance 110 establishes the "square" as the standard block and required sufficient open space for future growth:

> *. . . a plan for the site is to be made, dividing it into squares, streets, and building lots, using cord and ruler, beginning with the main square from which streets are to run to the gates and principal roads and leaving sufficient open space so that even if the town grows, it can always spread in the same manner.*

Main Plaza

At the center of Spanish urban life was the plaza—a center for secular, religious, political, social, and other activities having ceremonial overtones. It served as the point of convergence of main streets but was also the point at which civic identity, the feeling of belonging in the town, was expressed.[25] Figure 1-8 illustrates the dominance of Saint Francis Cathedral near the plaza.

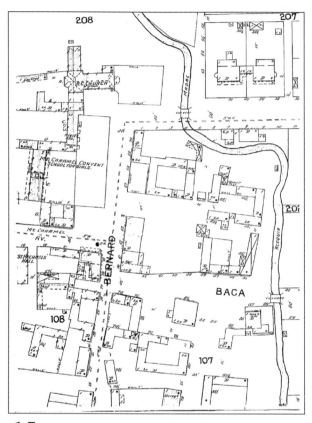

1-7 Socorro, New Mexico, 1893. The plaza lies at the center of the map. The streets do not run perfectly perpendicular.

Ordinance 112 directs the plaza to be at the center of the town and to be shaped in a square or rectangular form, preferably with a 1:1.5 ratio of length to width, given that this was best for fiestas in which horses are used. Ordinance 113 suggests that the size is further proportioned taking into account the size of the town, and that a minimum size was 200 by 300 feet, but that the best proportion was 400 by 600 feet wide.

Initially, the main plaza of Santa Fe was approximately 400 by 800 feet, slightly smaller than the suggested maximum size of 532 by 800 feet.[26]

1-8 Santa Fe, New Mexico, sometime between 1905 and 1915. View of Saint Francis Cathedral, looking down East San Francisco Street. The plaza is on the left.

Rebuilding and encroachment over time have reduced the plaza to approximately 200 by 240 feet today, slightly smaller than recommended (Figure 1-9). The plaza of Isleta Pueblo maintains the ratio of 1:1.5 established by the recommended 400 by 600 feet dimension.[27] Santa Fe's smaller square functions very well. Christopher Alexander observes in *A Pattern Language* that the tendency to make public squares large results in places that look and feel deserted.[28]

Climate and Solar Orientation

Accommodating climatic conditions was considered paramount. Without the technological ability to control climate as we do today, town-site and building location were the most important considerations in dealing with the negative effects of climate. Sites were to be selected that were not too windy, yet were sufficiently high in elevation to avoid potentially unhealthy lowlands, as identified in Ordinance 40:

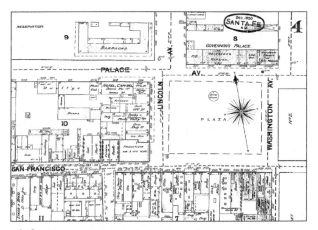

1-9 The 1890 Santa Fe Sanborn fire map shows a plaza that is substantially similar in size to the contemporary dimensions.

Do not select sites that are too high up because these are affected by winds, and access and service to these are difficult, nor in lowlands, which tend to be unhealthy; choose places of medium elevation that enjoy good winds, especially from the north and south . . . and in case that there should be a need to build on the banks of a river, it should be on the eastern bank, so when the sun rises it strikes the town first, then the water.

It is believed that siting a town on the eastern bank of a river would avoid the problem of sunlight blinding early morning marketgoers.[29]

Ordinance 114 sought to minimize exposure to the winds by forcing winds to enter the plaza from the northeast, southwest, and so forth, rather than from the four principal directions, which are believed to be stronger. Thus, streets were to enter the plaza at the corners rather than the center of the sides, as typically done in the "Old World" (Figure 1-10).

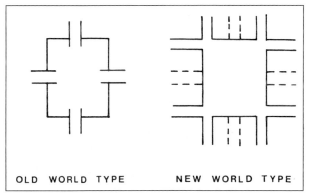

OLD WORLD TYPE   NEW WORLD TYPE

1-10 Old and New World Plazas. In the Old World plazas (left), streets would penetrate the middle of the sides; such plazas had to be carved out of the existing urban fabric, which was sometimes done in the 17th century, or might be added to the town by being placed outside the walls. In the New World (right), by contrast, the streets usually branch off from the corners, at right angles; the town planning ordinances call for important streets to enter at the center of each side, but this has not been practiced. Note that the corners of the plaza were supposed to point toward the cardinal directions, so that the winds would enter the square from northeast, southwest, and so forth, as did the streets, thus mitigating their harshness.

As required by Ordinance 115, portals (typically referred to as canopies today) were placed around the plaza to protect from the elements the merchants, shoppers, and others doing business near the plaza.

The hot climate of Santa Fe prompted the construction of streets only 22 feet wide, a narrow width suggested by Ordinance 116 which states:

. . . In cold places the streets shall be wide and in hot places narrow; but for the purposes of defense in areas where there are horses, it would be better if they are wide.

Narrow streets provide greater protection from the sun when buildings shade the majority of the street (Figure 1-11).

1-11   Narrow street in Santa Fe, New Mexico, approximately 1912.

Source: Denver Public Library, Western History Collection, Jesse Nusbaum, N-316

Instruction with respect to wind required buildings to enjoy both south and north winds (Ordinance 133), which were believed to be the best. Hospitals for the poor (those not afflicted by contagious diseases) were to be constructed near the church cloister in such a way as to enjoy both the north and south winds as well (Ordinance 124).

Public Facilities

In keeping with the central focus of Spanish colonization and indoctrination into the Christian religion, a central and prominent church was required in every town. Ordinance 148 directs that natives be settled into towns, that the churches be used to instruct them in the Christian doctrine, and to live in good order.

The importance of religious instruction resulted in the requirement for smaller plazas in various places throughout the town (Ordinance 118). Additional churches were typically placed on these plazas as was done in Santa Fe. The laws on church placement are followed literally in Santa Fe, and the main church is located not directly on the square but off the east side of the plaza and separated from other buildings as required by Ordinance 124.

Various other public buildings were required by the ordinances, including a royal house, customhouse, arsenal, and a hospital (Ordinance 121). In Santa Fe, these were all located near or within the perimeter of the plaza.

Ordinance 129 required a town commons, for the purpose of recreation and pasturing cattle, that was to:

> *. . . be delimited, large enough that although the population may experience a rapid expansion, there will always be sufficient space where the people may go to for recreation and take their cattle to pasture without them making any damage.*

Early maps of Santa Fe reveal a substantial commons lying to the north of the central plaza.[30]

Aesthetics

Perhaps the most striking and memorable feature of Santa Fe's architecture, and that of many other Spanish and Native American towns of the Southwest, is the simplicity and similarity of the architecture. This aesthetic is enforced by Ordinance 134, which states that:

> They shall try as far as possible to have the buildings all of one type for the sake of the beauty of the town.

The architecture during this period was extremely simple, primarily making use of adobe brick and some stone, with room sizes based on lengths of available logs for ceiling beams. Rooms were grouped around a patio, which might or might not have a portico. Flat roofs were common and contours soft because of the use of adobe plastered over for protection against weather. The architecture was a mixture of Spanish and Native American ideas, suitable for the mixed population and the climate. Adobe is easy to use, not requiring the sophisticated techniques of masonry.[31]

Historical Western Patterns

Based upon the Spanish colonial settlement pattern, additional and expanded, adaptable lessons that we can derive and characterize as patterns for the rural West today include the following:

Regional Development Patterns

- *Locate towns and settlements near water for supply and access.*

Town

Public Places

- *Concentrate community facilities around public "squares" at the intersection of community pathways or roadways.*

- *Configure streets and plazas to reduce the effect of winds on the plaza.*
- *Construct promenades within the heart of the community with main points of attraction at both ends.*
- *Create public places appropriately sized for the community and within walking distance of all citizens.*

Streets/Access

- *Create an intimate relationship between buildings and the street by placing buildings very close to the public right-of-way.*
- *Use a gridiron street pattern to take advantage of sun in the winter and to create connections throughout the community, but do so without slavish dedication to perfectly perpendicular or parallel streets.*
- *In the central portion of towns, require that the majority of buildings be constructed immediately adjacent to the public right-of-way. When multiple buildings are constructed in this manner, a sense of enclosed, inviting space is created.*
- *Provide ample public open space to accommodate population growth.*

Architecture/Design

Form

- *Avoid building large, monolithic structures. Buildings should comprise a complex of smaller buildings or parts that manifest their own internal social realities.*
- *Build arcades at the edge of buildings to provide shelter from sun and rain, and to ease the transition between public and private space.*

Color and Materials

- *Use biodegradable, low energy-consuming materials, which are easy to cut and modify on site. For bulk materials, use earth-based materials such as earth, brick, and tile.*
- *Avoid the use of a multiplicity of building materials, colors, and architectural styles. Doing so*

also serves to produce a commonality of architectural style.

Culture/Community

- *Concentrate major civic buildings (e.g., government offices and churches) around or near public squares.*
- *Utilize easily accessible public squares/spaces for political, social, and religious gatherings.*

Site Design

- *Orient streets, buildings, and groups of buildings to take advantage of the sun for winter warmth and mitigation of summer heat. Place buildings to the north of outdoor spaces, and keep outdoor spaces to the south, with opportunities for dappled shade from trees or trellises.*
- *Connect buildings to create a compact community fabric.*

The Native American and Spanish Colonial Patterns: A Synthesis

Early American settlers in the West had difficulty discerning between the Spanish-built and Native American-built settlements. It is not surprising, given the close interaction between the two peoples for several centuries, during which time both cultures profoundly affected each other. Jojola, in his study of Pueblo Indian and Spanish town planning, suggests that, in fact, today's modern "Santa Fe" regional style is a result of the cross-assimilative and reciprocal nature of their interrelations.[32]

It is clear that both cultures had very well-defined traditions and pattern languages for constructing buildings and towns, representing thoughtful responses to the natural environment and an integration with their religion and culture, which for both peoples was central to their lives.

3. AMERICAN SETTLEMENTS

Up until the American westward expansion, the extent of human settlement and its impact on the western landscape was infinitesimal—even the Spanish colonies in what is now California, Arizona, Nevada, and New Mexico, over a period of 250 years, never achieved a significant population.

Mapping and Exploration of the West

In 1805, President Thomas Jefferson and the United States Congress sent Merriweather Lewis and William Clark on the first American mapping and exploration expedition of the West with the goal of discovering a water passage to the west coast. Congress was not convinced at the time that Americans should settle the land. Lewis, however, believed that the natives could become gentleman farmers as a means of pacifying them and securing American boundaries.[33]

As reservations were established, the Bureau of Indian Affairs pursued a twofold program: to control tribes and keep them away from the corridors of westward expansion and the white settlements, and to "civilize" the tribes and transform them into Christian farmers embracing the values of the 19th-century white Americans. The goal, as one bureau head phrased it with unconscious irony, was to "make the Indian feel at home in America."[34]

Additional surveys of the West were commissioned in the 1860s and 1870s, and the land was photographed to show the folks back east the vast country that had not yet been conquered. In 1871, William Henry Jackson photographed Yellowstone. The awesome scenery encouraged Congress to create Yellowstone National Park, the first national park in the world.[35]

Jackson subsequently took numerous photographs throughout Colorado. A hundred years later, a good number of these exact scenes have been rephotographed by John Fielder, a prominent Colorado photographer.[36] In many cases, the changes are substantial and less than desirable, illustrating the often negative impact of recent development on the landscape.

Settlement

Despite early congressional prohibitions against settlement to land west of the Mississippi, the lure of western land proved too great for some, and Americans began homesteading on the west side of the Mississippi. Early settlement was slow, however. In 1820, Major Stephen Harriman Long led an exploring party across the Great Plains region of Nebraska and Colorado to the Rockies and pronounced all of it unfit for white people: "uninhabitable by a people depending on agriculture." Mapmakers called it the "Great American Desert" and for 40-odd years pioneers avoided settling on it.[37]

The Homestead Act of 1862 changed all that. It promised 160 acres of public land to any person who filed a claim for $10 and agreed to work the land for five years.[38] Between 1863 and 1890, nearly one million people filed homestead applications.[39] The famed Oregon Trail, stretching from Independence, Missouri to the Willamette Valley in Oregon, lured thousands of homesteading families to the West beginning in 1843. By 1860, an estimated 53,000 had journeyed the trail to settle in the West.[40]

In the 1850s, Congress granted the railroad companies six sections of public land for each mile of track they built. During the next 20 years, the federal government would give away 180 million acres of land in railroad construction grants. The impact was significant: settlement increased dramatically and the pace of life quickened. A generation earlier, a pioneer family might have taken six months to sail from the east coast to California or cross the West by wagon train. Now, they could travel by railroads coast to coast in eight short days.[41] Towns appeared along the rail lines approximately every 70 miles.[42]

Passed in 1877 as an amendment to the Homestead Act of 1862, the Desert Land Act was designed to encourage settlement in the desert areas of the West. Although drafted with good intentions, it was a major instrument of fraud for cattle ranchers looking to acquire large amounts of land from the government at little cost. The law stated that a settler could purchase a section of land (640 acres) with the proviso that the land would be irrigated within three years.[43] The seeds of the ubiquitous and contentious western theme of water use were planted.

The Timber and Stone Act passed by Congress in 1878 made additional land available to farmers. Corporations and timber companies who stripped millions of acres of western forests exploited the act. A staggering 15 million acres of the finest timberland were accumulated by a few large companies.[44]

Locked in their east coast mentality, Congress wished to use the Colorado River to supply "a million forty-acre farms in the West."[45] In his 1893 report on the *Lands of the Arid Region of the United States,* Major John Wesley Powell, the second director of the United States Geological Survey, warned: "It can't be done . . . Gentlemen, you are piling up a heritage of conflict, for there is not enough water to supply the land."[46] Congress ignored him and passed the New Lands Act, creating the Reclamation Service (later named the Bureau of Reclamation), and put the federal government in the dam-building business.[47] His words were prophetic, for the conflict over water of the Colorado River continues to this day.

Water, in fact, is a major issue in most of the arid western states. All army posts, cattle trails, farms, towns, and ranch locations were based on the availability of water. Acquiring water rights is an ever-present problem. There doesn't seem to be enough of it where it's needed, and it is not always distributed to proper advantage. Ironically, too much water is often gulped up, resulting in the irreversible depletion of aquifers and silt buildup in dammed rivers with adverse consequences on the natural environment.[48]

The dominant view accompanying early western settlement was of land mainly as a resource, a commodity to be used to fuel national dreams of progress and an ever-growing gross national product, as well as personal dreams of wealth and power.[49] In this frontier mentality, even the most beautiful land was essentially subservient to human needs.

Complementing this view was the belief by many that Americans had a "manifest destiny" granted by "Providence" to grow and expand over the entire continent. The phrase was first coined in 1845 by New York editor John L. O'Sullivan, who wrote in his newspaper, the *Democratic Review*, of the nation's "manifest destiny to overspread the continent allotted by Providence for the free development of our yearly multiplying millions."[50] This view was a combination of both altruism and greed. The former grew out of a belief of the superiority of American civilization; the latter was a rationalization of God's will decreeing that the enterprising, freedom-loving American people should exploit the riches of the wilderness.

By 1900, 1.67 million people lived in the Rocky Mountain States of New Mexico, Arizona, Nevada, Colorado, Montana, Idaho, Utah, and Wyoming.[51]

Gridiron Towns

The first towns of the American settlement were generally platted in a gridiron pattern of wide streets by engineers and surveyors from the East. This template was extensively used in laying out towns across the West irrespective of the topography. It was quick, easy, and had all the appearances of great things to come. The wide streets were a reflection of the wide, open landscape and broad vistas. From a practical standpoint, the wide streets also facilitated the easy movement and turnaround of teams of oxen.

While many professional planners today decry wide streets because of their supposed antipedestrian character, many people in fact admired places like Salt Lake City for the reason that there were no narrow streets and sunlight penetrated everywhere.[52] Most western towns, in fact, did not attempt to first accommodate the pedestrian

and create walkable distances between places. In many cases—such as in Billings, Montana—within a year of its founding, horsecars began running to the various dispersed parts of the city.[53] The early introduction of the latest technology was a hallmark of many western towns.

The grid pattern extended throughout all town districts, including the central business district, industrial, and residential areas. In places such as Greeley, Colorado, the 100-foot street width was consistently applied, even in single-family residential areas (Figure 1-12). Street widths commonly ranged from 60 to 100 feet, and as much as 132 feet in the case of Salt Lake City.

In downtown commercial districts, the fronts of all buildings were constructed to the edge of the street right-of-way. Combined with the tendency to make full use of narrow lots, a positive urban space was created at the street level. Salida, Colorado, provides a good example (Figure 1-13). Further accentuating this effect was the tendency for many western buildings to be constructed with "false" storefronts, designing them at the street level to make it appear as if they were much larger than they actually were.

The gridiron pattern was less successful in the numerous mining towns that appeared almost overnight throughout the West during the various gold and silver rushes. Idaho Springs, Colorado, and Burke, Idaho, are good examples of places where the topography was not well suited to this model. Many lots in Idaho Springs are on very steep ground and are virtually unbuildable, even today. In Burke, Idaho, the main street was so narrow that the awnings had to be raised to let the train go by.[54]

Despite the relatively low-density sprawl of the new western towns, the vast lands of the West encouraged people to settle in towns rather than in a dispersed manner throughout the countryside—a paradox of dispersed concentration. The pattern, in fact, is similar to that identified by Christopher Alexander in *A Pattern Language*

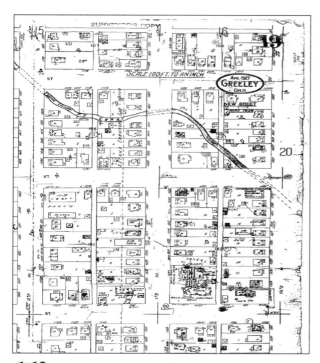

1-12 Greeley, Colorado, 1927. Street right-of-way widths of 100 feet were common throughout the city, in both commercial and residential areas. Today, the neighborhoods with these wide streets are lined with mature trees and convey a sense of stately spaciousness.

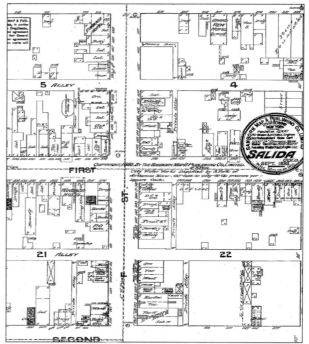

1-13 Salida, Colorado, 1883. Note that the 60-foot rights-of-way are significantly narrower than those of Greeley.

wherein towns and cities of various sizes are evenly dispersed and separated with relatively wide, open spaces between them.[55]

Railroad Towns

The Pacific Railroad Act of 1862 empowered the Central Pacific Company of California to build a transcontinental railway from California to the east, and chartered a new company—the patriotically named Union Pacific Railroad—to build west from the Nebraska Territory into Nevada.[56] The railway received right-of-way through public domain as well as a grant of half the land on a strip 10 miles wide on both sides of the track for each mile of railway built—an equivalent of 10 square miles per mile of track.[57]

During the course of construction, occurring between 1863 and 1869, both railway companies followed the uniform pattern of town planning and development established earlier by Illinois railways during the mid-1800s. Centering the railway depot within a grid pattern of streets, Illinois railway towns were laid out uniformly in a manner that allowed for growth. The philosophy that every town could become an important metropolis soon prevailed in the West. The case of Natrona, Illinois (platted by Conklin and Company in 1857 along the Chicago, Alton, and St. Louis Railroad), provided an ingenious street-naming solution to the problems of uninhibited expansion. The plan reveals Eleventh and Sixteenth and I and P as the outermost streets. With 10 more streets to the east, one-third of the alphabet to exhaust north and south, and infinity to the west, the town seemed well equipped for future growth.[58]

The Central Pacific and Union Pacific Railways quickly realized that town development and railroad company profits went hand-in-hand. Towns were needed initially to serve the needs of construction crews and ultimately as shipping points for agricultural and mining products to eastern markets. The increasing concentration of population in railroad towns inevitably would lead to an increase in the value of railroad-owned land and a ready market for rail passenger and freight services.[59]

Cheyenne, Wyoming

Cheyenne, Wyoming, began as an "end of the line" temporary town in 1867. The town site was named for an Native American tribe that roamed the area. Settlement came so fast that the nickname "Magic City of the Plains" was adopted.[60] The original 4-square-mile plat was surveyed by General Grenville Dodge, a surveyor for the Union Pacific Railway, who laid out many of the towns along the railway. In a manner similar to other railway towns, the railroad reserved most of the blocks within the center for tracks, a train depot, and service facilities such as a roundhouse. Many of these blocks are still owned by the Union Pacific Railroad.

The initial plat comprised streets with 80-foot rights-of-way in a grid comprising blocks of 264 feet by 280 feet with 18-foot-wide alleys. The entire grid of streets was angled 23 degrees toward the northwest to maximize sun penetration on buildings and public spaces in winter months (Figure 1-14). The benefit was the provision of both increased solar heat and daylight.

Other towns surveyed by General Grenville Dodge for the Union Pacific Railway in a similar fashion with respect to the sun included Grand Island and Ogallala, Nebraska; Rawlins and Rock Springs, Wyoming; and Elko, Nevada.

The earliest buildings comprised primarily residential and commercial establishments. The primary commercial area centered along 16th Street, a block north of the train depot on 15th Street. East/west roads were called "streets" and given numbers, with numbers ascending toward the north. North/south roads were called "avenues" and were given names.[61]

Union Pacific constructed one of its most elaborate western train stations in Cheyenne. By 1882, Cheyenne was already able to portray itself as a full-service city complete with municipal buildings, hotels, churches, and a hospital. An early visitor made the following remark:

> *On the Platte, where the central line across the continent often advances at the rate of two miles a day, town-making is reduced to a system. The depot at the end of the line is only moved every two or three months; and . . . the town usually moves also, while nothing remains to mark the spot where thousands lived, but a station, a name, and a few acres of bare earth. Last winter, Cheyenne was the terminal depot on this route, and increased in size to 5,000 inhabitants.*[62]

Other Railroad Towns

Towns planned by the Union Pacific's parent company, the Central Pacific Company of California, also followed a "stock" plan. In Fresno, California, for example, the initial plat comprised 150 rectangular blocks, measuring 320 by 400 feet with 80-foot rights-of-way and 20-foot alleys. Each block comprised 32 lots measuring 25 by 150 feet. The railway depot was placed in the center blocks of the plat. The only deviation in the plan was the central commercial street, "Fresno," with a 100-foot right-of-way.[63]

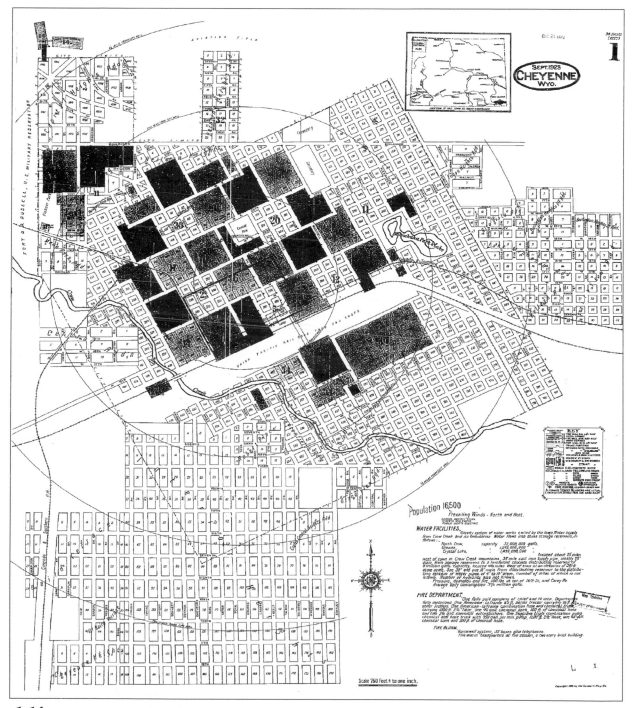

1-14 Historical map of Cheyenne, Wyoming, reveals the original 4-square-mile town site surveyed at a 23-degree angle to the northwest.

Source: Darcie White

Historical Western Patterns

History teaches us that early western towns had both positive and negative aspects in their design and layout. Many of these early communities survive today and are valued for their livable, attractive environments. Others, particularly the early mining towns, are stark warnings about the long-term impacts of unbridled exploitation of the land. On the positive side of the equation, these early western towns teach some lessons regarding the appropriate patterns for the rural West today, including:

Regional Development Patterns

- *Encourage the growth of new, self-contained towns in a dispersed manner across the countryside, allowing ample open space between them.*

Town

Public Places

- *In the central portion of towns, require that the majority of buildings be constructed immediately adjacent to the public right-of-way. When multiple buildings are constructed in this manner, a sense of enclosed and inviting space is created.*
- *Orient streets in such a manner so as to take advantage of distant views.*

Streets/Access

- *In places where the winters are long and cold, construct wide streets for maximum sunlight penetration.*
- *Establish a connected fabric of streets that respect topographical constraints. Allow for future expansion—don't choke new town growth areas with cul-de-sacs and dead-ends.*
- *Orient streets in such a manner as to take advantage of the solar heat and light provided by the sun during winter months. Align streets in a northwest/southwest and northeast/southeast fashion to achieve the maximum effect.*

- *Establish public transportation systems within and between towns.*

However, there are obviously some significant negative aspects that caution against slavish copying of older town development patterns. These include:

- avoiding adopting a "one size fits all" mentality—assuming that a town or development layout that works in one landscape (e.g., the plains) will work equally well everywhere (vs. the mountains)
- a general lack of respect and understanding for the natural terrain or other environmental conditions
- at times, a sprawling development pattern with houses scattered far and wide, increasing travel distances and times

Mormon Settlement and Community Planning

Perhaps the most significant, and often overlooked, American settlement in the West is that of the Mormons. A sizable part of the West bears the impress of Mormon culture. Hundreds of settlements, extending from Canada to Mexico, were founded in the 19th century under the aegis of Brigham Young.[64] It is worth our attention to examine their contributions to western town planning and rural architecture.

In 1847, the first settlers from the East arrived in the Salt Lake Valley. By 1852, more than 20,000 were living in the Great Basin; 100,000 by 1877. During the latter half of the 19th century, more than 360 planned settlements were established in Utah, Idaho, Arizona, Nevada, and California under the influence of Mormon settlers.[65]

The wellspring of Mormon civic design lies deep within the Mormons' doctrine that identifies a New Jerusalem referred to as Zion that would be located in the western hemisphere. This city is described in Revelation 21:16 as being a four square city.[66] Eventually, Salt Lake City would represent Zion to the Mormons. Perhaps equally important is the Mormons' "agrarian ethic." The family farm was presumed to be the mainstay of society. Synthesizing the urban view of Zion with an agrarian way of life, Mormon farmers were expected to live in town and commute to their fields to work. In his study of early Mormon community planning, Charles L. Sellers states that the rationale for this was the social advantages that village living entails: schools and churches can be more easily provided and more intensively used. Perhaps more importantly, Sellers suggests, is that the Mormons had faith in the rules of order of their religion's founder and prophet, Joseph Smith.[67]

Others further suggest that the concept of Zion was a new order contrary to gentile (non-Mormon) society: "If gentile society preferred a dispersed settlement pattern; Zion would be a nucleated community."[68] This important feature of the City of Zion, evident in nearly all Mormon communities, is a simple but powerful concept: an opposition between group and individual values, visually defining the Mormon western landscape.[69]

Joseph Smith, who was only 28 years old at the time, had devised a master plan for the City of Zion in 1833 that ultimately was used as a template for hundreds of Mormon towns, including Salt Lake City (Figure 1-15).

The plan can be summarized as follows:

- compact, nucleated farming community
- 1 mile square in physical dimension
- divided into 10-acre blocks of 660 by 660 feet
- further subdivided blocks into house lots of equal size
- streets 132 feet wide
- no more than one house on any one lot
- uniform setback of 25 feet for each house
- houses constructed of brick and stone
- each home site to have shade trees, orchards, and garden plots
- 24 central blocks reserved for public buildings and temples

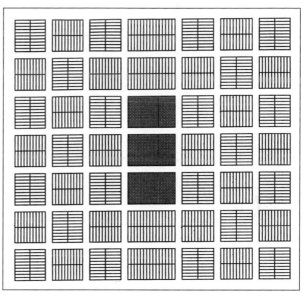

1-15   Joseph Smith's plan for the City of Zion.

Source: James van Hemert; graphic prepared by James van Hemert based upon Charles L. Sellers' "Early Mormon Community Planning," *Journal of the American Institute of Planners* 28 (1): 28.

- no street to have houses facing upon it throughout its entire length: houses would face north/south and east/west alternatively
- barns and stables to exist near, but outside of, town boundaries[70]

The model city was intended to accommodate a population of 15,000 to 20,000 people. Once this number had been reached, a new city would be laid out in a similar fashion. The population was further divided into wards (a secondary social group, similar to a Roman Catholic parish, in which all members of the denomination attended the same church). An unidentified rural Utah town shown in Figure 1-16 reveals the large blocks and wide streets of this pattern. The Sanborn fire map of Bountiful, Utah, provides a plan view of a typical Utah town laid out in the pattern of the City of Zion (Figure 1-17). The wide streets and their orientation, while not designed to take advantage of solar energy, clearly reflect a desire

1-16 Rural Utah town. Residential structures are interspersed with orchards, gardens, and various agricultural outbuildings.

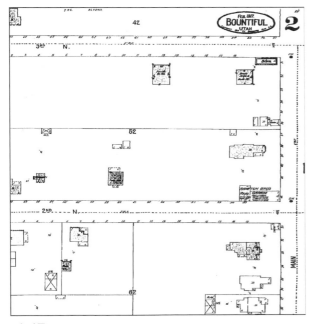

1-17 Bountiful, Utah, 1917. The main street has 99 feet of right-of-way; secondary streets, 49½ feet. Lots are large and structures are relatively dispersed.

to maintain distant views and create a sense of internal spaciousness within the town.

The City of Zion concept was never fully implemented in its pure form, but it served as the basic model for hundreds of Mormon communities.[71] Smith, in fact, was far ahead of his time in establishing an optimum city size, provision for public buildings' needs, zoning against undesirable uses, wide streets, density limits, and aesthetic controls.

There are some similarities between the concepts of community by Joseph Smith and by the 19th century English planner and father of the Garden City movement, Ebenezer Howard. Three key elements of the English garden city are all present to some extent within the Mormon towns: (1) use and density zoning; (2) ward or neighborhood planning unit; and (3) agricultural greenbelts to control urban size. Smith's City of Zion predated Howard's garden city by some 65 years. Given the utopian leanings of both and the desire to build strong, socially cohesive communities, it is perhaps not surprising that similarities in their pattern languages evolved.[72]

The Sanpete Valley—a rich agricultural area 75 miles south of Salt Lake City—provides a worthy study of Mormon pioneer architecture and town planning (Figure 1-18). Each of the Sanpete towns conforms to the nucleated structure of the City of Zion: at the heart, a block was set aside for the church meeting house; nearby, the tithing yard was placed (where in-kind tithing was collected and stored). The church tithing office, barn, and granary became distinctive features of each Sanpete town. Each town differed somewhat with respect to the width of their streets, the acreage of their blocks, and the number of homestead lots on each block. A typical town lot contains barns, granaries, and other farm-related outbuildings (Figure 1-19), contrary to Joseph Smith's original dictates.

Today, in the small towns of the Sanpete Valley, the rural town lot based on the historic principles

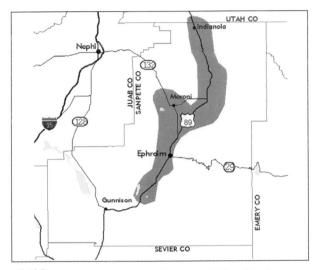

1-18   General location of Sanpete Valley, Utah.

Source: Darcie White

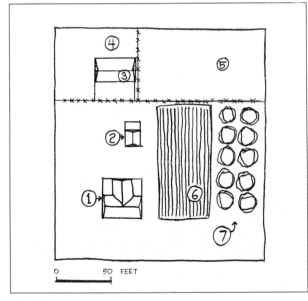

1-19   Typical rural town lot with outbuildings placed behind dwelling: (1) one-and-one-half-story stone dwelling; (2) one-story frame granary; (3) two-story log hay barn with one-story frame lean-to animal stable; (4) corral; (5) pasture; (6) vegetable garden; and (7) orchard.

Source: Drawing by James van Hemert based on Thomas Carter's "Building Zion: Folk Architecture in the Mormon Settlements of Utah's Sanpete Valley, 1849-1890" (Dissertation, 1984), p. 71.

is still very evident, as illustrated in the photo of a home in Centerfield (Figure 1-20).

The most common dwelling type in the Sanpete Valley, and viewed as the quintessential Mormon house in the West during the 19th century, was the hall-parlor house. This two-room house shares the asymmetrical internal arrangement of the rectangular cabin form, yet may be distinguished both by its size and compositional flexibility. Typically, they were 30 to 34 feet wide and about 18 feet deep. Most examples have original or added rear kitchen wings.[73]

Due to the scarcity of lumber, the most widely used wall material in the area was unfired adobe brick. Adobe was a cheap and readily available resource. It is believed that the origins of this Mormon adobe craft arose from church members who served in New Mexico and California during the Mexican War. One contemporary observer concludes that transcending the subtle building and community variations is an overriding visual continuity originating from their initial identity as planned communities.[74]

Historical Western Patterns

The Mormon settlement and community planning traditions offer a number of additional lessons that can help shape new development in the rural West in a more appropriate fashion.

Regional Development Patterns

- *Limit rural communities to 15,000 to 20,000—a size that provides a critical mass for services and amenities, before creating new towns or major developments.*

Town

- *Locate employment within close proximity to housing.*

- *Develop towns in a compact form surrounded by agricultural land in close proximity to town dwellers.*

Streets/Access

- *Establish a connected fabric of streets that respects topographical constraints without resorting to dead-ends.*

- *Create wide streets or public rights-of-way to preserve distant views and create a sense of spaciousness.*

Public Realm

- *Reserve sufficient space within the core of each neighborhood or town for civic buildings and facilities; at least one should serve as a visually prominent civic focal point.*

Community

- *Where possible, establish neighborhoods within towns built on a foundation of common social, political, or cultural interests.*

Environmental

- *Require the planting of native, drought-resistant trees to provide shade.*
- *Encourage planting of fruit trees to provide food for residents and an attractive environment.*

Architecture/Design

Color and Materials

- *Create a sense of quality and stability by utilizing building materials such as brick and stone.*

Site Design

- *Create a sense of unity and continuity by utilizing uniform setbacks in residential and commercial areas.*

1-20 View of home and agricultural buildings in Centerfield, Utah, today reflecting the historical rural town lot.

Source: James van Hemert

NOTES

1. Herman Kahn, William Brown, and Leon Martel, *The Next 200 Years: A Scenario for America and the World* (New York: Morrow, 1976), p. 1.

2. Sherry Dorward, *Design for Mountain Communities* (New York: Van Nostrand Reinhold, 1990), p. 23.

3. William M. Ferguson, *The Anasazi of Mesa Verde and the Four Corners* (Niwot, CO: University Press of Colorado, 1996), pp. 13-14.

4. *Spruce Tree House* (Colorado: Mesa Verde Museum Association, undated).

5. Theodore S. Jojola, "Pueblo Indians and Spanish Town Planning in New Mexico: The Pueblo of Isleta, chapter in Proceedings: Pueblo Style & Regional Architecture," eds. Baker Morrow and V.P. Price (Albuquerque: University of New Mexico Press, 1997), pp. 177-179.

6. Robert M. Utley, *Encyclopedia of the American West*, s.v. "Adobe" (New York: Wings Books, 1996), p. 3.

7. Fr. Francisco Atanosio Dominguez, *The Missions of New Mexico*, translated by Eleanor B. Adams and Fr. Angelico Chavez (Albuquerque: University of New Mexico Press, 1962), p. 110. Cited in Marc Simmons, "Settlement Patterns and Village Plans in Colonial New Mexico" in *New Spain's Far Northern Frontier*, ed. David Weber (Albuquerque: University of New Mexico Press, 1979), p. 108.

8. William M. Ferguson, *The Anasazi of Mesa Verde and the Four Corners* (Niwot, CO: University Press of Colorado, 1996), pp. 13-14.

9. Sherry Dorward, *Design for Mountain Communities* (New York: Van Nostrand Reinhold, 1990), pp. 21-24.

10. Theodore S. Jojola, "Pueblo Indians and Spanish Town Planning in New Mexico: The Pueblo of Isleta, chapter in Proceedings: Pueblo Style & Regional Architecture," eds. Baker Morrow and V.P. Price (Albuquerque: University of New Mexico Press, 1997), p. 179.

11. Dora P. Crouch and Axel I. Mundigo, "The City Planning Ordinance of the Laws of the Indies Revisited," *Town Planning Review* 48 (3): 247.

12. Dora P. Crouch, Daniel J. Garr, and Axel I. Mundigo, *Spanish City Planning in North America* (Cambridge, MA: MIT Press, 1982), p. 3.

13. *Ibid.*

14. All citations of ordinances from the "Laws of the Indies" are taken from Dora Crouch and Axel I. Mundigo, "The City Planning Ordinance of the

Laws of the Indies Revisited," *Town Planning Review* 48 (3): 249-259.

15. Nina Veregge, "Transformations of Spanish Urban Landscapes in the American Southwest, 1821-1900," *Journal of the Southwest*, Winter 1993, p. 46. digital.library.arizona.edu/jsw/3504/veregge/veregge.htm.

16. Antonio Padilla-Corona, "The Urban Layout of Old Town San Diego." English translation by Suzette Falk. *The Journal of San Diego History* 43 (3): 1.

17. www.san-juan-bautista.ca.us.

18. Dora P. Crouch, Daniel J. Garr, and Axel I. Mundigo, *Spanish City Planning in North America* (Cambridge, MA: MIT Press, 1982), p. 70.

19. Theodore S. Jojola, "Pueblo Indians and Spanish Town Planning in New Mexico: The Pueblo of Isleta, chapter in Proceedings: Pueblo Style & Regional Architecture," eds. Baker Morrow and V.P. Price (Albuquerque: University of New Mexico Press, 1997), p. 174.

20. *Ibid.*

21. Dora P. Crouch, Daniel J. Garr, and Axel I. Mundigo, *Spanish City Planning in North America* (Cambridge, MA: MIT Press, 1982), p. 69.

22. Theodore S. Jojola, "Pueblo Indians and Spanish Town Planning in New Mexico: The Pueblo of Isleta, chapter in Proceedings: Pueblo Style & Regional Architecture," eds. Baker Morrow and V.P. Price (Albuquerque: University of New Mexico Press, 1997), p. 181.

23. Marc Simmons, "Settlement Patterns and Village Plans in Colonial New Mexico" in *New Spain's Far Northern Frontier*, ed. David Weber (Albuquerque: University of New Mexico Press, 1979), p. 15.

24. Ralph L. Knowles, *Energy and Form* (Cambridge, MA: MIT Press, 1978), p. 26.

25. Dora P. Crouch, Daniel J. Garr, and Axel I. Mundigo, *Spanish City Planning in North America* (Cambridge, MA: MIT Press, 1982), p. 42.

26. *Ibid.*, p. 77.

27. Theodore S. Jojola, "Pueblo Indians and Spanish Town Planning in New Mexico: The Pueblo of Isleta, chapter in Proceedings: Pueblo Style & Regional Architecture," eds. Baker Morrow and V.P. Price (Albuquerque: University of New Mexico Press, 1997), p. 182.

28. Christopher Alexander, *A Pattern Language* (New York: Oxford University Press, 1977), pp. 311-313.

29. Dora P. Crouch, Daniel J. Garr, and Axel I. Mundigo, *Spanish City Planning in North America* (Cambridge, MA: MIT Press, 1982), p. 35.

30. *Ibid.*, p. 80.
31. *Ibid.*, p. 70.
32. Theodore S. Jojola, "Pueblo Indians and Spanish Town Planning in New Mexico: The Pueblo of Isleta, chapter in Proceedings: Pueblo Style & Regional Architecture," eds. Baker Morrow and V.P. Price (Albuquerque: University of New Mexico Press, 1997), p. 171.
33. For a detailed and stirring account of their adventures, see Stephen Ambrose, *Undaunted Courage: Meriweather Lewis, Thomas Jefferson, and the Opening of the American West* (Simon and Schuster: New York, 1996).
34. Robert M. Utley, *Encyclopedia of the American West*, s.v. "Bureau of Indian Affairs" (New York: Wings Books, 1997), p. 55.
35. Geoffrey C. Ward, *The West: An Illustrated History* (Boston: Little, Brown and Company, 1996), p. 256.
36. William Henry Jackson, *Colorado: 1870-2000. Photography by William Henry Jackson and John Fielder; essays by Ed Marston et al.* (Englewood, CO: Westcliffe Publishers, 1999).
37. Geoffrey C. Ward, *The West: An Illustrated History* (Boston: Little, Brown and Company, 1996), p. 264.
38. *Ibid.*, p. 265.
39. Robert M. Utley, *Encyclopedia of the American West*, s.v. "Homestead Act" (New York: Wings Books, 1997), p. 208.
40. Judith Austin, *Encyclopedia of the American West*, Volume 3, s.v. "Oregon Trail" (New York: Wings Books, 1996), pp. 1242-1243.
41. Robert M. Utley, *Encyclopedia of the American West*, s.v. "Railroads" (New York: Wings Books, 1997), p. 359.
42. Geoffrey C. Ward, *The West: An Illustrated History* (Boston: Little, Brown and Company, 1996), p. 222.
43. Robert M. Utley, *Encyclopedia of the American West*, s.v. "Desert Land Act" (New York: Wings Books, 1997), p. 126.
44. *Ibid.*, s.v. "Timber and Stone Act," p. 431.
45. T.H. Watkins, *The West: An Illustrated History* (Boston: Little, Brown and Company, 1996), p. 326.
46. *Ibid.*
47. *Ibid.*
48. Robert M. Utley, *Encyclopedia of the American West*, s.v. "Water" (New York: Wings Books, 1996), p. 457.
49. T.H. Watkins, *The West: An Illustrated History* (Boston: Little, Brown and Company, 1996), p. 324.
50. Robert M. Utley, *Encyclopedia of the American West*, s.v. "Manifest Destiny" (New York: Wings Books, 1997), p. 271.
51. www.demographia.com/db-state1900.htm.
52. Carol A. O'Conner, "A Region of Cities," in *The Oxford History of the American West.* eds. Clyde A. Milner II, Carol A. O'Conner, and Martha A. Sandweiss (New York: Oxford University Press, 1994), p. 540.
53. *Ibid.*, p. 542.
54. Wendell Brainard, *Golden History Tales from Idaho's Coeur d'Alene Mining District* (Wallace, ID: Crow's Printing, 1990), p. 52.
55. Christopher Alexander, *A Pattern Language* (New York: Oxford University Press, 1977), p. 19.
56. William L. Withuhn, *Rails Across America* (New York: Smithmark Publishers, 1993), p. 31.
57. Mavry Klein, *Union Pacific: The Birth of a Railroad 1862-1893, Vol. 1* (Garden City, NY: Doubleday & Company, 1987), p. 14.
58. John W. Reps, *The Making of Urban America: A History of City Planning in the United States* (Princeton, NJ: Princeton University Press, 1965), p. 397.
59. *Ibid.*, p. 389.
60. www.cheyennecity.org/history.htm.
61. Interview with Chuck Lanham, Administrative Assistant for Cheyenne Historic Preservation Board, May 3, 2001.
62. William A. Bell, "New Tracks in North America" (personal journal, London, 1869, Vol. I), pp. 17-18.
63. Richard Harold Smith, "Towns Along the Tracks: Railroad Strategy and Town Promotion in the San Joaquin Valley, California" (Ph.D. Dissertation, University of California at Los Angeles, 1976), p. 158.
64. Charles L. Sellers, "Early Mormon Community Planning," *Journal of the American Institute of Planners* 28 (1): 28.
65. Robert M. Utley, *Encyclopedia of the American West*, s.v. "Mormons" (New York: Wings Books, 1996), p. 299.
66. Charles L. Sellers, "Early Mormon Community Planning," *Journal of the American Institute of Planners* 28 (1): 25.
67. *Ibid.*
68. Thomas Carter, "Building Zion: Folk Architecture in the Mormon Settlements of Utah's Sanpete Valley, 1849-1890" (Dissertation, 1984), p. 51.
69. *Ibid.*, p. 2.
70. Charles L. Sellers, "Early Mormon Community Planning," *Journal of the American Institute of Planners* 28 (1): 24.
71. *Ibid.*, p. 26.
72. *Ibid.*
73. *Ibid.*, p. 148.
74. *Ibid.*, p. 250.

2

Setting the Stage: Rural Architecture and Site Elements

The more living patterns there are in a place
—a room, a building, or a town—
the more it comes to life as an entirety,
the more it glows,
the more it has that self-maintaining fire
which is the quality without a name.[1]
—Christopher Alexander, *The Timeless Way of Building*

Historical western town development patterns can provide important clues and guidance to local officials in their planning and development review efforts. To get a complete picture, however, it is also important to examine development on a site level:

- What do buildings look like?

- How are they arranged on a site?

- What is the character of fences and outbuildings?

This chapter examines important historical rural architectural and site elements and distills lessons from them.

1. EARLY SETTLEMENT UNTIL WORLD WAR II

Homes

It is difficult to imagine the rural West without log cabins. Many still stand today, often in various states of disrepair. They were often limited in size by the height of the trees used to build them, but they could be enlarged by adding rooms, thereby taking on a greater complexity of roof forms that suggested the social purpose of the parts. Log cabins were built both in rural areas and in towns. Agricultural settlers and miners, however, built most cabins (Figure 2-1).

2-1 The first house in Poverty Gulch, Cripple Creek, Colorado (1892–1895). Note the sod roof.

Source: Denver Public Library, Western History Collection, X-707

2-3 Kimm Family Farm House in Amsterdam (Gallatin County, Montana). Recent addition maintains the ranch vernacular of more shallow roof pitches at the outer edges. Note the "telescoping" addition on the left.

Source: James van Hemert

2-2 Home in Del Norte, Colorado, built of board-and-batten siding, 1873.

Source: Denver Public Library, Western History Collection, X-7965

Settlers with lesser means on the prairies often began their homestead with "soddies"—homes constructed of earthen blocks. Later, as they acquired greater wealth, they were able to purchase logs or sawn wood and construct a cabin or wooden house. Many ranchers and miners, perhaps as a result of their close ties with the land, developed a simple, domestic architecture with the extensive use of vertical board-and-batten siding (Figure 2-2).

Ranches developed as clusters of buildings and additions, reflecting increasing wealth and availability of materials over time. A defining characteristic of these clusters is the varying roof pitches, often with the steepest roof pitches in the center of a building or group of buildings. In almost all cases, the ranch cluster was located within a relatively flat meadow and near a stream. Homes almost always were located on level ground at lower elevations for protection from the wind, with rows of trees planted around the perimeter where possible as additional protection. Typically, a source of convenient water for animals would also be nearby. Rarely were homes built on ridges or steep slopes due to access difficulties and exposure to the wind and elements.

Over the years, as families grew and became wealthier, natural additions in the form of lean-tos, secondary or tertiary wings, or simple telescopic extensions were constructed. These types of additions are pervasive across the rural West, and reflect an organic architectural vernacular borne of necessity and modest means (Figure 2-3).

2-4 Farm cluster in Gallatin County, Montana. The predominantly metal barns fit appropriately in the landscape on the edge of the meadow and below the toe of the background slopes.

Source: James van Hemert

While many of the homes were still constructed with simple, land-hugging architecture and readily available materials, increasing wealth, technology, and improved means of transportation permitted a greater range of architectural styles (as witnessed by Victorian homes) and a broader range of materials. The result was an eclectic mix of rural design; yet, for the most part, negative impacts on the environment and on community aesthetics were minimal. Almost without fail, buildings were sited modestly and off the tops of ridges. Larger homes were usually built on large acreages, reducing their prominence and apparent size (Figure 2-4).

Barns and Outbuildings

Ranches and farms require a variety of barns and storage sheds for crops and animals. Typically, they would be built in close proximity to the home. Often a cluster of buildings with varying roof pitches would be built over the years to accommodate new crops or increased livestock. The varying roof pitches of a barn in Montana actually serve as a counterpoint to the mountains in the background (Figure 2-5). Farm and ranch

outbuildings would be located in proximity to the home and be protected from the harsh winds by placement in valleys or at the toe of a slope.

In some cases bright, contrasting colors were used for barns, providing a fitting contrast to the often monochromatic landscape. A Douglas County, Colorado, barn is painted red (Figure 2-6).

Barns in southern Colorado and northern New Mexico have a decidedly vernacular flavor. A synthesis of Spanish and American cultures produced a simple structure comprising latia-based walls supported by simple post-and-beam construction (Figure 2-7).

Fencing and Other Site Elements

Barbed wire fencing dominates the rural West, because it is relatively inexpensive and easy to construct (Figure 2-8). Given the large extent of many western ranches, it is the most sensible and economical means of fencing in livestock. An unintended consequence is that wildlife has difficulty crossing the fence without being injured.

Before the introduction of barbed wire fencing, latia fences were common in northern New Mexico and southern Colorado. Such fences are constructed out of locally available, woody materials. They are constructed of cedar posts, spaced 6 to 8 feet apart, with some sort of connection between them for fastening the latias, plaited between aspen poles or two strands of wire (Figure 2-9). There are miles of these fences in northern New Mexico, built of readily available material.[2]

Log post-and-rail fences were used when timber was readily available. Typically, post-and-rail fencing was used for smaller enclosures such as those for animals or small fields (Figure 2-10). Only barbed wire fencing could traverse vast expanses economically.

Historical Western Patterns

The manner in which houses, outbuildings, and fences were built before World War II offers some important lessons for local officials who want

2-5   Flikkema family farm, Gallatin County, Montana. The barn's roof outline mimics that of the mountains in the background.

Source: James van Hemert

2-6   Douglas County, Colorado, barn. The bright red contrasts with the yellow and brown vegetation, yet the location and the scale of the barn remain subservient to the landscape.

Source: Chris Duerksen

2-7   Circa 1890 Spanish American barn. Posts were sunk into the ground to support roof structures; walls were often made of little more than latia fences.

Source: This image from *Rural Architecture of Northern New Mexico and Southern Colorado* (1989) by Myrtle Stedman appears courtesy of Sunstone Press, Box 2321, Santa Fe, NM 87504-2321.

2-8   Barbed wire fence, Sweet Ranch, Carbondale, Colorado, 1900-1910.

Source: Denver Public Library, Western History Collection, L.C. McClure, MCC-1118

2-10   Log post-and-rail fence near Fraser, Grand County, Colorado, between 1899 and 1904.

Source: Denver Public Library, Western History Collection, H.H. Lake, L-82

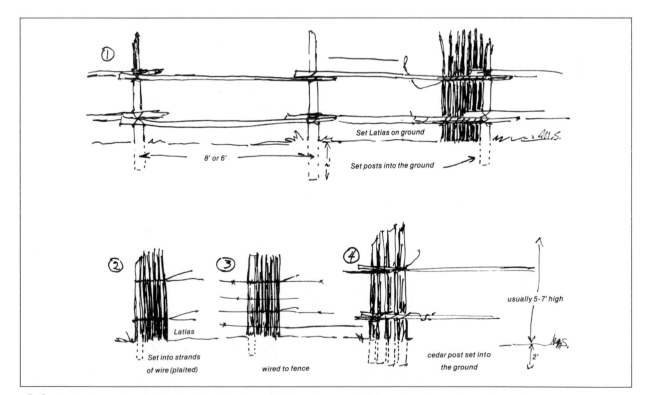

2-9   Latia fence constructed of locally available woody materials, predominant in northern New Mexico and southern Colorado.

Source: This image from *Rural Architecture of Northern New Mexico and Southern Colorado* (1989) by Myrtle Stedman appears courtesy of Sunstone Press, Box 2321, Santa Fe, NM 87504-2321.

developments that fit better with their surroundings. These include:

Dispersed Rural Settlement

Visual

- *Avoid siting buildings on prominent ridges to reduce visual impact.*

Architecture/Design

Form

- *Arrange roofs so that each distinct roof corresponds to an identifiable social entity in the building. Place the largest roofs—those which are highest and have the largest span—over the largest, most important, and most communal spaces; build the lesser roofs off these largest and highest roofs. Allow for and expect additions to be made over time.*
- *Design buildings that profile the natural landscape: in steep, mountainous areas, steeply pitched rooflines are appropriate; in areas that are flat or rolling, a lower profile is fitting (Figures 2-11 and 2-12).*
- *Vary roof pitches, with shallower outer pitches.*
- *Expect that a building or complex of buildings is never complete, leaving room for organic future growth.*

Color and Materials

- *As a first choice, use natural, earth-tone colors; however, do not do so exclusively. With an appropriate building profile, bright historical colors such as red, green, or ochre may serve as a beautiful counterpoint to the natural landscape.*
- *Use natural materials in a manner that reflects an organic integrity and harmony with the natural surroundings. Stone and wood are often appropriate as the primary construction materials. Muted natural colors are particularly important to help buildings in prominent locations blend in with the landscape.*

2-11 and 2-12 Two examples in South Park, Colorado, of homes that fit the landscape—one nestled in trees and the other a single-story home hugging the ground.

Source: Chris Duerksen

Site Design

- *Build homes, outbuildings, and villages in a clustered manner, creating natural, organic courtyards or "common" areas.*
- *Locate buildings at the toes of slopes and edges of meadows in a manner that allows for natural windbreaks and creates a feeling of shelter (Figure 2-13).*

Other Elements

- *Construct fences of historical materials that are unobtrusive and use locally available natural*

2-13   Ranch and outbuildings near Gunnison County, Colorado.

Source: Chris Duerksen

materials when possible. Avoid fence types that have no historical precedent or are made from foreign materials (e.g., chain link or plastic).

2. POST-WORLD WAR II DEVELOPMENT AND THE CHALLENGE WE FACE TODAY

Rural and town residential development in the West following World War II is predominantly characterized by tract housing in towns; trailer, ranch-style, and "starter castle" homes on acreages in rural areas; and second "vacation" homes in recreation-oriented areas. New technologies and tremendous growth combined to dramatically alter the cultural landscape in ways that often ignored the historic context and natural environmental constraints.

Rural Areas

In rural and exurban areas, the introduction of relatively inexpensive trailer homes provided affordable housing for many and the opportunity to settle on rural acreages. Trailer homes quickly

became a ubiquitous feature of the western landscape (Figure 2-14). Mixed in with these "mobile" homes were stick-built, "ranch-style" homes. The single-story or split-level ranch-style home became popular on rural acreages as an outgrowth of postwar, suburban-style architecture.

The A-frame became a popular, inexpensive, postwar vacation home during the 1950s and 1960s, particularly in ski areas where its relatively cheap construction made it popular for use as a second home. Few of these relatively small dwellings are constructed today, as skyrocketing land prices have led to larger and more elaborate homes in a style similar to urban areas.

A recent phenomenon is the construction of so-called "starter castles" of gargantuan proportions—often 15,000 square feet and larger—and their slightly downsized wannabes on large acreage lots. These large homes often dominate the landscape, particularly when placed atop significant ridgetops to capture the best all-round views (Figure 2-15). In many cases, significant amounts

2-14 Trailer homes in Costilla County, Colorado. Although many do not view these as attractive additions to the landscape, their long-term environmental impact is usually minimal.

Source: Sandra Dallas, Colorado Homes. Copyright 1986 by the University of Oklahoma Press. Reprinted by permission.

2-15 Ridgetop development in Castle Rock, Colorado. Public outcry over this development, visible from I-25, led to the establishment of the Town of Castle Rock's Skyline/Ridgeline Protection Overlay Zoning District.

Source: James van Hemert

of vegetation must be disturbed or eliminated in order to provide road and driveway access.

Little consideration is given to the high winds that often occur on hilltops or the difficulty in providing adequate water and fire protection services. In many cases, in fact, such homes are in very high wildfire hazard areas. Materials and colors are sometimes used that are artificial and foreign to the natural environment. Size and ersatz grandeur appear to be the primary principles in design. Also introduced is a multiplicity of designs, many of which bear little or no relation to the land, the historical context, or any type of architectural genre whatsoever.

Their appearance comes at a time of substantially increased wealth, relatively cheap electricity to produce enough heat and air conditioning to counteract any climatic conditions, a desire by many to have majestic views in beautiful and nat-

ural areas, and an increasing shortage of easily developable land. Laissez-faire land use policies have fueled the flames of this conflagration, resulting in dispersed, single-family developments with inadequate emergency access, substandard utility and emergency services, and, in many cases, irreparable ecological damage.

Towns

The West had a population of only 13.9 million before World War II.[3] Population grew rapidly in many areas with the introduction of relatively inexpensive suburban tract housing, the construction of the interstate system, and the expansion of resort towns in the mountains. In their expansions, many pre-World War II towns adopted the curvilinear and cul-de-sac street pattern from larger urban areas (Figure 2-16).

2-16 Sprawling cul-de-sac subdivisions on the outskirts of Phoenix, Arizona.

Source: Alex S. McLean/Landslides

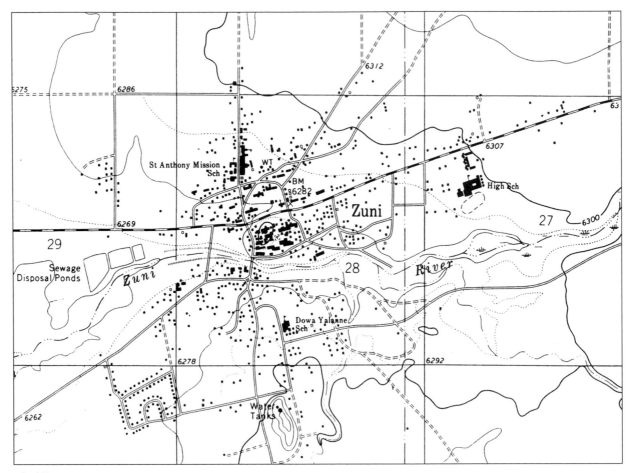

2-17　Zuni and suburbs, New Mexico, 1972. At the center lies the historical dense core. Newer subdivisions spread out from the center in typical post-World War II fashion. The impact of the automobile has been immense, and virtually all exterior space, except for the small dance plaza used for religious ceremonies, has been modified so that it can be used as a roadway.

Source: U.S. Geological Survey

The forerunners of tract housing so prevalent after World War II had already appeared in company mining towns before the turn of the century. They were simple, all the same, and without lawns, but they did provide adequate shelter for the workers. Much of the tract housing constructed after World War II was labeled "ranch," yet bore little resemblance to the architecture of western ranches. Little of this housing, in fact, bore any relationship to historical architectural forms.

In more traditional towns that predate even the Spanish occupation, such as Zuni, New Mexico, the impact of growth and new technology, such as the automobile, has had a significant impact. Zuni, for example, had already undergone a radical architectural transformation at the turn of the century with the abandonment of the old pueblo and resettlement into the suburbs in single-family homes[4] (Figure 2-17).

2-18 Contemporary view of Zuni pueblo.

Source: James van Hemert

With the exception of the small dance plaza used for religious ceremonies, all exterior space has been modified so that it can be used for roadways and parking. New masonry styles, gabled roofs, and building materials such as cinderblock have become popular, and the new construction has tended to obscure the old terraces that were formerly such a prominent part of Zuni architecture[5] (Figure 2-18).

Far worse, however, was the thoughtless manner in which so many semiurban density subdivisions appeared in rural and "exurban" areas where no historic settlements previously existed. The wide, open western landscape is now studded with haphazard, "cookie-cutter" residential development, with nary a thought given to the historical, cultural, and environmental context in which they find themselves. Development standards were nonexistent, substandard, or uselessly excessive and introduced urban-style amenities such as curbs and gutters where they simply are not needed.

This development pattern is neither rural nor urban, exhibiting none of the redeeming features and benefits of either. Accepted historical and cultural pattern languages for human settlement are lost and ignored.

In south central Colorado, in a high mountain valley of uncommon beauty, Chaffee County is becoming a poster child for how *not* to do it. The county seat is Salida—a compact, attractive community of about 5,000 people. Once a railroad town, the older parts of Salida are laid out in a regular grid pattern modified where it borders the Arkansas River. An historic downtown thrives but is challenged by a miles-long commercial strip south of downtown along U.S. 50, the main east/west artery in the county. While the city has made some strides in taming this commercial sprawl, the strip bleeds out into the county despite an adopted county policy to require all commercial development to locate in municipalities. There are few connections between businesses, except by automobile. Crossing U.S. 50 can be a harrowing adventure for tourists staying in local hotels.

The track record with residential development is even more depressing. While Salida has been able to maintain a fairly compact form, some recent developments approved by the city look like they parachuted in from the east coast with their cul-de-sacs and curvilinear street patterns. (Compare Figures 2-19 and 2-20.) They peter out quickly, however, into "ranchettes" of 3 to 20 acres in the county that sprawl west toward the Town of Poncha Springs (almost 5 miles away) and north up the banks of the Arkansas River, a gold-medal trout stream. Houses are built so close to the river in some places that fly-casting from the porch is a possibility. Not surprisingly, ranches in the county have been fragmented, and the county's costs for providing emergency services such as fire protection and road maintenance have skyrocketed. At night, numerous twinkling lights document the sprawl that has enveloped and despoiled this quintessential western landscape. Fortunately, a new county board of commissioners is making progress in tackling these challenging issues that were neglected for many years.

Further fueling this population dispersion into the towns and rural hinterlands of the West today is an explosion of wealth and technology. An increasing percentage of homes in western counties are second and third vacation homes (Figure 2-21), which often drive up land costs and make housing unaffordable for locals. With the vast utility of the Internet, a growing number of business people are no longer limited by geographical constraints. They can work and live anywhere they please and tele-commute via the Internet. Remote, but desirable, geographical locations are now plausible. Jet service to western towns is steadily increasing to accommodate this new pattern of settlement.[6]

The Challenges We Face

We now have greater knowledge, more training, more wealth, and more sophisticated technology, yet many citizens of the West still ask, "Why aren't we doing better? Why aren't we building better communities?" It can be argued that our attitudes of manifest destiny, viewing the land and what it

provides as a resource primarily for our use, and free market laissez-faire capitalism are similar to those of the early American settlers whose settlements, while not perfect, were more in harmony with their context.

The primary difference, it would seem, is that our wealth, technological sophistication, and sheer numbers have tipped the balance. Technology has in many ways pushed the settlement envelope to the extreme, allowing us to live in places characterized by features such as steep slopes and ridgetops that simply weren't possible 100 or even 50 years ago. Inaccessible by even four-wheel drive vehicles, some land in the mountains is being marketed for sale as getaways for the ultra-rich who can arrive by helicopter or snowmobiles.

Furthermore, it appears that our predominant attitudes today are very different from that of the Native Americans, Spanish colonizers, and Mormons who thoughtfully constructed homes and towns with limited resources in simple ways that responded to the land, the climate, and their religious beliefs and culture.

The increasing sophistication of technology, and the growth in wealth and population, will continue largely unabated. The answer is not in having any less of these; rather, it is to re-establish an appropriate land and development ethic that fits the western landscape. This ethic must view land and the natural environment as intrinsically valuable. We are the caretakers—the stewards, if you will—of this incredible gift of creation. An ethic of the built environment must value harmony, integrity, quality, community, and simplicity. Concurrently, we must learn from historical patterns and from current-day successes.

3. AN HISTORICAL FOUNDATION FOR A WESTERN RURAL DEVELOPMENT PATTERN LANGUAGE

Drawing on the best of the past, interpreted and influenced by modern understanding of the environment, we propose a preliminary list of the fol-

2-19 and 2-20   Salida, Colorado. Despite the town having a well-defined street and development pattern, some new subdivisions, with their cul-de-sacs and curvilinear streets, look like they have parachuted in from the East.

Source: Denver Public Library, Western History Collection, X-13256 (2-19); Chris Duerksen (2-20)

2-21   Demand for second homes is driving up land prices and redefining the term "affordable housing" in the West.

Source: Chris Duerksen

lowing preferred development patterns. They serve as an historical foundation for a modern rural western development pattern language. These patterns comprise all those distilled in Chapters 1 and 2 and provide a point of reference for the discussion of contemporary development case studies in Chapters 3 and 4. The case studies build on this foundation with additional development principles, all of which are then synthesized in Chapter 6.

Regional Development Patterns

- *In the face of development pressure, preserve existing country towns and villages and their established development patterns.*

- *Encourage the growth of new, self-contained towns in a dispersed manner across the countryside, allowing ample open space between them.*

Concentrate development in a compact manner within the towns.

Town

Public Places

- *Orient streets in such a manner so as to take advantage of distant views.*
- *Create an intimate relationship between buildings and the street by placing buildings very close to the public right-of-way.*
- *In the central portion of towns, require that the majority of buildings be constructed immediately adjacent to the public right-of-way. When multiple buildings are constructed in this manner, a sense of enclosed urban space is created.*

Streets/Access

- *Establish public transportation systems within and between towns.*

- *In places where the winters are long and cold, construct wide streets for maximum sunlight penetration.*
- *In hotter climates, construct narrow streets to maximize shade in public areas.*
- *Create wide streets or public rights-of-way to preserve distant views and create a sense of spaciousness.*
- *Establish a connected fabric of streets that respects topographical constraints without resorting to dead-end.*

Public Realm

- *Provide and incorporate common areas within clusters of homes.*
- *Concentrate community facilities around public "squares" at the intersection of community pathways or roadways.*
- *Construct promenades within the heart of the community with main points of attraction at the ends and at other key midpoint locations.*
- *Create public places appropriately sized for the community and within walking distance of all citizens.*

Community

- *Where possible, establish neighborhoods built on a foundation of common social or cultural interests.*
- *Reserve sufficient space within the core of each neighborhood or town for civic buildings and facilities; at least one should serve as a visibly prominent civic focal point.*

Environmental

- *Maintain access to agricultural land in proximity to town-dwellers.*
- *Limit the population size and geographical extent of towns in a sustainable manner suggested by the natural and cultural geography of the region.*
- *Require the planting of native, drought-resistant trees to provide shade.*

Dispersed Rural Settlement

Environmental

- *Locate buildings at the toes of slopes and edges of meadows in a manner that allows for natural windbreaks and creates a feeling of shelter.*
- *Plant windbreaks of native vegetation to conserve energy and provide wildlife habitat.*

Architecture/Design

Form

- *Design building profiles that mimic the profiles of the natural landscape: in steep, mountainous areas, steeply pitched rooflines are appropriate; in areas that are flat or rolling, a lower profile is fitting.*
- *Limit the majority of buildings to four stories high or less. Taller buildings in small towns and rural areas should be exceptional and reserved for cultural or civic purposes.*
- *Draw on historic building styles and elements found in the community.*
- *Avoid building large, monolithic structures. Buildings should comprise a complex of smaller buildings or parts that manifest their own internal social facts.*
- *Arrange roofs so that each distinct roof corresponds to an identifiable social entity in the building. Place the largest roofs—those that are highest and have the largest span—over the largest and most important and most communal spaces; build the lesser roofs off these largest and highest roofs. Allow for and expect additions to be made over time.*
- *Build arcades at the edge of buildings to provide shelter from sun and rain, and to ease the transition between public and private space.*
- *Vary roof pitches, with shallower outer pitches.*
- *Harvest and conserve water through simple and ingenious methods, and incorporate them into the design of buildings.*

- *Expect that a building or complex of buildings is never complete, leaving room for organic future growth.*

Color and Materials

- *Use natural materials in a manner that reflects an organic integrity and harmony with the natural surroundings. Use natural materials such as stone and wood as the primary construction material.*
- *Use relatively thick, well-insulated exterior walls.*
- *Use biodegradable, low energy-consuming materials, which are easy to cut and modify on site. For bulk materials, use earth-based materials such as earth, brick, and tile.*
- *Avoid the use of a multiplicity of building materials, colors, and architectural styles. Doing so also serves to produce a commonality of architectural style.*
- *As a first choice, use natural, earth-tone colors; however, do not do so exclusively. With an appropriate building profile, brighter historical colors such as dark red and green may serve as a beautiful counterpoint to the natural landscape (Figure 2-22).*

Site Design

- *Orient buildings and groups of buildings to take advantage of the sun for winter warmth and mitigation of summer heat. Place buildings to the north of outdoor spaces and keep outdoor spaces to the south, with opportunities for dappled shade from trees or trellises.*
- *Build homes, outbuildings, and villages in a clustered manner, creating natural, organic courtyards or "common" areas.*
- *Construct buildings immediately adjacent to one another to create a compact fabric of connected buildings.*

2-22   Sometimes design review can be pushed a bit too far (e.g., "teal arches" in Sedona, Arizona).
Source: Chris Duerksen

Other Elements

- *Construct fences of historical materials that are unobtrusive; use locally available natural materials when possible. Avoid fence types that have no historical precedent or are made from foreign materials (e.g., chain link or plastic).*

NOTES

1. Christopher Alexander, *The Timeless Way of Building* (New York: Oxford University Press, 1979), p. x.

2. Myrtle Stedman, *Rural Architecture of Northern New Mexico and Southern Colorado* (Santa Fe: Sunstone Press, 1989), p.11.

3. 1940 U.S. Census. quickfacts.census.gov/qfd/states/00000.htm.

4. A.L. Kroeber, "Zuni Houses and Clans, 1916," in *A Zuni Atlas* by T.J. Ferguson and E. Richard Hart (Norman, OK: University of Oklahoma Press, 1984), p. 81.

5. Perry E. Borchers, "Zuni Houses and Clans, 1916," in *A Zuni Atlas* by T.J. Ferguson and E. Richard Hart (Norman, OK: University of Oklahoma Press, 1984), p. 121.

6. William E. Riebsame, *Atlas of the New West: Portrait of a Changing Region* (New York: W.W. Norton & Company, 1997), pp. 68-71.

3

Contemporary Development Cases

The nation behaves well
if it treats the natural resources as assets
which it must turn over to the next generation increased;
and not impaired in value.[1]
—THEODORE ROOSEVELT

In this chapter, we examine in depth a selection of seven contemporary development cases as a means to illustrate the evolution and implementation of development projects that fit appropriately in the western landscape. In several cases, both the implementing regulations and development design are reviewed in depth. With the exception of Case Study 6, "Santa Cruz County, Arizona: Private Initiative," local regulations have played an important and positive role in shaping project design or regional development patterns. In Case Study 7, "City of Claremont, California," we review the evolution of plans and regulations since the town's founding, and illustrate it with a variety of historical and contemporary examples.

While the case study developments uniformly have exemplary features, they are by no means perfect. For example, while the project elements of both Rancho Viejo near Santa Fe and Melody Ranch near Jackson, Wyoming, both maintain significant open space and compare quite favorably to other recent developments in those locales, critics might question whether creating significant new population centers some distance from town limits is a desirable growth pattern. Nevertheless, we believe that the positive aspects significantly outweigh the negative, and that the case studies offer some important lessons for local officials and developers alike.

Case study review involved site visits; interviews with key players including developers, designers, and local planning staff; and analysis of the regulatory framework under which the project was approved. Inquiry focused on the role of development standards, approval process, and market economics in shaping the design and success of the development.

For ease of comparison, we have organized each case study generally along the following lines:

- **Geographical, Climatic, and Social Setting**
- **Regulatory Standards and Planning Processes**
  — introductory overview
  — history of regulations and process
  — desired goals of the standards
  — benefits and noteworthy implementing features
  — development review process
  — support and implementation of legislation
- **Individual Project**
  — project description
  — lay of the land and context
  — key features and elements that relate to the western landscape
  — open space preservation
  — process of design and approvals
  — market review
  — success relative to the intent of local government regulations
  — evaluation
- **Western Rural Development Pattern Language**

CASE STUDY 1

Douglas County, Colorado: Rural Site Plan Process

LAMBERT RANCH

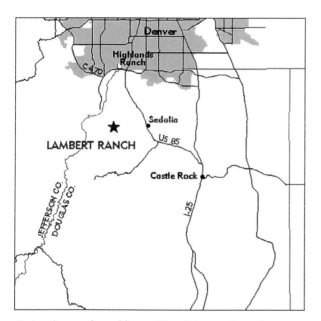

Lying in a vulnerable position between two pincers of rapid urban growth—Denver and Colorado Springs—Douglas County seeks to maintain its attractive rural character through a creative and user-friendly land development process, the Rural Site Plan. Without public hearings and an extended review process, owners of agricultural zoned land may as much as double the allowable residential density in exchange for conserving visually significant open space, maintaining critical wildlife habitat, preserving valuable historic resources, and providing paved road access.

Geographical, Climatic, and Social Setting

In a growth category all its own, according to the U.S. Census, Douglas County sustained a double-digit growth during the entire decade of the 1990s, growing from 60,000 in 1990 to 165,000 in 2000.[2] Located between Denver and Colorado Springs, the county's rolling ranchland and majestic buttes have increasingly attracted urbanites looking for a rural lifestyle. Most residents work outside the county in Denver and Colorado Springs' burgeoning business parks. Receiving less than 15 inches of rain per year, the county's upland Ponderosa pine forests and lower level Gambel oak shrubland are slow growing and irreplaceable in most residents' lifetimes.

Cattle ranching, exurbanites' "ranchettes," and large-lot suburban sprawl have eclipsed the county's historical economic base. Despite these changes and ongoing dramatic growth, large land holdings of historic ranches remain, thus maintaining the wide, open geographical character of the land. Wildlife, particularly large mammals such as elk and deer, are attracted to the verdant river valleys and open fields. The lure of the landscape and its wildlife, however, is threatening its very charm and ecological viability.

Regulatory Standards and Planning Processes

Introductory Overview

The Douglas County Rural Site Plan (RSP) process was devised as a voluntary land development alternative to traditional 35-acre development, which is allowed to proceed with little control under Colorado subdivision law. The RSP process requires no change in zoning and no public hearings aside from a meeting before the Board of County Commissioners to approve a subdivision exemption plat. The process is incentive based, offering density bonuses of up to 100% for preservation of environmentally and visually significant open space, sensitive design, paved roads, and wildlife-friendly fencing. The review process is almost entirely administrative with an emphasis on negotiation to apply standards to site-specific situations.

History of Regulations and Process

The State of Colorado's Senate Bill 35, enacted in May 1972, requires a formal subdivision review process for all land divisions that result in parcels of less than 35 acres. To avoid the process of subdivision, many landowners simply divided their holdings into 35-acre tracts or larger without the benefit of the formal subdivision review process; in many cases, they ignored basic public health and safety standards with respect to sufficient water supply and safe public road access.

Douglas County was plagued with numerous, private, 35-acre-plus tract developments, some of them overlying steep mountain slopes. Deteriorating private roads and low water pressure placed some homeowners in a position of being unable to obtain basic fire and police protection and snow plowing. Often, roads were placed with extensive "cut and fill," and homes were placed in visually sensitive meadows and on prominent ridgetops. In response, the county in 1995 initiated the RSP process to entice landowners away from 35-acre tract development and toward a more appropriate land-based design approach with assistance and review by county staff.

Desired Goals of the Standards

Beyond meeting basic public health and safety standards, the RSP regulations seek to focus design on appropriate environmental and aesthetic principles. At a minimum, plans must be accompanied with a set of detailed, restrictive covenants governing fencing, outbuildings, building materials, and color—all subject to review by a local architectural review board. Home sites are carefully selected to enhance the open, rural landscape typical of Douglas County.

Where possible, existing ranching operations are encouraged to continue, and preservation of historical sites is considered in achieving density bonuses. Various levels of density bonuses may be achieved, depending on the benefits obtained by the proposed design. The 40% density bonus may be achieved through a combination of paved roads, set-aside of 50% open space, and wildlife-friendly fencing. To achieve a 100% bonus, two-thirds of the land must remain in open space outside of individual home parcels and be subject to a conservation easement. Additionally, the county may require financial participation in off-site improvements such as road paving and dust mitigation. Road paving may be perceived by some as contrary to maintaining rural character; however, in Douglas County, fugitive dust is a serious environmental problem and, accordingly, paving of heavily traveled rural roads is a priority.

Benefits and Noteworthy Implementing Features

The RSP process provides significant environmental, visual, and cultural benefits to the county. Specifically, these include the following:

Environmental

- *protection and enhancement of wildlife habitat and movement corridors*
- *protection of riparian and other significant ecological complexes*
- *preservation of vegetation*
- *limited land disturbance*

Cultural

- *preservation of historic sites including ranch buildings*
- *preservation of ranching activities*
- *preservation of historic landscapes*

Visual

- *protection of roadway view sheds*
- *protection of ridgelines and meadows*

• *use of building color and materials that blend with the natural environment*

Additionally, the RSP process is intended to provide a user-friendly approach to limited land development while offering the landowner the opportunity to maintain ownership and operation of their traditional ranching livelihood. In some cases, through the use of conservation easements, individuals may further benefit with respect to tax credits. As an alternative to 35-acre tract development, the RSP offers the added benefit of county-maintained roads, snow plowing, and public school bus service—none of which is available on 35-acre tracts because all access is on private roadways.

Development Review Process

The process begins with an informal meeting between staff and the landowner and/or prospective developer. In some cases, there may be no more than a hand-drawn sketch presented to illustrate an idea. Early on in the process, county staff make a site visit to provide an early evaluation of the proposal's feasibility. County staff reserve the right to conclude that a piece of land or a proposal is not worthy of development under the RSP process if no significant benefits can be discerned.

The next step is a formal submittal that includes a formal plan, floodplain study, and a design summary sheet for negotiation purposes. No fees are required. Roadway design and drainage studies are not required at this time in an effort to simplify the process and the early stages.

A 21-day referral process includes at a minimum the County Building Division, the applicable fire district, the State Division of Wildlife, and County Engineering. Comments from all agencies are considered in what typically requires several rounds of negotiations to achieve a plan that supports both county and landowner objectives.

Approval criteria include the following:
• minimized development on ridgelines and in highway corridor view sheds, as identified in the County Master Plan;
• minimized tree, vegetation, and soil disturbance or removal, and no scarring of hillsides with roads and utilities;
• protected and preserved wetlands and riparian areas, critical wildlife habitats, and natural features and landmarks; and
• preserved significant archaeological and historical features or structures, and adaptive reuse where feasible.

Upon being granted county staff approval for the plan, an exemption plat is forwarded to the Board of County Commissioners for approval. Recordation must occur within 30 days of exemption approval. Road, grading, and drainage plans are subsequently approved by County Engineering prior to issuance of building permits.

Support and Implementation of Legislation

Colorado Revised State Statutes 30-28-101 (10), 31-23-201(2), and 31-23-214(1) exempt from the statutorily defined subdivision review process the creation of land parcels of 35 acres or more. Coloradoans refer to this statute as "Senate Bill 35." Many citizens are concerned about the detrimental impact of 35-acre parcel proliferation, and the inability of most jurisdictions to effectively address the adverse visual, economic, and public safety concerns associated with such developments. The granting of well permits by the State Engineer's office is on the basis of an appropriately approved subdivision with sufficient water rights or the 35-acre exemption in accordance with state statute (every 35-acre parcel has the right to drill one well for domestic use).

Recent legislation (C.R.S. 30-28-401), referred to as the "Cluster Bill," allows for greater flexibility in this regard by allowing well permits for divisions of land that have a minimum overall density of one unit per 17½ acres—a substantial increase in density from the previous 35-acre rule. The legislation requires that at least two-thirds of the total area of the tract be reserved as open space. It is in the context of this legislation that the RSP process establishes a viable alternative—one that provides an incentive via increased density and flexibility in exchange for preservation of open space or the achievement of other county objectives. Home rule cities in Colorado may allow clustering in other forms, although those that result in smaller lots must still receive well permits from the State Engineer, which typically requires a water augmentation plan if existing water rights are not available.

Individual Project—Lambert Ranch

Project Description

Encompassing what was once the largest apple orchard west of the Mississippi, the Lambert Ranch RSP preserves the ranch home, several outbuildings, and an abandoned mining rail line corridor. The plan provides for 37 home sites on parcels ranging from 7 to 15 acres. Open space tracts set aside for wildlife habitat comprise 499 acres, or 54% of the site (Figure 3-1).

Lay of the Land and Context

A small creek traverses the land, forming a flat valley that is bordered on the east and west by hillsides that retain hints of the former orchard.

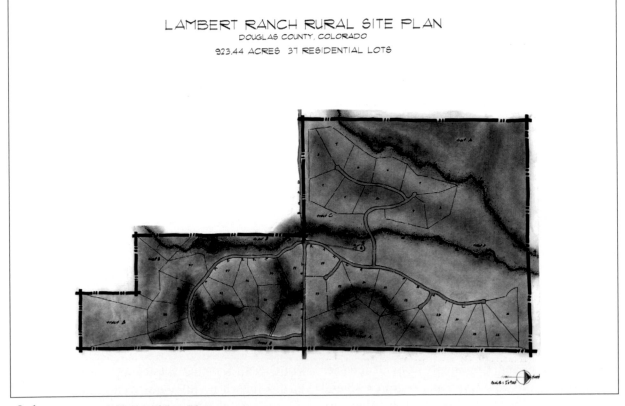

3-1 Lambert Ranch Rural Site Plan.

Source: Douglas County Community Development; drawing by Paul Whalen

Land to the west has been divided into 35-acre tracts; to the south is a 2½-acre lot subdivision. The Colorado Division of Wildlife holds a large parcel of land to the north, and an active farm serves as the eastern border. A dead-end, unpaved rural road provides the only access.

Key Features and Elements That Relate to the Western Landscape

The land's vegetation is primarily characterized by grassland and Gambel oak, a slow-growing shrub with a dense branching habit and a typical height of 15-20 feet. The hills rising from the valley form several prominent, treeless ridges. The creek's floodplain provides for an attractive, naturally irrigated meadow—a unique feature in Douglas County's arid and primarily nonirrigated rural landscape. The development plan preserves this meadow and allows for its continued irrigation (Figure 3-2).

A brick ranch home and outbuildings, dating from the early 1900s, are preserved as a feature of the RSP. The historical settlement pattern is apparent: the central location of the home adjacent to Indian Creek, the mature trees surrounding the home planted by the original settlers, and the close and intimate relationship of the outbuildings. The RSP maintains the cluster of buildings and their visual identity in the center of the ranch by preserving sufficient open space surrounding the cluster (Figure 3-3).

To protect the landscape's character, building envelopes are used to keep home sites off all the ridgelines and outside of the stands of Gambel oak. The limited vegetation on the site does not permit most homes to be hidden; instead, the design focuses on restrictive covenants requiring the use of natural building materials and earthtone colors (Figure 3-4).

Open space is configured to maximize the preservation of wildlife habitat and to facilitate wildlife movement across and within the site.

3-2 Lambert Ranch, viewing south, the central irrigated meadow. In the background is a neighboring subdivision with the Rocky Mountain foothills as a backdrop.

Source: James van Hemert

3-3 Lambert Ranch. 1902 home and outbuildings.

Source: James van Hemert

3-4 Lambert Ranch. Home sites nestled into the side of the hill amidst Gambel oak.

Source: James van Hemert

Open Space Preservation

Open space is preserved in two ways: (1) designation of restricted areas within privately owned parcels; and (2) under a conservation easement held by Douglas County overlying tracts owned by a homeowners' association. A total of 803 acres, or 90% of the project, is preserved as open space, of which 499 acres lie within tracts owned and maintained by a homeowners' association; the remaining acreage comprises a no-build zone within individual residential parcels.

Sufficient open space was preserved within the riparian corridor to satisfy the U.S. Fish & Wildlife's requirements for habitat protection of the threatened Preble's meadow jumping mouse.

Process of Design and Approvals

Prior to formal submittal, the applicant—a real estate developer—requested a site visit with planning staff to evaluate the potential for development either under an RSP or standard rezoning and subdivision. Staff concluded that the land would not qualify for a rezoning to a higher residential density than the current 35-acre density afforded by the Agricultural District zoning. They concluded, however, that the land provided several important features worth preserving within the context of an RSP. Planning staff provided general design direction and encouraged formal submittal of a plan.

From start to finish, the process took 10 months with several unexpected hurdles to overcome. The first hurdle began with the county's Engineering Division. Concerned with the amount of review time required for the roadway design, the legitimacy of the process was questioned by engineering staff. Furthermore, the unpaved access road proved to be a potential deal-breaker. A solution was reached whereby the developer agreed to participate financially in off-site road paving. This cost was not initially contemplated but was ultimately and willingly absorbed by the developer.

Negotiations on design specifics lasted several months, and concluded in a plan that preserved 90% of the land as open space, protected significant wildlife corridors and important historical elements, and kept home sites away from ridgelines and the irrigated river valley. A surprise was in store, however, for all parties. During the final stage of the project approval at a public meeting to approve the exemption plat, neighbors from the adjoining 2½-acre subdivision to the south complained that the proposal would have a negative impact on them. They further expressed concern over the fact that the design was now very different from the one they saw at the beginning of the process.

To the commissioners, it was clear that these neighbors were not consulted in the final stages of the design process, and the meeting was rescheduled for a later date, at which time a solution was expected to be found. The RSP design was reworked to accommodate the neighbors' concerns; unfortunately, a significant area of prime, upland open space was sacrificed to provide the necessary distance from the southern neighbors.

Market Review

According to the developer, parcels are selling significantly faster than anticipated and at prices comparable to standard 35-acre tracts. The absorption rate has been three times faster than anticipated: rather than a two-year time frame, all the lots have sold within nine months. For example, a typical 10-acre site is being reserved at between $160,000 and $225,000. The developer is actively seeking another RSP opportunity in the county.

Success Relative to the Intent of Local Government Regulations

By all accounts, the Lambert Ranch RSP is a design success. However, two major processing hurdles had to be overcome: (1) the Engineering Division's recalcitrance in spending large amounts of time on a low-fee, relatively low-impact project; and (2) the surprise opposition of neighbors. Thus, the intent to provide an easy, low-cost processing mechanism was significantly off the mark.

As a result of the lessons learned in this process, the county changed the regulations to allow for developer contributions for off-site improvements in exchange for greater density (up to 100%). Furthermore, to save processing time in advance of final commissioner exemption plat approval, final engineered road design is no longer required until *after* commissioner approval. It also became clear that local neighborhoods that may be affected by the design should remain at the negotiation table throughout the entire process.

Evaluation

Since its inception in 1995, seven RSP projects have been formally reviewed, approved, and recorded—encompassing 5,543 acres and providing 221 home sites. An additional eight RSPs are currently under review.

An unexpected reality is that one of the larger approved RSP projects was never recorded, and was instead carved up through the sale of several large parcels, leaving just over half of the remaining land area within the original RSP. This land remains at risk for 35-acre tract development, and the attendant lack of control over ridgeline development and intrusion into sensitive riparian areas. The county and various conservation funds have aggressively negotiated with the landowners to ensure that, regardless of the ultimate manner of land division, critical wildlife habitat and visually important mountain ridgelines remain intact.

With one exception, all RSPs have been submitted by developers and real estate interests, not the resident landowner or rancher, as originally envisioned. Despite the low fee structure, reduced and simplified processing time, and delayed submittal of expensive roadway design documents, the design process remains sufficiently costly and intimidating to discourage resident landowners and ranchers from pursuing plans independently. The county recognizes that successful RSPs require considerable expenditures and time, typically best afforded by experienced land developers.

Because the RSP is a voluntary program, the standard 35-acre tract land divisions remain a simpler, quicker, and less expensive option for resident landowners.

The county continually evaluates and revises the RSP in response to hands-on experience with development projects. Significant changes and lessons learned include the following:

- Greater incentives are needed to attract interested developers.
- Benefits to the county, including mitigation of off-site impacts such as road dust, need to be clearly evident.
- The process is more attractive and successful for developers and real estate interests than for resident landowners.
- It is a time-intensive process regardless of the size of the proposal.
- Neighboring homeowners must be involved throughout the entire process.
- It is an effective means of preserving open space and critical wildlife habitat at little cost to the county.
- A collaborative approach is the most successful.
- The primarily administrative process requires strong political support and high trust level of planning staff.

Western Rural Development Pattern Language

A number of significant historical western development patterns may be distilled from the Douglas County/Lambert Ranch case study. Moreover, the project teaches some important lessons and suggests additional patterns that respond to modern land use planning and environmental concerns and objectives. Both these historical and contemporary lessons are summarized and categorized below with explanatory comments provided as appropriate.

Dispersed Rural Settlement

Environmental

- *Locate buildings at the toes of slopes and edges of meadows in a manner that allows for natural windbreaks and creates a feeling of shelter.*

In the northern portion of Lambert Ranch, the homes are nestled at the edge of the meadow and along the side of the hills in a manner that evokes a strong sense of shelter. Homes are not placed on the ridges.

- *Plant native, drought-resistant trees to screen development and provide shade and shelter from the wind.*

The trees planted by the homesteaders are mature and provide significant shade.

- *Protect wildlife habitat and enhance wildlife movement corridors in a manner that allows for continued free movement of the broadest possible variety of species.*

Douglas County and the Colorado Division of Wildlife have identified this area as a critical wildlife habitat movement corridor between the Front Range foothills and the plains to the east. The plan preserves sufficiently wide swaths of open space in the most critical areas for wildlife movement. Most significantly, sufficient space was provided to protect the habitat of the federally listed and threatened Preble's meadow jumping mouse, which lives primarily along creeks. The vast majority of Gambel oak, which provides the most critical cover for animals in this area, is preserved.

- *Where fugitive dust is an air-quality concern, pave rural roads.*

Douglas County encourages the paving of rural roads. A paved road is not the rural visual characteristic that naturally comes to mind; however, in many western jurisdictions, the arid climate exacerbates the problems associated with fugitive dust. As traffic increases, paved roads are the most cost-effective and environmentally sound solution to minimizing this source of air pollution.

Cultural

- *Preserve and integrate historic ranching operations.*

Although the ranching operation has ceased to exist, the central meadow, ranch homestead, and several outbuildings are preserved as the focal point of the new development. Sensitive siting of homes has retained the historical visual character.

Architecture/Design

Form

- *Design buildings that mimic the profiles of the natural landscape: in steep, mountainous areas, steeply pitched rooflines are appropriate; in areas that are flat or rolling, a lower profile is fitting.*

The modestly pitched roofs of Lambert Ranch reflect the foothills and rolling land that provide the topographical context.

Other Elements

- *Use locally available natural materials in the construction of fences that are unobtrusive and reflect historic character.*

Fencing is limited to simple, open-rail type within limited building envelopes.

- *Construct fences that are wildlife-friendly.*

Wildlife-friendly fences allow for safe movement for the full range of animals that move within the area. For example, pronghorn crawl under fences and require a minimum of 16 inches of clearance with a wire fence (12 inches for a solid fence). Deer, which cross over fences, have difficulty with a wire fence over 40 inches in height or a solid fence over 45 inches. (See Chapter 4, Case Study 14, "Wildlife-Friendly Fencing.")

CONTACTS

Douglas County Planning Department
100 Third Street, Castle Rock, CO 80104
(303) 660-7460
www.douglas.co.us

Stan Brown
(303) 972-4919
www.dimensionsdiversified.com

SOURCES

Interviews with Betty Allen, Assistant Planning Director of the Douglas County Planning Department; and Stan Brown, project developer, 2000.

Douglas County Zoning Resolution, Section 3A, Rural Site Plan.

CASE STUDY 2

Fremont County, Idaho: Performance Development Code

JACOB'S ISLAND PARK RANCH

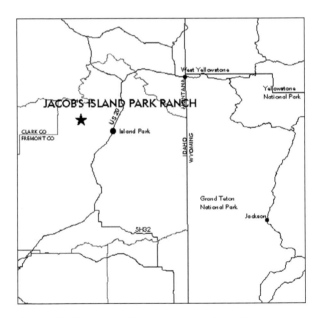

Located adjacent to the western reaches of Yellowstone National Park, Fremont County, Idaho, has established a flexible performance-based development code in order to accommodate growth while preserving agricultural land, protecting visual resources, and protecting critical wildlife habitat. Jacob's Island Park Ranch illustrates how the code works.

Geographical, Climatic, and Social Setting

Fremont County is located in the central west portion of Idaho, sharing its eastern boundary with Wyoming. Its farthest eastern reaches lie within Yellowstone National Park. The southern and western parts of the county lie over the basalt flows of the Snake River plain, an area of irrigated cropland and sagebrush steppes that also includes a belt of active sand dunes. The northern and eastern parts of the county are on the volcanic highlands of the Yellowstone Plateau, where the landscape features lodgepole pine forests, mountain meadows, streams, and the headwaters of the Henry's Fork of the Snake River. The steeply rising Centennial Mountains and Henry's Lake form a distinctive landscape on Fremont County's northern border. The county seat—St. Anthony, population 3,100, located in the southwestern portion of the county—is the only sizable town.

Average annual precipitation in Fremont County ranges from less than 10 inches in the western part of the county to more than 30 inches at higher elevations. Elevations in Fremont County range from 4,380 to 10,240 feet above sea level. Summers are brief; winters long and cold. Its economy is primarily agricultural and tourism-based, with an increasing number of year-round residents. With a population of 12,000 in 2000, it has experienced modest growth, with an annual rate of approximately 1% since 1990, when its population stood at 11,000.[3]

Slightly less than 32% of the county lies within private land ownership; the remainder comprises the Targhee National Forest, Bureau of Land Management lands, and various parcels managed by the State of Idaho.

Regulatory Standards and Planning Processes

Introductory Overview

The Fremont County Development Code is a unique, performance-based unified code that covers all matters pertaining to zoning and subdivision. Points are assigned based on achieving certain specified goals. Only developments that receive an overall positive score are approved. Density is not specified according to zone districts (as is traditional in most jurisdictions) but is calculated based on the environmental sensitivity of the land. Density bonuses are available to projects that accumulate a minimum number of points under the performance standard system. Subdivisions are processed in three stages beginning with a sketch plan reviewed by the Planning and Zoning Board, which offers suggestions and criticisms; a Preliminary Plat hearing before the Planning and Zoning Board; and final approval by the county commissioners.

History of Regulations and Process

A major public outcry over the development of a large, visually prominent meadow spurred the county to re-evaluate its development codes. A planning consultant, Lee Nellis, was hired to oversee the development of a new development code that would ensure the protection of valuable visual resources, preserve agricultural land, protect valuable environmental resources, and protect wildlife habitat. The Fremont County Comprehensive Plan and its implementing document, the Fremont County Development Code, were formally approved in 1997 following a series of well-attended town meetings.

Desired Goals of the Standards

Beyond meeting basic public health and safety standards, the Fremont County Development Code seeks to accomplish the following:

- maintain agricultural resources and preserve farms;
- assure provision of adequate public facilities;
- protect visual resources and enhance the community's image;
- maintain natural assets, including critical slopes;

- protect critical areas including stream, lakeshore corridors, and floodplains;
- protect critical wildlife habitat; and
- protect irrigation systems.

Benefits and Noteworthy Implementing Features

The implementation of the development code provides significant environmental, cultural, and visual benefits to the county. Specifically, these include the following:

Environmental

- *Protection of critical natural areas.*

  Recognizing the importance of the integrity of the riparian complex, setbacks beyond the 100-year floodplain, wetlands, and significant riparian vegetation are established for stream and lakeshore corridors varying from between 30 and 50 feet. Open space use of slopes over 15% is encouraged; development on slopes over 30% is generally forbidden.

- *Protection of wildlife habitat and corridors.*

  Development may not disturb more than 1 acre in or adjoining a critical wildlife habitat area, and proposals are encouraged to implement professionally prepared plans for the protection of wildlife values.

Cultural

- *Agricultural land preservation.*

  Agriculture is recognized as a way of life and as a part of the social economy of the region. As such, the development code encourages siting and design of developments in a manner that minimizes the conversion of productive agricultural lands to other uses and minimizes conflict with neighboring agricultural operations. Irrigation systems are also afforded protection. A high value is placed upon preserving the integrity of irrigation systems. For example, no development may channel storm water or snowmelt runoff into any irrigation system without the consent of the responsible irrigation entity.

Visual

- *Protection of important visual features.*

  Maintenance of the scenic qualities of visually sensitive areas is encouraged. This is implemented through the transfer of development densities from visually sensitive areas or through clustering development within a small portion of the visually sensitive area. The latter may be accomplished, for example, by placing structures against a forested background at the edge of the sensitive area, or by using architectural and landscaping techniques to minimize visual impact.

Development Review Process

The process begins informally with a sketch plan review by the Planning and Zoning Commission. The commission's initial review is not a regulatory proceeding but an opportunity for the commission to be made aware of the proposal and to provide a venue for possible questions, comments, and concerns to be raised. During this phase, the applicant has an opportunity to work with staff and neighboring property owners in determining the overall direction of the project and which environmental and visual criteria are most important. The relative point system of the code clearly provides flexibility to all parties involved in the design of a project. A particular feature or criterion may be traded off for one that is mutually

perceived as more important without "killing the deal."

Subsequent to this meeting, the applicant files a complete, formal preliminary plan application with supporting materials. The application goes out on a formal referral period to an established "hit list" of referrals, including the National Forest Service, U.S. Fish & Wildlife, State Fish & Game, school districts, emergency services, and any additional agency that is deemed to have an interest in the proposal.

Once comments are received and agreed-upon modifications are made, the application may be scheduled for a formal hearing before the Planning and Zoning Commission, which may approve, approve with conditions, or deny the application. Upon approval, the application may proceed for final plat review by the both the Planning and Zoning Commission and the Board of County Commissioners.

A comprehensive system of performance standards is utilized to evaluate development proposals. Full compliance is required for absolute performance standards. Relative performance standards address complex issues for which absolute standards are inappropriate. They encourage or discourage certain kinds of design in developments through the use of a point-scoring system, which uses a scale of –2 to +2, measuring both effort and success in achieving a range of criteria (Table 3-1).

Additionally, relative importance factors on a scale of 1-5 are assigned for each performance standard, with "1" being the least important and "5" the most. A final cumulative score of no less

Table 3-1. Point Scoring System

- –2 points are assigned when no effort is made to implement a particular performance standard.
- –1 point is assigned when the effort is inadequate.
- 0 points are assigned when the standards are not relevant or implementation is inadequate.
- +1 point is assigned for a successful effort in implementation.
- +2 points are assigned when effort in implementation is outstanding.

than "0" must be attained in order for an application permit to be approved.

The performance standard of visual features may illustrate the assignment of point values. Higher points are assigned when development maintains the scenic qualities of visually sensitive areas. An assignment of "+2" is granted only to developments using density transfer to leave the visually sensitive area undeveloped or establishing cluster development into a small portion of the visually sensitive area. An assignment of "+1" is granted when development is designed to retain scenic quality by placing structures against a forested background at the edge of the sensitive area and/or using architectural and landscaping techniques to minimize visual impact. No points are granted when the standard is either irrelevant or implementation is inadequate. Negative points are given when effort is inadequate (–1) or when no effort is made whatsoever (–2).

An average density is assigned to all undeveloped lands, as shown in Table 3-2.

The development rights permitted on each land type are added up to yield the number of dwelling units that may be constructed on a parcel. Development rights may be transferred from parcels of productive cropland, wetlands, stream corridors, wildlife habitat, or visually sensitive areas to lands of lesser value in respect to any of these items.

A density bonus of a dwelling unit for each increment of 10 cumulative points is granted for cluster development. Additionally, the number of dwelling units permitted by transfer from any critical area (wetlands, stream and lakeshore corridors, slopes over 15%, etc.), productive cropland,

or visually sensitive area may be doubled. Cluster development must have a positive score on its relative performance standards. In no case may the permitted density exceed one-half dwelling unit per acre.

Support and Implementation of Legislation

The Fremont County Development Code is adopted pursuant to the authority granted by the Idaho Local Planning Act of 1975, including provisions for the zoning ordinance required by I.C. 67-6511 and the subdivision ordinance required by I.C. 67-6513. The performance-based development code does not require any specific enabling legislation beyond the Local Planning Act.

Individual Project—Jacob's Island Park Ranch: Arrowwood and Blue River Subdivisions

Project Description

Jacob's Island Park Ranch is a 960-acre working ranch, which also provides commercial western entertainment and lodging on the weekends. It is the first development to follow the county's new development code. The developed portion will ultimately comprise 400 acres with 132 lots. The first 48 lots have been platted as the Arrowwood Subdivision (Figure 3-5).

Lay of the Land and Context

The land is characterized primarily by open grazing land on the southern portion and pine forest in the north. A riparian corridor traverses the land in a north/south direction. The topography is gently

Table 3-2. Density Calculation

Site Characteristics	Average Density, One Dwelling Unit Per:
Wetlands, slopes over 30%	25 acres
Stream corridors, critical wildlife habitat, slopes of 15-30%	10 acres
Other areas	2.5 acres

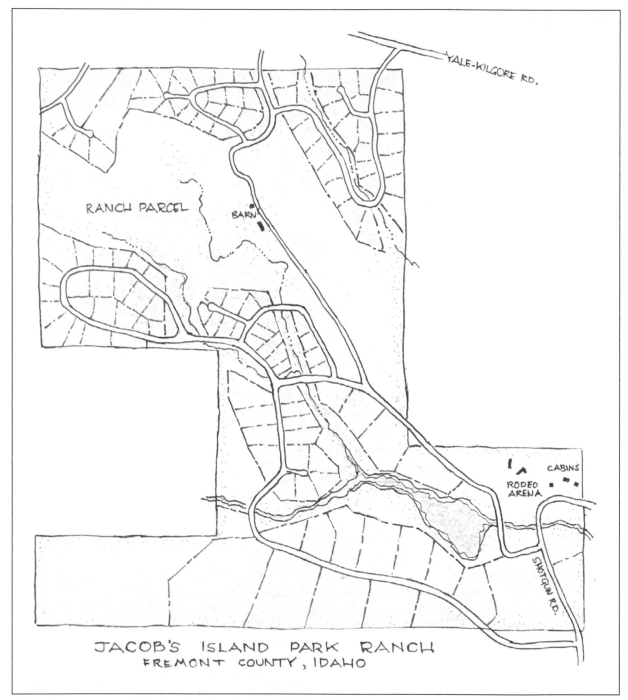

3-5 Jacob's Island Park Ranch, Fremont County, Idaho.

Source: James van Hemert

rolling. A significant portion of the ranch lies within a wildlife movement corridor.

Key Features and Elements That Relate to the Western Landscape

With mountains rising to the north, the pine forest and open cattle grazing land, bare wood barns and barbed wire fencing, the property represents a classic western landscape, both from a natural and cultural perspective. The character of the subdivision is subdued, allowing the features of the natural landscape and existing ranching operations to dominate. So subdued is the subdivision's character, in fact, that it is difficult to actually find the development (Figure 3-6).

Design standards are controlled by covenants that require all structures and fencing to be in harmony with surrounding structures and topography. Wire-mesh fencing is not permitted, nor may any fencing obstruct views of neighboring residences. Most homes have been constructed using mountain cabin-style architecture with natural colored logs and standing-seam metal roofing material the color of the sky or forest. Reflective finishes are prohibited. Permitted colors are low reflective shades of gray, brown, gray-greens, and brown-greens (Figure 3-7).

Lots do not have specified building envelopes, but the homes that have been built to date are carefully sited within their lots without any apparent undue disturbance to the land or excessive loss of trees. In many cases, the lots offer seclusion within the forest. As the project builds out, more homes will be built in open areas; however, these areas are generally of lower density. Virtually all the ground surrounding the homes is left in its natural state without any blue-grass turf or exotic landscaping. There are no restrictions on well-water use within the covenants.

All utilities are underground and the roads are relatively narrow and gravel-surfaced. No over-lot grading is required to accommodate development (Figure 3-8).

3-6   Arrowwood's low-key entrance blends with the ranch environment and doesn't call attention to itself.

Source: James van Hemert

3-7   Arrowwood homes are constructed of natural materials such as log and stone, which reflect the ranch vernacular.

Source: James van Hemert

3-8   Narrow gravel roads characterize Arrowwood and maintain the laid back, rural ranch atmosphere.

Source: James van Hemert

Open Space Preservation

The landowner desired to maintain cattle operations and weekend western-theme attractions; as such, a significant portion of open grazing land is preserved comprising 309 acres, or 32% of the ranch. An additional 89 acres, or 9%, of open space within riparian corridors is preserved.

Process of Design and Approvals

The design process began with one-on-one meetings with professional planning staff and the landowners. Initially, the owner only desired to develop a portion of the project, but was convinced that taking the whole property into account worked in the best interests of all concerned. The new development standards encourage this through the use of an average density calculation. In this particular case, 28 lots were awarded for 700 acres of wildlife habitat (at a rate of 1:25) and 104 lots were awarded for 260 acres of standard, unencumbered land (at a rate of 1:2.5). The first 48 lots were platted as the Arrowwood subdivision. Five homes have been constructed to date. A second filing of 26 lots, titled Blue River, has recently been approved. Lots range in size from 1 to 64 acres.

Market Review

Marketing began in earnest in 1999. Lots are selling from $30,000 to $140,000. As of August 2000, 29 lots had been sold and five homes had been built. Homes are selling within a range of $70,000 to $200,000. The unique nature of these lots makes any comparison with other lots elsewhere in the county problematic.

Success Relative to the Intent of Local Government Regulations

The zoning administrator believes that this project has become one of the choicest subdivisions in the county, even though waterfront property is generally taken up first. The process was slow because it was new; however, the intent of the county regulations was clearly met. Establishing a positive working relationship with the developer was very important and key in the success of the project.

Evaluation

The zoning administrator reports that approximately 20 subdivisions have been reviewed under the new development code. The only component of the process that is not working well is the lack of a strong requirement to provide adequate electrical and telephone utilities up front for smaller subdivisions.

Western Rural Development Pattern Language

A number of significant historical western development patterns may be distilled from the Fremont County/Jacob's Island Park Ranch case study. Moreover, the project teaches some important lessons, and suggests additional patterns that respond to modern land use planning and environmental concerns and objectives. Both of these historical and contemporary lessons are summarized and categorized below, with explanatory comments provided as appropriate.

Dispersed Rural Settlement

Environmental

- *Protect wildlife habitat and movement corridors.*

  Lay out developments and lots to protect large blocks of contiguous open space so as to preserve wildlife habitat and corridors. As development increasingly encroaches on critical wildlife habitat and movement corridors, wildlife is either disappearing altogether from areas they once frequented or their numbers are seriously diminished. For many animal species, the American West is one of the last places with sufficient unfragmented habitat. Jacob's Island Park Ranch accommodates wildlife movement corridors and preserves significant habitat in contiguous tracts.

- *Construct the narrowest rural roads possible, without undue negative impacts on public safety, in order to minimize impacts on vegetation, natural drainage patterns, and the natural terrain. In placing roadways, do so in a manner that minimizes the need for "cut and fill."*

The relatively low density of this project allows for narrow gravel roads that are characteristic of the existing ranch and the rural nature of Fremont County. The narrow gravel roads serve to minimize the amount of impervious surface.

Cultural

- *Preserve and protect historic ranching operations.*

Developments and lots should be configured to preserve significant parcels of land that can maintain economically viable agricultural operations. Integration of historic ranching operations provides a critical link with the past while preserving a cultural way of life unique to the American West. It further serves to maintain a distinct feature of the landscape. An added element that enhances the economic viability of the ranching operation are the tourist attractions programmed over the weekends.

- *Preserve irrigated agricultural lands.*

Irrigated agricultural land is a signature feature of many rural landscapes, even in the relatively arid West. From both a visual and cultural perspective, Fremont County appropriately encourages preservation of irrigated lands.

Architecture/Design

Form

- *Design buildings that mimic the profiles of the natural landscape: in steep, mountainous areas,* *steeply pitched rooflines are appropriate; in areas that are flat or rolling, a lower profile is fitting.*

Roof pitches of up to 12:12 reflect the mountainous background and complement the tall, thin evergreens.

- *Preserve significant historical buildings.*

Several historical ranch structures are preserved as part of continuing weekend recreation activities, thereby adding to the historical ambiance and connection to traditional ranching.

Color and Materials

- *Avoid the use of a multiplicity of building materials, colors, and architectural styles. Doing so also serves to produce a commonality of architectural style.*
- *Use natural materials in a manner that reflects an organic integrity and harmony with the natural surroundings. Stone and wood are often appropriate as the primary construction material.*
- *As a first choice, use natural, earth-tone colors that reflect the surrounding landscape; however, do not do so exclusively. With an appropriate building profile, brighter historical colors such as dark red and green may serve as a beautiful counterpoint to the natural landscape.*

A limited palette of natural materials is promoted by the Architectural Review Committee for the Arrowwood subdivision.

Site Design

- *Avoid planting nonnative vegetation and turn landscaping. Maintain existing vegetation, and minimize land disturbance and overlot grading.*

Native vegetation and existing landforms should retain their dominance. Additional landscaping should be native or native-complementary. Turf should be minimized or eliminated altogether. If turf is used, it should be drought-tolerant and reflect similar texture and color to that of native vegetation. Land disturbance should be limited to that necessary to provide access and a building footprint.

- *Minimize the size of building footprints.*

Jacob's Island Park Ranch teaches us that less is indeed more. The modest-sized homes limit the visual impact, and allow the forest and mountain backdrops to dominate. Modest footprints also require less land disturbance and artificial means of mitigation such as retaining walls.

Other Elements

- *Construct fences of historical materials that are unobtrusive and use locally available, natural materials.*

Homeowner covenants are an effective way to ensure appropriate fencing that doesn't obstruct neighbors' views and the visual flow of the landscape.

- *Avoid large entryway signs and monumentation. Allow the natural landscape to dominate.*

"Understatement" should be the guiding theme in designing any signage. Signage must clearly be subservient to the landscape.

- *Minimize privacy fencing to limited areas immediately adjacent to the home.*

Privacy fencing must be limited to allow the natural landscape to visually flow unimpeded.

- *Place all utilities underground.*

Overhead utilities are particularly obtrusive in the relatively sparsely vegetated West. Utility boxes should be painted in natural colors and placed in unobtrusive locations.

CONTACTS

Fremont County
Karen Lords, Zoning Administrator
Court House, 151 West 1st North, St. Anthony, ID 83445
(208) 624-4643
www.co.fremont.id.us

Lee Nellis, A.I.C.P.
(520) 290-0828

SOURCES

Interviews with Karen Lords, Zoning Administrator for Fremont County; Lee Nellis, planning consultant; and Connie Rowedder, Henry's Fork Realtors, February 2000.

Fremont County Development Code.

CASE STUDY 3

Santa Fe County, New Mexico: Growth Management Plan

RANCHO VIEJO

At the intersection of three cultures—Native American, Spanish, and Contemporary American— an interesting growth management model is being tested. Its expression is emerging in the Rancho Viejo development south of Santa Fe, New Mexico, providing an alternative to the 1- to 10-acre lot rural sprawl so common in today's West.

Geographical, Climatic, and Social Setting

Santa Fe County is located in the north central portion of New Mexico along the convergence of the Rio Grande River Valley and the southern Sangre de Cristo Mountains. The county encompasses 1,911 square miles of diverse terrain. Elevation in the county ranges from lowland riparian areas and the Caja del Rio (5,500 feet) to the Alpine Tundra (over 12,600 feet) in Santa Fe National Forest.

The unique variety of terrain and elevation creates different ecosystems and life zones that support various animal and plant species. Dry, sunny days and cold, dark nights characterize the climate. The arid climate makes water a scarce and important resource. Average annual precipitation is 14 inches. The population in 1999 was approximately 125,000, of whom 66,000 resided in the City of Santa Fe.[4] This represents an increase of more than 25,000, or 25%, over the 1990 population of 99,000. Significant growth has been occurring in the unincorporated portion of the county, often in a random, sprawling pattern that has fragmented open space and wildlife habitat, and for which it is costly for the county to provide basic services such as roads and police/fire protection (Figure 3-9).

3-9 Sprawling subdivisions can be seen around the edges of Rancho Viejo.

Source: Chris Duerksen

Regulatory Standards and Planning Processes

Introductory Overview

The Santa Fe County Growth Management Plan is a policy document that forms the foundation for the county's land use regulation. A more detailed plan was then created for the Santa Fe Community College District in which Rancho Viejo is located. It is, in effect, a "neighborhood" or "area" plan with very specific policies for development for this district, which lies immediately south of the incorporated limits of Santa Fe.

Parts of the district lying between Rancho Viejo and the city limits have already been developed with "rural" subdivisions, with small lots of from 1-5 acres, but several large, undeveloped tracts remain. The district is bordered to the east and south by large, suburban density subdivisions with curvilinear streets and cul-de-sacs. The plan recommends breaking away from both the rural sprawl and suburban, cookie-cutter subdivision development patterns to one where development takes place in traditional villages interspersed in the countryside and separated by large tracts of open space (Figure 3-10).

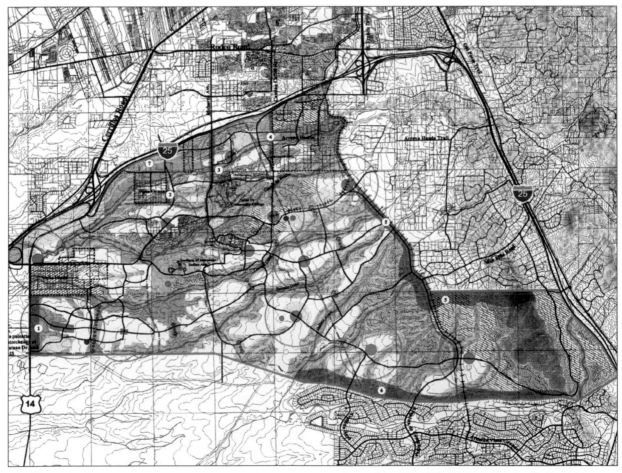

3-10 Santa Fe Community College District Plan.

Source: Santa Fe County, New Mexico

History of Regulations and Process

The Growth Management Plan was adopted by the county commissioners in October 1999 after an extensive community participation process lasting six years. Background studies examining public opinion, community values, water resources, population and housing, open space and trail resources, visual resources, economic development, infrastructure, and services were commissioned to serve as a foundation for the plan update. The Santa Fe Community College District Plan, which adds specific policies and detailed guidance for developers, was adopted in October 2000. It was followed in December 2000 by the adoption of comprehensive land use and zoning regulations for the district that embody and implement the plan's vision.

Desired Goals of the Standards

The overall intent of the Growth Management Plan is succinctly stated in the primary goal:

> Santa Fe County's land use and growth management policy is to promote development that **avoids sprawl; protect open spaces** and maintain the diverse character of the county through creative development design solutions; ensure the availability and diversity of housing and economic opportunities with adequate and economically efficient infrastructure and services; **and maintain and preserve traditional communities** and support their traditional economic structures [emphasis added].[5]

More specifically, with respect to the Community College District, the primary development objective is to create a pattern of development characterized by villages interspersed with open countryside:

> The heart of the Community College District planning effort has been to develop a new way to think about metro area edge problems and to develop a new set of rules and regulations for developments in the non-urban areas near the City of Santa Fe. It became clear early in the planning process that the basic premise of the Plan is that the land, the remarkable countryside, should determine the patterns. The patterns of development should be the patterns of the land, not the other way around. It was obvious that our present rules and regulations do not necessarily fit and encourage this notion. In a most real sense, our present is in conflict with our past. We need to change the norm.
>
> The traditional land use pattern in the region—village—followed the features of the land with agriculture and governance as the organizing principle. The Community College District Plan proposes to follow the features of the land with community centers and connections supporting modern economic development as the organizing principle. The plan seeks to create neighborhoods and a community which can sustain itself over time by building protection of resources. . . .[6]

Benefits and Noteworthy Implementing Features

Implementation of the Community College District Plan promises to provide significant visual, cultural, and fiscal benefits to the county when compared to the random, sprawling development patterns permitted by the county in the past. Specifically, these include the following:

Visual

- Limit development to villages interspersed by open space with a minimum overall ratio of 60% open space to 40% development.
- Establish village character and design as follows:
  - Define its edges clearly;
  - Establish entrance and exit points (gateways);
  - Utilize traditional New Mexican communities to influence community and architectural design;

- Establish a compact development pattern;
- Use human proportions in building scale and height; and
- Use unifying elements such as color, texture, portales, roof design, landscaping, pedestrian amenities, and places for recreational and special events.

Social-Cultural

- *Density within approved new villages:* Must be at a minimum density of 3.5 dwelling units per acre. Minimum lot size is 1,500 square feet in the Village Zone.
- *Creation of a central place of up to 2 acres in size with seating and placement of institutional buildings, businesses, and employment:* This may be in the form of a main street, crossroads, or plaza.
- *Establish inclusionary housing provisions that require a mix of housing types:* Single-family, multi-, manufactured homes, apartments, "mother-in-law" units or guest houses, town or row houses, and compounds as well as a specified percentage of affordable units.
- *Larger lots may be platted on the perimeter to ease transition:* This is in keeping with the larger agricultural and ranching lots that are frequently found at the periphery of traditional communities.

Development Review Process

The development review process for Rancho Viejo, which was approved prior to adoption of the Community College District land use and zoning regulations, involved significant negotiation and numerous variances, because the then-applicable Rural District Zoning required larger lots (2+ acres) and contained other provisions that would have rendered the development as envisioned in the Community College District Plan infeasible.

Subsequently, the county adopted new, detailed zoning regulations to govern all development in the district. These regulations are applied during the normal development review process set forth in the development code applicable to other developments in the county. All development within the district is required to submit a master plan, a preliminary development plan, and a final development plan.

In addition, the requirements of the subdivision regulations apply. The applicant must submit various reports, phasing schedules, and impact analyses (e.g., school impact study). The project may be approved if it conforms to the county growth management plan and district plan as well as all of the district land use regulations. While these regulations are very specific in many regards (e.g., road circulation, irrigation, open space, and other requirements), a significant amount of negotiation will continue to take place to work out the details of development proposals.

Support and Implementation of Legislation

New Mexico state-enabling legislation provides broad authority for the county to plan and regulate development within its borders.[7] To implement the Community College District Plan, the Board of County Commissioners adopted detailed zoning and use regulations, a zoning matrix that contains density and other standards, and a series of detailed maps delineating subdistricts. These regulations were an outgrowth of the negotiated development standards and regulations for Rancho Viejo.

Individual Project—Rancho Viejo

Project Description

Rancho Viejo is 21,000 acres, of which some 5,000-6,000 acres lie within the Santa Fe Community College District. The remaining 15,000 acres lie within the Rural District zone, which allows only larger lot developments. The current development construction comprises approximately 2,500 acres and two villages. The first village includes 334 units on 350 acres of land. Each village is intended to be a contemporary version of a traditional New

3-11 The first two villages at Rancho Viejo are under construction.

Source: Chris Duerksen

Mexico village based on a pattern of town building prescribed in the Spanish "Laws of the Indies" promulgated in 1653. Villages are defined and separated by open space, and are characterized by a variety of housing types and a central core that serves as a community focal point for social, recreational, cultural, and institutional purposes (Figures 3-11 and 3-12).

Lay of the Land and Context

Lying about 1 mile south of the City of Santa Fe, the Rancho Viejo project is situated within a landscape of rolling piñon; juniper-covered hills; broad, open grasslands; and wide, dry arroyos. At the time the project was conceived, the land was zoned Rural District within Santa Fe County. Because of limitations inherent in the former zoning regulations, the project was subject to intense negotiation and was approved with numerous variances to accommodate the vision of a traditional New Mexico village. The project also enjoys proximity to the Santa Fe Community College, which will serve as an anchor for development in the area. This has further served to entice the Institute of Native American Art to locate in the vicinity, just south of the first village in Rancho Viejo.

A number of traditional larger lot subdivisions have already sprung up between Rancho Viejo and the city limits (e.g., Vista Ocasa and Arroyo

Hondo); to the east and south, major residential subdivisions have been carved out that stand in stark juxtaposition to the development patterns envisioned in the Community College District Plan.

Key Features and Elements That Relate to the Western Landscape

The Community College District Plan and the Rancho Viejo master plan contain a number of innovative features that echo some of the historic Spanish and Native American village development patterns discussed in Chapter 1:

- Village boundaries are defined by open space, which, in turn, provides connections to the larger region of villages via trail linkages.
- Each village will be organized around a central square and gathering space formed by two-story buildings, including civic uses and commercial space with second-floor live/work lofts or studios.
- The plan proposes to establish a meaningful housing-to-employment ratio.
- High concentrations of development are located on the level, open meadow. Low-density, single-family houses are carefully sited on wooded slopes between the village and the arroyos.
- Density is concentrated in the central core to provide the greatest number of people within the shortest walking distance to the village center and future transit.
- Streets are generally aligned to provide solar orientation and to focus on distant mountain views.
- Buildings reflect a contemporary version of Santa Fe pueblo architecture, and most homes will be single story to blend into the piñon-juniper forest.
- Indigenous landscape materials are used throughout.
- Water harvested from streets, drainage ways, and rooftops will be reused to irrigate

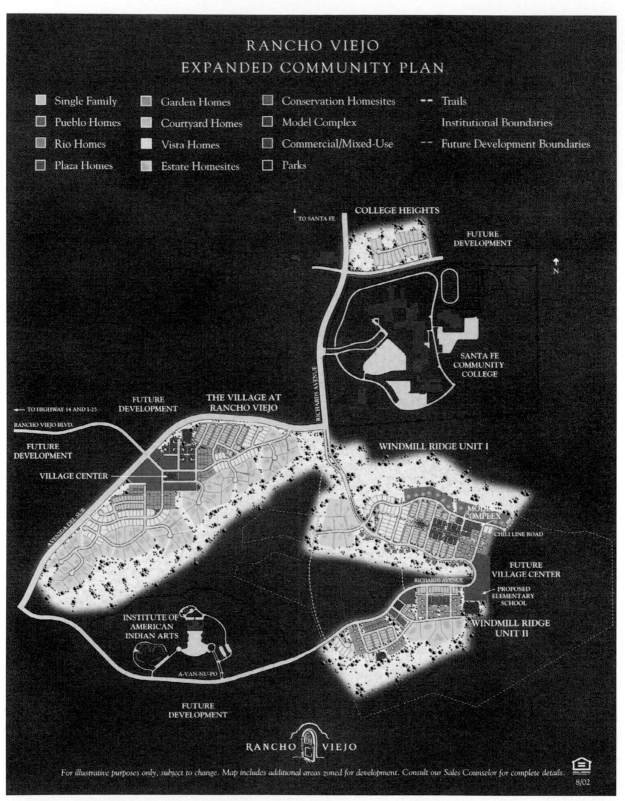

3-12 Large blocks of open space ring Rancho Viejo's villages.

Source: Rancho Viejo, SunCor Development Corporation (2000)

common areas, playfields, and commercial/industrial areas (Figures 3-13, 3-14 and 3-15).

Open Space Preservation

Approximately 50% of the project is contiguous open space, forming a clear edge surrounding the village and providing future separation of additional villages. Trails run through the open space,

3-13   Rancho Viejo has an extensive trail system that links neighborhoods and villages.

Source: Chris Duerksen

3-15   Natural landscaping and street trees are drought-tolerant and add much to the development's curb appeal.

Source: Chris Duerksen

3-14   The town squares at Rancho Viejo echo the "Laws of the Indies" and will provide a centrally located community focal point.

Source: Chris Duerksen

3-16   Rancho Viejo's trail system receives kudos from residents (and their pooches).

Source: Chris Duerksen

providing for recreational opportunities and linking the villages and the community college campus (Figure 3-16).

Process of Design and Approvals

The Rancho Viejo project was proposed in advance of the adoption of the 1999 Growth Management Plan under the then-existing "rural" zoning, which would have allowed 750 dwelling units with a 2½-acre minimum lot size. Clustering was not allowed under the zoning regulations.

The vision of the current landowners and the county was much different from this rural sprawl scenario, and the concept for Rancho Viejo developed in a symbiotic way, which resulted in a project that currently is substantially in conformity with the policies of the Community College District Plan and zoning regulations. According to the developers, the project served as a model for what the county envisions for development in its plan.

Initially, the first village required numerous variances from the then-applicable Rural District zoning. However, with adoption of the Community College District Plan and implementing zoning regulations, subsequent villages should no longer require extensive variances from development standards or extended negotiations. Many of the concepts embodied in the Rancho Viejo master plan regarding open space, uses, landscaping, affordable housing, and other key issues are directly reflected in the zoning regulations.

According to the developers, key factors in the successful design review process were an experienced community developer and clearly articulated community values, which were derived from an extensive visioning process with citizens, landowners, and consultants. The design consultants emphasize that a smart business plan was key in ensuring a quality design project. The business plan allows the owners to continue operating the property as a working ranch, and participate in development profits as land for the villages is taken out of the ranch and developed according to the master plan. This arrangement avoids the typical prohibitive carrying costs of large-scale land development.

Market Review

Homes are marketed to a broad segment of the population, ranging from starter homes that are priced in the low $100,000s to high-end production models at $280,000 and estates in the $300,000-$400,000 range. First-year sales projections have exceeded expectations by 40%. The developers believe this is due largely to the fact that no other comparable development is offering as much in terms of community amenities. The developer anticipates that future sales will be in the range of 120-150 units per year.

Success Relative to the Intent of Local Government Regulations

County planning staff evaluate the Rancho Viejo project in terms of how it successfully measures up to the county policies and vision, as well as a project that favorably helped shape the direction of the county policy with respect to its vision and policies for countryside development. It is viewed as a model project and in many ways embodies the policies of the county.

Evaluation

The Rancho Viejo project embodies a number of appropriate western development patterns from Native American, Spanish colonial, and American settlement as detailed below. It is clearly preferable to the scattered large-lot (2.5+ acres) rural development that has been the predominant form of rural development in the county. Rancho Viejo provides substantial amounts of contiguous open space, and employs a variety of environmentally sensitive practices such as the use of drought-tolerant native vegetation and water recycling. The general form of the villages, with development oriented around small public squares, echoes Spanish and Native American development patterns.

However, some observers question whether the entire Community College District represents an appropriate development pattern. The community college campus was built several miles from any existing development outside city boundaries with relatively poor access. It has become a magnet for more outlying edge development like Rancho Viejo. They argue that a more appropriate development pattern would be denser, more compact growth contiguous with existing development in the City of Santa Fe.

Moreover, given the overall low density of the Rancho Viejo development, the county's goals of significant employment and commercial development within the villages to serve residents may be extremely difficult to realize due to market realities, despite the best of intentions. Additionally, while portions of the villages are laid out in a traditional grid pattern with interconnections, others look suspiciously like typical suburban cul-de-sacs dressed up in Santa Fe pueblo-style architecture, with little resemblance to development patterns in old Santa Fe neighborhoods.

Western Rural Development Pattern Language

A number of significant historical western development patterns may be distilled from the Santa Fe County/Rancho Viejo case study. Moreover, the project teaches some important lessons and suggests additional patterns that respond to modern land use planning and environmental concerns and objectives. Both these historical and contemporary lessons are summarized and categorized below, with explanatory comments provided as appropriate.

Regional Development Patterns

- *In the face of development pressures, preserve country towns and villages, and emulate their development patters in growth areas.*

The Santa Fe County Growth Management Plan explicitly seeks to preserve traditional villages while encouraging new growth to incorporate historical patterns.

- *Encourage the growth of new, self-contained towns in a dispersed manner across the countryside, allowing ample open space between them. Concentrate development in a relatively compact manner within the towns.*

Rancho Viejo represents a vision for relatively self-contained towns with commercial services and employment opportunities, although it is not clear whether the market will respond. The village boundary is sharply defined by open space that the preferred development pattern envisioned in the Community College District Plan. However, existing and approved large-lot rural subdivisions between city boundaries and Rancho Viejo will to a certain extent blur this vision.

Town

Public Places

- *Create public places appropriately sized for the community and within walking distance of all citizens.*

The centrally located plazas of the first two villages are within easy walking distance of the majority of residents. The plazas are sized and oriented in the tradition and dictates of the "Laws of the Indies."

- *Concentrate community facilities around public "squares" at the intersection of community pathways or roadways.*

A defining feature of Rancho Viejo is the central community public plazas that will incorporate community civic, market, and employment functions. However, no civic buildings are yet planned or constructed and, as noted above, it is questionable whether the market will support any substantial commercial or employment uses within the villages. This is a challenge confronting even existing neighborhood commercial uses in more densely populated urban areas, and not just a problem unique to Rancho Viejo.

- *Reserve sufficient space within the core of each neighborhood or town for at least several public community facilities; at least one should serve as a visibly prominent civic focal point.*

Land and building space is reserved for future community functions. The developer has "jumpstarted" this process by locating the sales office in the central core, although it is still questionable whether there is sufficient population in the villages to justify any government offices or civic uses. The community college campus is not within easy walking distance of either of the first two villages.

Streets/Access

- *In hotter climates, construct narrow streets to maximize shade in public areas.*

The development has much narrower streets than surrounding suburban subdivisions, and street trees have been planted to provide shade in the future. These elements are required for future development in the zoning regulations for the Community College District.

Public Realm

- *Provide and incorporate common areas for clusters of homes.*

All homes have easy access to the main village plazas, as well as to the surrounding open space, through an extensive trail network.

- *Create an intimate relationship between buildings and the street by placing buildings close to the public right-of-way. In the central portion of towns, require that the majority of buildings be constructed immediately adjacent to the public right-of-way; when multiple buildings are constructed in this manner, a sense of enclosed urban space is created.*

The central buildings will be two stories high and built with little or no setbacks to the street. In most of the residential areas, houses are close to the street as well, in the tradition of Santa Fe neighborhoods. Overall, the feeling of the villages is much more "village" than suburban and provides a welcome contrast to other development in the county.

Community

- *Provide diverse housing opportunities, including primary housing.*

Another term to describe this pattern is "inclusionary housing." This concept is promoted as a conscious strategy in Santa Fe County and is evident in the Rancho Viejo project. The villages have a wide mix of housing types and prices, which should result in a very diverse community. This is consistent with the traditional New Mexico village model, and stands in contrast to surrounding subdivisions in which most of the homes are of similar size on similar lots with similar prices. The new zone district regulations require a mix of housing types and inclusion of affordable housing in that mix.

- *Establish public transportation systems within and between towns.*

The Community College District is served by the regional Santa Fe public transit system, although the area itself has relatively poor access via a two-lane road that has no interchange with nearby Interstate 25 at the present time. Given the low overall density of the Rancho Viejo development, service by public transit is questionable. The auto will remain the primary form of transit.

Environmental

- *Limit the population size and geographical extent of towns in a sustainable manner suggested by the natural and cultural geography of the region.*

The limits of natural geography are respected in the siting of Rancho Viejo. The cultural geography of New Mexico strongly suggests a dispersed village settlement pattern. The villages represent a manageable size from an environmental and cultural perspective but, as noted above, it remains to be seen whether the goal of providing neighborhood commercial services and some employment opportunities in the villages will pan out.

- *Maintain agricultural land in close proximity to town dwellers.*

The open space surrounding the village presents an opportunity for managed cattle grazing as well as recreational opportunities. It is one of the strongest points of the development.

- *Harvest and conserve water through simple methods and incorporate them into the design of buildings and developments.*

Water is collected from roadways and rooftops to irrigate common and commercial landscaping in the villages. Moreover, drought-resistant landscaping is utilized. These features are embodied in the new zone district regulations.

- *Protect wildlife habitat and movement corridors.*

The open space surrounding the village preserves large blocks of contiguous land for wildlife habitat as well as providing recreational opportunities for residents.

- *Plant trees to provide shade in the hot summer months.*

Street trees have been planted throughout the villages, and drought-tolerant species have been used. The zone district regulations require planting of street trees in future villages.

Architecture/Design

Form

- *Design building profiles that mimic the profiles of the natural landscape: in steep, mountainous areas, steeply pitched rooflines are appropriate; in areas that are flat or rolling, a lower profile is fitting.*

Residential structures have low-pitched or flat roofs that reflect the relatively low-profile rolling hills.

- *Limit the majority of buildings to four stories high or less. Taller buildings in small towns and rural areas should be exceptional and reserved for cultural or civic purposes.*

No buildings will exceed four stories.

- *Build arcades at the edge of buildings to provide shelter from sun and rain, and to ease the transition between public and private space.*

The inclusion of portales ("arcades"), a traditional New Mexico building feature, is encouraged.

- *Reflect indigenous architectural patterns in contemporary construction as a way to connect with the region's cultural history.*

The use of the Spanish pueblo style and natural colors/materials ensures that the village has an authentic character (Figure 3-17).

Color and Materials

- *Use natural materials in a manner that reflects an organic integrity and harmony with the natural surroundings. Stone and wood are often appropriate as the primary construction material.*
- *Avoid the use of a multiplicity of building materials, colors, and architectural styles. Doing so also serves to produce a commonality of architectural style.*
- *As a first choice, use natural, earth-tone colors; however, do not do so exclusively. With an appropriate building profile, brighter colors may serve as a beautiful counterpoint to the natural landscape.*

The entire development embraces these principles, and the sum is a visually harmonious village character. It stands in stark contrast to the often hodgepodge development that characterizes other edge rural areas of the county.

3-17 Rancho Viejo's common architectural style gives the development a familiar, traditional character.

Source: Chris Duerksen

Site Design

- *Orient buildings and groups of buildings to take advantage of the sun for winter warmth. Place buildings to the north of outdoor spaces and keep outdoor spaces to the south, with opportunities for dappled shade from trees or trellises.*

Some of the main streets in the villages are oriented to capture the sun in winter, although others are in a more random suburban pattern. To date, no special effort appears to have been made to orient homes or clusters of homes to take advantage of sun for winter heating. The new district zoning regulations do include what is termed a "Sustainable Village Development" option that provides incentives for placing structures on south-facing slopes that are designed to use passive solar gain (Figure 3-18).

3-18 Some of Rancho Viejo's houses take full advantage of sun for passive heating.

Source: Chris Duerksen

CONTACTS

Santa Fe County
Jack Kolkmeyer
102 Grant Ave., P.O. Box 276, Santa Fe, NM 87504
(505) 986-6336
www.co.santa-fe.nm.us

Rancho Viejo de Santa Fe
Bob Taunton
(505) 983-6921
www.ranchoviejo.com

Design Workshop
Faith Okuma (505) 982-8399
Joe Porter (970) 925-8354
www.designworkshop.com

SOURCES

Interviews with Jack Kolkmeyer, Planning Director for Santa Fe County; Bob Taunton, project developer; Faith Okuma and Joe Porter, planning consultants, February 2000.

Site visit, June 2002.

The Santa Fe Community College District Plan, October 2000.

CASE STUDY 4

Teton County, Wyoming: Land Development Regulations

MELODY RANCH

In Wyoming's high country, an innovative set of land development regulations is helping to shape residential development to coexist with and complement the area's spectacular scenery, traditional ranching activity, and wildlife habitat, while providing badly needed affordable housing. The Melody Ranch development illustrates how it can work.

Geographical, Climatic, and Social Setting

Teton County, located in northwest Wyoming, is mountainous and heavily forested, with several broad river valleys, the most well known containing the Snake River. At its center is the town of Jackson. It has some of the most stunning scenery in the world and a high concentration of critical wildlife habitat. At an average elevation of well over 6,000 feet above sea level, winters are long and cold in most of the county. Its lower valleys provide wintering ground for a wide range of wildlife.

The rise of the Teton Range, as well as the erosion caused by eons of glaciation, have created the conditions that allow several plant communities to thrive—from ribbons of green riparian plants bordering rivers and streams, to sagebrush flats, lodgepole pine and spruce forests, subalpine meadows, and alpine stone fields. The wide range of plant communities creates habitat for a variety of animals, including larger mammals such as black bear, grizzly bear, elk, moose, deer, and bison. The Trumpeter Swan, a threatened species, finds important habitat here.

The highest elevation is Grand Teton at 13,766 feet above sea level and the lowest elevations are at 6,200 feet. Average annual rainfall is 17 inches and snowfall 150 inches. The county encompasses a portion of Yellowstone National Park and all of Grand Teton National Park. All told, the federal government owns 97% of the county. The remaining private land is under very intense development pressure. Not surprisingly, its economy is primarily tourist-based. The county has an estimated 2000 population of 18,250—an increase of 7,250, or approximately 80%, over the 1990 population of 11,000.[8]

Regulatory Standards and Planning Processes

Introductory Overview

The Teton County Land Development Regulations are a unified development code that implements both land subdivision and zoning functions. Development review is mandatory and subject to approvals by the Planning Commission and the Board of County Commissioners. Some projects qualify for internal review only.

History of Regulations and Process

The current process was adopted in 1994 as part of the Land Development Regulations and new Comprehensive Plan. The community embarked upon adopting a new plan and regulations in 1990 in response to a transportation plan study that indicated the zoning in effect at that time would allow too much development in a pattern necessitating huge roadway projects, along with other character-damaging impacts. The Town of Jackson and Teton County partnered and hired a consultant to produce a new Comprehensive Plan and a new set of Land Development Regulations. Four years of public meetings and public hearings involving the town and county staff, consultants, planning commissions, and elected officials produced the current process.

Desired Goals of the Standards

The Land Development Regulations implement two broad priorities: the protection of natural resources and scenic resources. The Natural Resources Overlay (NRO) District is essentially a composite of mapped critical winter habitat for elk, moose, grizzlies, and deer, plus habitat for bald eagles. Teton County's elk herd is one of the largest in North America with approximately 15,000 animals. Teton County is also home to approximately 215 Trumpeter Swans.

Specifically, the purpose of the NRO District is to protect and maintain the following:

- the migration routes and crucial winter ranges of elk and mule deer;
- the crucial winter habitat of moose;
- the nesting areas and winter habitat of Trumpeter Swans;
- the spawning areas of cutthroat trout;

- the nesting areas and crucial winter habitat of bald eagles; and
- the natural resources and biodiversity that supports the wildlife population.

The Scenic Resources Overlay (SRO) District identifies scenic views and areas of the county judged to be "image-setting." The SRO District identifies areas in which ridgetop development (skylining) is prohibited. These areas are protected by standards requiring that development be located out of the foreground of a scenic view (meadows) or off ridgelines. The standards also provide guidelines for development that cannot be located outside of protected areas.

From a social-cultural point of view, the purpose of the overlays is to protect areas of the county that are critical to community character, both for quality of life and preservation of the tourist economy.

Benefits and Noteworthy Implementing Features

The Land Development Regulations provide significant environmental, wildlife, visual, and cultural benefits to the county. Specifically, these include the following:

Environmental

The regulations prohibit development in 10-year floodplains and wetlands. Wetlands may be reconfigured in a limited manner in some cases, and on-site mitigation must be provided wherever possible at a ratio of 1½ acres of new wetland for every acre filled. Stream buffers are intended to protect the riparian plant community. Buffers must be no less than 50 feet, and up to 150 feet in some instances. Buffers for natural lakes and ponds are based on the same criteria. Buffer setbacks from specified resources are as follows:

- *Rivers:* 150 feet
- *Streams and the riparian plant community:* 50 feet
- *Natural lake/pond:* 50 feet

• *Wetlands:* 30 feet

Wildlife

• *Protection of crucial elk and mule deer migration routes and winter ranges:* No development may occur within these identified areas unless the applicant can demonstrate the project will not have any detrimental effect.

• *Protection of crucial moose winter habitat:* No development within such areas unless it can be demonstrated that it will have no detrimental effect.

• *Protection of Trumpeter Swan's nests:* No development may occur within a radius of 300 feet.

• *Protection of Bald Eagle's nests:* No development may occur within a radius of 400 meters of a standing/occupied, active, or inactive Bald Eagle's nest.

• *Fencing:* All fencing must comply with wildlife-friendly fencing standards.

Visual

There are several options for locating development: (1) at the rear of the foreground; (2) at the edges of the foreground; (3) behind existing stands of vegetation; (4) behind or built into a natural topographic break; or (5) clustered in meadows. Specific scenic areas are identified in the land use regulations, and development is subject to the following standards, which recognize and address a variety of scenarios:

1. For development located at *rear edge of foreground* behind meadow or pasture:
   • Locate it at the greatest possible distance from a major public road, and where applicable, adjacent to existing development.
   • Locate it at the rear edge of a meadow or pasture, where such meets the toe of the hillside, or on a relatively less steep, lower hillside area behind the meadow.
   • Separate developed areas such that the maximum continuous piece of open space is preserved.
   • Supplementary vegetation must be provided where the proposed development is located within 1,320 feet of a state highway or county-designated scenic road. Native vegetation shall be planted to mimic either the existing species composition and pattern of growth or traditional farm and ranchstead planting patterns of the American West.

2. For development at the *edges* of the foreground where there is an open meadow or pasture, developed areas should preserve the maximum continuous piece of open space and provide supplementary vegetation within a quarter mile of a state highway or county-designated scenic road.

3. For development located *behind existing stands of vegetation*, the scale of development shall not interrupt or obscure the existing occurring stand of vegetation behind which it is located, and supplementary vegetation shall be added as needed. Existing vegetation must be preserved to the maximum extent possible.

4. For development *behind or built into a natural topographic break*, the scale must be subordinate to the natural change in topography, and earth moving must be minimized to extend a naturally occurring topographic change and screen the development, but not create a new, man-made landform.

5. For development within *irrigated pasture or meadows*, it must not preclude view of designated vistas from the public road to the rear portions of the foreground view.

It must provide clustered design, and native vegetation must be planted that mimics either the existing species composition and pattern of growth, or traditional farm and ranchstead planting patterns of the American West.

Additional guidelines related to the reduction of visual impacts include the following:

- *Earth-tone materials shall be used.*
- *Use of traditional ranch colors, which may include shades of red or brown, may be approved for ranch compound-type developments.*
- *Roof colors shall be similar to that of surrounding vegetation or land features.*
- *Reflective roof materials shall not be used.*
- *Avoid dividing meadows and pastures with roads or driveways.*
- *Utilize soft edges. Avoid straight-line corridors created by roads or driveways that are incongruous with the natural setting.*

Skyline

The regulations prohibit penetration of the skyline on buttes and hillsides, as viewed from any public road. In the case of an existing lot where, if no other siting alternative is available that complies with the standards, development may penetrate the skyline if:

- it does not exceed 20 feet above the original grade;
- the mass is broken into distinct, smaller forms;
- the roof form mimics the natural form of the hillside or butte;
- earth-tone materials and colors are used; and
- landscape screening is provided where appropriate.

Cultural

Ranching and farming are agricultural uses that formed the original basis for the com-munities in Teton County. A large part of the private lands in Teton County are still used in agriculture. Agriculture is crucial to the wildlife and scenic qualities and western atmosphere of Teton County, and therefore to the tourist-based economy. Every major wildlife species is dependent on habitat provided by ranch lands. The county views the maintenance of agricultural lands as the most efficient and inexpensive method to preserve open space, which is crucial to the wildlife and scenic resources. The ranchers will keep their land undeveloped and unpopulated, control trespassing and poaching, maintain waterways and water rights, and manage vegetation—all with no expense to the public.

Development Review Process

The development plan process comprises four steps:

1. *Preapplication conference* with staff and, on occasion, with the Planning Commission and Board of County Commissioners;
2. *Sketch plan review with public hearings* before both the Planning Commission and the Board of County Commissioners;
3. *Final Development Plan review with public hearings* before both the Planning Commission and the Board of County Commissioners; and
4. *Plat review and approval at a hearing* with the Board of County Commissioners. Internal review processes and shortened public review processes are provided based on project size.

An Environmental Analysis is required for all land development applications that are in the NRO and/or SRO Districts, and for any application that disturbs an area of 1 acre or more, and at a minimum must comprise the following four components:

- on protected resources, containing review of water bodies, 10-year floodplains, wetlands, mesic and nonmesic habitats, and mitigation plans for any impacts;
- a wildlife component required for all lands within a development that fall within the NRO District and must identify critical winter habitat or migration routes;
- lands within the SRO District that must contain a visual component, which includes a visual analysis; and
- an agricultural component that identifies the location of agricultural land and describes related agricultural operations, such as irrigation practices, that occur on the land.

Support and Implementation of Legislation

State-enabling legislation for land use planning in Wyoming is modest. When working on the adoption of these regulations, many believed that a transfer of development rights (TDR) system would accomplish much of what the community is trying to achieve in land resource preservation and patterns of land development. However, the enabling legislation was deemed too vague to guarantee the viability of a TDR program, thus the county did not adopt an entire land protection scheme based on a mechanism that may or may not be legislatively viable. Instead, it relied on a more traditional zoning/subdivision regulation approach.

Individual Project—Melody Ranch

Project Description

Located 2 miles south of the incorporated boundaries of Jackson, Melody Ranch is a purely residential development of 893 acres (Figure 3-19). It will ultimately accommodate a total of 401 dwelling units, of which 11 represent existing ranch dwellings, 262 are market-rate housing, and 128 are affordable in accordance with the county definition. Lot sizes within the market portion of the

development range from 0.22 acres to 4.79 acres. The affordable housing component comprises both single-family homes and townhouses, of which several were built by Habitat for Humanity.

Lay of the Land and Context

Melody Ranch lies primarily within a flat valley that falls away gently from U.S. Highway 191/89. Much of the land currently continues as a working ranch and is largely hay meadow. As such, it is a highly visible feature of the landscape south of Jackson. A large portion is cleared of vegetation (except for crops). Mature deciduous trees in the typical pattern of western ranch clusters surround the ranch buildings.

The dominant features of the land include the meandering Snake River and various stream tributaries lying within a broad meadow, all of which lie in the foreground of a dramatic mountain backdrop. The riparian habitat adjacent to the Snake River is largely intact. Several ranch-building clusters dot the meadow. The land is largely free of significant vegetation. Two wetland areas are adjacent to Flat Creek. Critical habitat is identified for Trumpeter Swans at two locations along the creek. A major elk migration corridor emanates from Horsethief Canyon to the west.

Key Features and Elements That Relate to the Western Landscape

The ranch is typical of those in the area, providing broad vistas across the valley floor to the steeply rising mountains. Scattered across the land are various clusters of ranch buildings connected by ranch roads, and fencing constructed of barbed wire and post-and-pole. The ranch contains sizable critical wildlife habitat and movement corridors that are preserved in accordance with the county's NRO District.

Scenic views from the highway are preserved by ranching operations and fields in the foreground; intense development is placed in the northern portion of the ranch with intervening

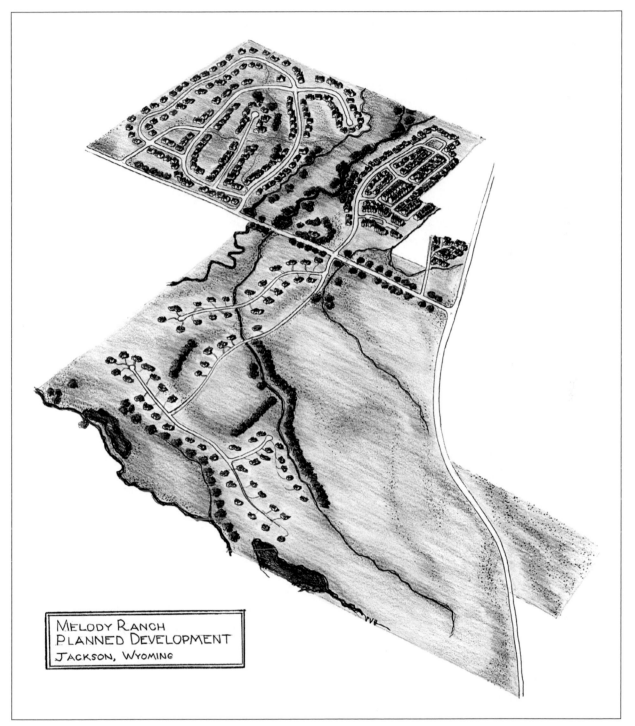

3-19 Melody Ranch Planned Development, Teton County, Wyoming.

Source: James van Hemert

3-20   Melody Ranch's preserved foreground, looking west from U.S. Highway 191/89.

Source: James van Hemert

3-21   Melody Ranch's preserved foreground looking southwest. Several home sites will ultimately be scattered beyond the trees.

Source: James van Hemert

fields in the foreground (Figure 3-20). Low-density development is placed in a subservient position to the topography at a considerable distance from the highway view. Final development in this portion of the ranch will appear similar to the existing ranch cluster pattern (Figure 3-21).

3-22   Melody Ranch workforce housing. Note the varying roof pitches and traditional ranch colors. The aggregate roofline profile mimics that of the mountains in the background.

Source: James van Hemert

The workforce housing cluster is an exception: it lies immediately adjacent to the highway but consistent with existing development immediately to the north. The impact, however, is mitigated with appropriate architecture reflecting the color, varying roof pitches, and clustered appearance of local ranches. The end result is a pleasing, aggregate-building profile that mimics the mountainous background (Figure 3-22).

Specific criteria found within the covenants include:

- building design features compatible with the existing ranches characteristic of the area;
- materials compatible with the high alpine environment;
- low, rambling, and informal structures relative to the terrain;
- exterior materials of rough or resawn natural wood, peeled log, stone, exposed aggregate concrete, or other similar rough-textured, natural materials;
- exterior colors for wall and roof surfaces subdued and in the earth-tone range; tradi-

tional ranch colors of deep barn red, forest green, and ochre where appropriate;

- maximum height of 28 feet; and
- minimum roof pitch of 6:12; all primary roofs with a minimum overhang of 2 feet.

Open Space Preservation

Open space is preserved primarily within the foreground of the highway viewshed and comprises agricultural, environmentally significant land, as well as important winter wildlife habitat. These lands comprise 463 acres, or 52% of the land. An additional 15% has been preserved as recreational and equestrian open space benefiting the residents of the development.

Process of Design and Approvals

The proposal as approved is zoned Neighborhood Conservation–Planned Unit Development District and falls within both the NRO and SRO Zone Districts. The NRO and SRO were drafted when Melody Ranch was first submitted as a development proposal, but they were not adopted at that time. They were adopted, however, by the time the final development plan for Melody Ranch was approved. The entire property falls within the SRO Zone, and the extreme southeast corner also falls within the NRO Zone, representing significant winter elk habitat.

The base density under the previous Land Development Regulations allowed 255 dwelling units. A density bonus of 57% was granted for an additional 146 dwelling units (128 affordable and 18 market rate). Final approval netted 401 dwelling units. A primary development objective is to cluster residential development in order to maintain an active ranch operation on the southern portion of the property.

The initial development proposal was less dense—with 229 market dwelling units—but included a village commercial center and 75% open space. Through the process review and hearings, the project grew to 273 market dwelling units, encompassing 893 acres, dropped the village commercial center, and added 128 affordable housing units, meeting an important county objective to provide a full range of housing. A smaller percentage of open space represented a trade-off for affordable housing.

Market Review

The development is doing very well from a market standpoint. It has built and sold all the affordable units anticipated in Teton Sage, the development on the exaction parcel for Melody Ranch. However, there are three other lots that will eventually be conveyed to the county for affordable housing development, as Melody Ranch continues to develop under its phasing plan.

The county has already built and sold all of its affordable housing units. Two more affordable components are expected to be developed by entities other than the Melody Ranch Development Company. A number of the lots are also being sold as "attainable" lots, which are priced a little higher than the county's definition of affordable but still below the market. The developer reports that sales are doing at least as well as other similar developments in the area, and in fact may be doing better at later build-out stages because of the overall amenity package, particularly the open space and architectural appeal of the homes.

Success Relative to the Intent of Local Government Regulations

Strictly from visual and natural resource points of view, the development as it is planned and being executed is apparently falling within both the intent and the letter of the regulations. Large tracts of open space and a working ranch have been preserved.

However, county planning staff point out that Melody Ranch was planned and approved prior to the community fully coming to terms with the fact that a single-use, residential, suburban, density land use pattern that is prevalent in the county—one that Melody, to some degree, perpetuates—places serious demands on the county transportation system and other community services. The community is attempting to change the old pattern by encouraging integrated, mixed-use developments featuring both housing and neighborhood commercial services that can be served by transit and other transportation modes.

Evaluation

County staff observe that implementation of its Land Development Regulations is going very well. Some relatively simple development applications seem to get caught up in a longer and more complex review process than warranted, and some larger scale projects warrant greater review than the requirements set forth.

When the regulations were originally adopted, digital mapping and visual simulation were not required. The regulations will likely be amended in the near future to require such critical and helpful information for developments of over an acre or any development within the NRO and SRO Districts.

Western Rural Development Pattern Language

A number of significant historical western development patterns may be distilled from the Teton County/Melody Ranch case study. Moreover, the project teaches some important lessons and suggests additional patterns that respond to modern land use planning and environmental concerns and objectives. Both these historical and contemporary lessons are summarized and categorized below with explanatory comments provided as appropriate.

Town

Streets/Access

- *Establish public transportation systems within and between towns.*

The concentrated pattern of development in the northern portion of Melody Ranch allows for future efficient expansion of public transit. However, the location of a substantial number of housing units 2 miles from the population center in Jackson means that the project will generate significant auto traffic and place further demands on an already strained local transportation system.

Environmental

- *Maintain agricultural lands in close proximity to town dwellers.*

Significant Melody Ranch acreage is preserved in active agricultural production in perpetuity adjacent to the Town of Jackson.

- *Limit the population size and geographical extent of towns in a sustainable manner suggested by the natural and cultural geography of the region.*

The Melody Ranch development respects and is limited by the natural geography and wildlife habitat of Teton County.

Dispersed Rural Settlement

Environmental

- *Protect wildlife habitat and enhance wildlife movement corridors in a manner that allows for continued free movement of the broadest possible variety of species.*

As development increasingly encroaches on critical wildlife habitat and movement corridors, wildlife are either disappearing altogether from areas they once frequented or their numbers are seriously diminished. For many animal species, the American West is one of the last places with sufficient unfragmented habitat. Melody Ranch accommodates wildlife movement and preserves a sufficiently significant portion of habitat to protect the regional integrity of the habitat.

Cultural

- *Preserve and integrate historic ranching operations.*

Integration of historic ranching operations provides a critical link with the past while preserving a cultural way of life unique to the American West. It further serves to maintain a distinct feature of the landscape.

Visual

- *Locate buildings at the toes of slopes and edges of meadows in a manner that allows for natural windbreaks and creates a feeling of shelter.*

With the exception of the workforce housing cluster, the foreground and middle-ground meadows are preserved. This pattern also serves to protect visually significant open space.

- *Preserve and protect significant foreground views along significant "viewing platforms or passageways" such as public gathering places and major roadways.*

Melody Ranch provides a good example of preserving important signature views that characterize a geographical region.

Architecture/Design

Form

- *Design buildings that mimic the profiles of the natural landscape: in steep, mountainous areas, steeply pitched rooflines are appropriate; in areas that are flat or rolling, a lower profile is fitting.*

Required minimum roof pitches of 6:12 establish a significant angular element in the roof form reflecting the mountain background. The 28-foot height limitation is consistent with traditional ranch architecture.

- *Avoid building large, monolithic buildings. Buildings should comprise a complex of smaller buildings or parts that manifest their own internal social facts.*

The architectural form of the workforce housing cluster clearly reflects the various functions within the homes.

- *Arrange roofs so that each distinct roof corresponds to an identifiable social entity in the building. Place the largest roofs—those that are highest and have the largest span—over the largest, most important, and most communal spaces; build the lesser roofs off these largest and highest roofs. Allow for and expect additions to be made over time.*

The roof forms of the workforce housing clearly illustrate this pattern, with the central portion of the structures having the largest, most prominent roof.

- *Vary roof pitches, with shallower outer pitches.*

The roof pitches of the workforce housing are steepest for the central portion of buildings, while lesser, adjacent "lean-tos" have shallower pitches and are visually subservient. This style mimics historic ranch architecture.

Color and Materials

- *Use natural materials in a manner that reflects an organic integrity and harmony with the natural surroundings. Stone and wood are often appropriate as the primary construction material.*

Traditional board-and-batten siding is used for the workforce housing. Covenants governing design of single-family homes require the use of natural materials, with a focus on rough lumber and stone.

- *As a first choice, use natural, earth-tone colors; however, do not do so exclusively. With an appropriate building profile, bright historical colors such as red, green, or ochre may serve as a beautiful counterpoint to the natural landscape.*

The covenants require first and foremost earth-tone colors; however, historic ranch colors of deep red and forest green are also permitted.

Other Elements

- *Use locally available natural materials in the construction of fences that are unobtrusive and reflect historic character.*

The traditional ranch fencing remains.

CONTACTS

Teton County Planning Department
Teresa de Groh
P.O. Box 1727, Jackson, WY 83001
(307) 733-3959
ww.tetonwyo.org

Melody Ranch Development Company
David Quinn
(307) 733-3559
www.melodyranch.com

SOURCES

Interviews with Teresa de Groh, Teton County Planning Department staff, and David Quinn, project developer, February 2000.

Teton County Land Development Regulations, Natural Resources Overlay District, and Scenic Resources Overlay District.

CASE STUDY 5

Larimer County, Colorado: Rural Land Use Process

LUDWICK FARM

Free of the use of financial subsidies and complex regulatory mechanisms, the Larimer County Land Use Process maximizes private initiative through an incentive-based land development program that seeks to preserve productive agricultural land while allowing for limited development. This program helps to ensure a financial return to the landowner. The Ludwick Farm Rural Land Use Plan illustrates the success of this approach.

Geographical, Climatic, and Social Setting

Larimer County lies in north central Colorado, extending from the plains to the Continental Divide. The county encompasses ranch land, mountainous forest, and irrigated farmland. Over 50% of Larimer County's land is publicly owned, a significant portion of which includes Rocky Mountain National Park. The climate is arid, with 14 inches of precipitation in an average year on the plains and foothills. Higher levels of rain and snowfall occur in the mountains. In 2000, the population was estimated at 256,000, a 35% increase over the 1990 population of 186,000.[9] Its diversified economy includes strong agriculture, tourism, education, and high-tech industry sectors.

Regulatory Standards and Planning Processes

Introductory Overview

The Rural Land Use Process is an alternative to traditional 35-acre parcel development, a process over which Larimer County has very little review authority due to statutory limitations on subdivision review. (See "Support and Implementation of Legislation" below.) The program invites landowners to submit to county review in exchange for additional development rights, or "density bonuses," subject to specific criteria. The process relies on a cooperative approach to review with the lure of incentives to encourage development that promotes rural land preservation. The process is voluntary, user-friendly, and flexible. In exchange, a formal, multistage subdivision process is waived. The process may be used in the context of any residential zone district in the county.

History of Regulations and Process

The process was developed by a diverse and broad stakeholder group of Larimer County citizens in response to an ever-increasing loss of prime agricultural land and scenic open space to 35-acre land divisions. The county commissioners in 1996 formally adopted the process. The program is managed by the Rural Land Use Center, under the supervision of the Planning and Building Division, and is staffed by three planning professionals.

Desired Goals of the Standards

The standards seek primarily to achieve preservation and protection of contiguous agricultural land in a manner that both allows for continued, economically viable agricultural practices as well as limited development. Secondarily, the process seeks to preserve and protect critical lands such as forests, watersheds, wildlife habitat, riparian areas, scenic views and corridors, and historic and archeological sites.

Under the process, two-thirds of a property can be maintained in agricultural production or as private open space utilizing conservation easements, or protective covenants. The process enables homes to be carefully sited: either clustered in areas of the property to accommodate more homes; or dispersed on sites well suited for individual homes, on lots that are 2 acres or larger, depending on the soil's ability to handle on-site septic systems. This specific site planning maintains open space, reduces infrastructure needs, retains land for agricultural uses, and provides wildlife habitat. The preserved land must remain free of development for a minimum of 40 years. In many cases, the preservation is for perpetuity.

Benefits and Noteworthy Implementing Features

The benefits of the Rural Land Use Process can be summarized as follows.

Environmental

Critical natural areas and wildlife habitat may be restored, preserved, and enhanced in a comprehensive manner.

Visual

Land may be creatively developed in a manner that preserves the rural character of the county.

Cultural

The program achieves preservation of contiguous and economically viable agricultural operations.

Process

Development review process is faster and less restrictive than other county development processes and offers property owners a more predictable outcome.

Economic

In return for efforts and increased costs to retain unique land characteristics, owners avoid a multistage subdivision review process. In most cases, additional "bonus" housing units may be granted. The majority of development engineering work occurs after preliminary project approval. Sites planning for cluster development can better utilize existing infrastructure and potentially reduce total infrastructure costs.

Development Review Process

The process for preliminary approval takes approximately three to five months. Upon approval, a landowner or developer has up to 365 days to complete the final plat. The steps in the process are itemized as follows:

1. The landowner meets with the director of the Rural Land Use Center to discuss objectives and alternatives. A site visit is conducted for the purpose of developing an initial development idea.
2. Upon completion of a conceptual plan, a discussion-oriented meeting is held with the Rural Land Use Board.

3. The plan is reviewed by interested governmental agencies, utilities, and service districts that may be affected by the development.

4. The conceptual plan is presented at a community meeting with a request for comments. Neighboring property owners are notified of this meeting by mail.

5. After comments are received, adjustments to the conceptual plan might be requested.

6. A proposal is sent to the Board of County Commissioners for preliminary approval.

7. Full development plans and documents must be submitted for final approval within 365 days of the commissioner's preliminary approval.

8. On-site improvements may begin immediately after final approval.

Approval criteria include the following:

1. To be eligible for the process, a minimum of 70 acres of land is required. It may be combined with neighboring ownership.

2. At least two-thirds of the total land is preserved for agriculture, wildlife, and open space. It must remain free of development for a minimum of 40 years through a conservation easement or protective covenant.

3. A management plan must be provided that defines the roles and responsibilities for managing residual land.

4. Preserving rural character includes attention to ridgelines, riparian areas, meadows, and hillsides.

Support and Implementation of Legislation

Colorado Revised State Statutes 30-28-101 (10), 31-23-201(2), and 31-23-214(1) exempt from the statutorily defined subdivision review process the creation of land parcels of 35 acres or more. Coloradoans refer to this statute as "Senate Bill 35." Many citizens are concerned about the detrimental impact of 35-acre parcel proliferation, and the inability of most jurisdictions to effectively address the adverse visual, economic, and public safety concerns associated with such developments. The granting of well permits by the State Engineer's office is on the basis of an appropriately approved subdivision with sufficient water rights, or the 35-acre exemption in accordance with state statute (every 35-acre parcel has the right to drill one well for domestic use).

Legislation enacted by the state in the late 1990s, C.R.S. 30-28-401 (referred to as the "Cluster Bill"), allows for greater flexibility in this regard by allowing well permits for divisions of land that have a minimum overall density of one unit per 17½ acres—a substantial increase in density from the previous 35-acre rule. The legislation requires that at least two-thirds of the total area of the tract be reserved as open space. Home rule cities in Colorado may allow clustering in other forms, although those that result in smaller lots must still receive well permits from the State Engineer, which typically requires a water augmentation plan if existing water rights are not available.

It is in the context of this legislation that the Rural Land Use Process establishes a viable alternative—one that provides an incentive via increased density and flexibility in exchange for preservation of open space.

Individual Project—Ludwick Farm Rural Land Use Plan

Project Description

Ludwick Farm Rural Land Use Plan (RLUP) comprises 160 irrigated acres with seven new residential sites ranging in size from 3½-10 acres, for a total of 33 acres; one pond/greenspace tract of 5 acres; and one farm parcel of 122 acres, including the original homestead lot of approximately 2½ acres. Approximately 127 acres, or 79% of the land, is protected in perpetuity by restrictive covenant (Figure 3-23).

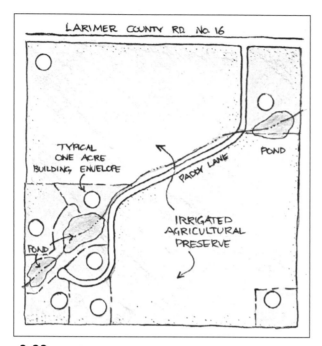

3-23 Ludwick Farm Rural Land Use Plan, Larimer County, Colorado.

Source: James van Hemert

Lay of the Land and Context

The irrigated Ludwick Farm is located approximately 10 miles southeast of Fort Collins in the southern part of Larimer County. It is in active agricultural production with cattle, alfalfa, and sugar beets. The land slopes up gently to the south boundary. Land on two sides has experienced residential development, with portions of the surrounding land having been developed as 5- to 35-acre parcels. However, there are many operating farms remaining in the vicinity that sustain the area's agricultural economy and character.

The current zoning is FA-Farming, which allows for a maximum density of one residential lot per 2.29 acres if municipal or Metropolitan District sewer is not used. (If municipal or District sewer is used, a density of one residential unit per ½ acre is possible in this zone.) Theoretically, under this scenario, the property could

yield 70 home sites; however, such a plan would require very expensive entitlement and infrastructure development costs in addition to a lengthy and costly public hearing process. In the end, an agricultural livelihood and way of life would be lost.

Key Features and Elements That Relate to the Western Landscape

The management plan and restrictive covenants will ensure that the following key features and elements of the local western landscape are preserved:

- maintenance of irrigated lands, ensuring the integrity of the farm (Figure 3-24)
- installation and care of perimeter and agricultural fencing
- maintenance of meadows, ponds, and open space
- architecture that fits within the agricultural context
- clustering of homes in an area that subordinates structures with the southern horizon and county road viewshed. It is important to note that homes are located at the far extreme of the open meadow. No trees or forested areas exist to "hide" development (Figure 3-25).
- plat notes and other disclosure documents that alert future residents that they are in a rural agricultural community and may experience odors, noise, and dust as a part of normal agricultural operations
- rural private roads that require only a 20-foot minimum width, with narrower widths permitted for short distances to accommodate topographical constraints (Figure 3-26)
- open space preservation

Nearly 80% of contiguous open space, the majority being irrigated farmland, is preserved in perpetuity with a restrictive covenant. Additionally, each residential lot is further restricted with the application of building envelopes and fence

3-24 Original farmstead (in the background) remains as a residence and working operation.

Source: James van Hemert

3-25 Ludwick Farm. New homes in the center-far middle ground do not dominate the landscape, despite lack of screening.

Source: Larimer County Rural Land Use Center

3-26 View across preserved working farm to new homes. Narrow roadway without curbs and gutters preserve rural farm character.

Source: James van Hemert

restrictions. The land is guaranteed a 10-year water lease for irrigation. Should that not be renewed, the management plan requires that appropriate native and "dry land" vegetation be planted.

Process of Design and Approvals

The landowner approached the Rural Land Use Center in November 1996 to discuss the alternatives available through the Rural Land Use Process. The FA-Farming zoning would allow for one dwelling unit per 2.29 acres without central sanitary sewer services under the traditional multi-stage subdivision review scenario. As a result of these initial discussions and visits to the site, a conceptual plan was developed and a neighborhood meeting was held in July 1997, with 18 residents in attendance. The meeting resulted in general approval of the preliminary plan by the Rural Land Use Board, with concerns raised over the following issues:

- change in the agricultural character of the area;
- long-term enforcement of the management plan;
- alterations and/or compromise of neighbors' views; and
- concern relating to nearby oil and gas wells.

Concerns were ultimately addressed satisfactorily, and the preliminary plan was brought back to the Rural Land Use Board and approved by consensus. The plan was given final approval by the Board of County Commissioners in September 1997. The process ultimately took nearly a year, which was longer than anticipated in accordance with the Rural Land Use Center's goal.

Market Review

Once placed on the market, the lots sold quickly. A knowledgeable realtor in Larimer County, who has marketed a number of Rural Land Use developments, remarks that today lots are sold in advance of final plat approval. The latest lots sold command prices in the neighborhood of $150,000-$200,000 for 2- to 3-acre sites, representing 80-85% of the price fetched by 35- or 40-acre parcels.

Success Relative to the Intent of Local Government Regulations

According to county staff, the Ludwick Farm RLUP is one of the better examples of a project that meets the intent of the regulations.

Evaluation

As of August 2000, 24 RLUPs had been given preliminary approval since the program's inception in 1996. Of these, 15 have been given final approval, representing 136 dwelling units and approximately 2,400 protected acres. Of these, 10 provide open space and agricultural land protection in perpetuity; the remainder provides protection for 40 years.

The process was amended in 1999 to accommodate concerns that the process was too slow, particularly for projects with a small number of building lots, and to remove an economic equivalency analysis (comparing profitability of RLUP projects with profitability of a 35-acre split) requirement so that this would no longer be a review criterion.

The county has evaluated and revised the RLUP program in response to finding ways to better serve the citizens of Larimer County, the landowners, and the land. In general, the RLUP has been very successful and well received, and the county is pleased with the initial successes. Some changes have been necessary to clarify terms or provisions found to be ambiguous during the actual application of the regulation. There have been situations where questions or circumstances have come up that were not originally contemplated or addressed by the regulation. Some changes were necessary to make the process more efficient, predictable, and user-friendly.

Additionally, the county has learned that land conservation is an imprecise science, particularly in the chaotic environment of Colorado today. The Rural Land Use Process is a "work in progress," and more changes are likely.

Western Rural Development Pattern Language

A number of significant historical western development patterns may be distilled from the Larimer County/Ludwick Farm case study. Moreover, the project teaches some important lessons, and suggests additional patterns that respond to modern land use planning and environmental concerns and objectives. Both of these historical and contemporary lessons are summarized and categorized below, with explanatory comments provided as appropriate.

Regional Development Patterns

- *Encourage the growth of new, self-contained towns in a dispersed manner across the countryside allowing ample open space between them. Concentrate development in a compact manner within the towns.*

  A repetition of the Ludwick Farm pattern creates a concentrated yet dispersed settlement pattern. The development pattern is preferable to the scattered, large-lot development that has been typical in Larimer County in the past, which fragments open space and is costly for the county to service. On the other hand, changing the state-enabling legislation to allow counties to better regulate 35-acre lot splits, or action by the county to rezone agricultural areas with true rural zoning as Weld County, Colorado, has done (instead of the approximately one unit per 3 acres allowed in most areas of the county) might be an equally or more effective way to preserve agricultural areas, open space, and wildlife habitat.

Town

Public Realm

- *Provide and incorporate common areas for clusters of homes.*

  While the scale is too large for intimate courtyards, the clustering of homes does provide a neighborly village "feel."

Environmental

- *Maintain agricultural lands in close proximity to town dwellers.*

  Agricultural land is preserved through the Rural Land Use Process in areas threatened by large-lot exurban development.

Dispersed Rural Settlement

Environmental

- *Locate buildings at the toes of slopes and edges of meadows in a manner that allows for natural windbreaks and creates a feeling of shelter.*

  Homes are clustered at the far edge of the meadow. In this case, however, no natural windbreaks are present.

Cultural

- *Ensure that new development respects and complements existing agricultural land use through the use of appropriate fencing, setbacks, and overall placement of structures.*

  The management plan, fence controls, setbacks, and clustering are intended to minimize future conflicts between rural residents and agricultural operations.

Visual

- *Where natural vegetation or topography do not allow for "hiding" development, locate structures such that they are subordinate to the horizon and any significant viewsheds.*

Homes are clustered at the extreme far edge of the meadow, and they are not hidden by any existing plantings. This is consistent with the historical placement of ranch buildings; however, it bears singling out today as a new additional pattern because its scale is likely to be broader, and existing ranches and farmsteads are associated with substantial mature vegetation introduced by the original settlers. New vegetation will mature over time.

- *Construct the narrowest rural roads possible, without undue negative impacts on public safety, in order to minimize impacts on vegetation, natural drainage patterns, and the natural terrain. In placing roadways, do so in a manner that minimizes the need for "cut and fill."*

Larimer County's private rural road standards allow for roadways as narrow as 12 feet in particular circumstances.

Architecture/Design

Form

- *Design buildings that mimic the profiles of the natural landscape: in steep, mountainous areas,* *steeply pitched rooflines are appropriate; in areas that are flat or rolling, a lower profile is fitting.*

Homes maintain the relatively low profile of the surrounding plains.

Other Elements

- *Construct fences of historical materials that are unobtrusive; use local, natural materials.*

New fencing is severely limited. Only fencing consistent with agricultural practices is permitted.

CONTACTS

Larimer County Rural Land Use Center
Jim Reidhead, Director
(970) 498-7686
www.co.larimer.co.us/planning

Ken Ludwick (landowner/developer)
(970) 669-2003

SOURCES

Interviews with Jim Reidhead and Brenda Gimeson of the Larimer County Rural Land Use Center; Ken Ludwick, developer; and Ted Yelek, real estate agent, 2000.

Larimer County Land Use Code, Section 5.8, Rural Land Use Process.

CASE STUDY 6

Santa Cruz County, Arizona: Private Initiative

CASAS ARROYO DE SONOITA

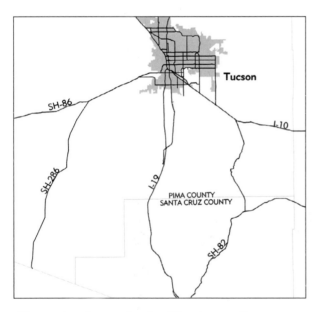

Illustrating the maxim that "less is more," a private development initiative seamlessly blends development into the attractive, rolling hills of Santa Cruz County, Arizona, southeast of Tucson. The development was conceived and built with little influence by local development regulations. Restrictive covenants administered by a homeowners' association ensure that new development will follow established design guidelines.

Geographical, Climatic, and Social Setting

Santa Cruz County lies approximately 50 miles southeast of Tucson in the southernmost portion of the state, adjacent to Mexico. The highest point in the county, Mt. Wrightson at 9,452 feet, dominates the horizon. The average elevation in the Sonoita area is 5,000 feet. The landscape is characterized by high, rolling savanna, the oak-dotted Canelo hills, and the spectacular Patagonia Mountains and canyons. Public lands cover 61% of the county land area.

Average temperatures range from the low 40s in the winter to the mid-70s in the summer. Average annual precipitation is 18 inches; however, most of it falls in the late summer "monsoon" season. Winters are primarily dry. The county had a 2000 population of 38,381, a 29% increase over the 1990 population of 29,676.[10] Several major development projects are anticipated in the next few years, guaranteeing future growth. The economy is based upon a mix of ranching, second homes, and recreation-based tourism.

Regulatory Standards and Planning Processes

Introductory Overview

Casas Arroyo de Sonoita, a residential subdivision, was developed in the 1970s independent of any local development regulations addressing design or environmental protection. This particular case study provides an example of sensitive accommodation to the western landscape completely in the context of private initiative (Figure 3-27).

Individual Project— Casas Arroyo de Sonoita

Project Description

Casas Arroyo de Sonoita encompasses just over 200 acres, situated along State Highway 82 to the southwest of Sonoita, Arizona. The subdivision of

3-27   Homes at Casas Arroyo nestle in the landscape.

Source: Chris Duerksen

3-28   Trees are preserved and respect the landscape.

Source: Chris Duerksen

39 home sites was recorded in 1972 and, to date, 30 lots have been developed. The homes are clustered on lots of approximately ½ acre each with 190 acres held in common. It was planned as an exclusive development, but has no prominent gate or entryway features that often announce upscale developments today. The subdivision falls under the somewhat antiquated county zoning category of Planned Area Development, which is similar to a Planned Unit Development. The homeowners' association operates its own central water system, maintains the roads, and enforces the covenants, including architectural review.

Lay of the Land and Context

The land is hilly with short 15- to 20-foot oak trees dotting the savanna. The surrounding area is rural in character with ranching being the primary agricultural activity. There are good views of the mountains to the west. Despite its location south of Tucson, the area receives more moisture and has a much lusher aspect to it. Other development in the area has been more traditional large-lot, scattered development patterns (Figure 3-28).

Key Features and Elements That Relate to the Western Landscape

Homes blend well with the landscape and are nestled sensitively in draws and among the trees on the site. Only limited native landscaping is permitted to augment a home site. The earth-tone colors and natural materials of the homes further embrace the natural landscape in a manner that complements rather than detracts. Narrow gravel roads wend gently through the hilly terrain, following the natural topography (Figure 3-29).

3-29   Trees and topography screen homes and outbuildings.

Source: Chris Duerksen

Open Space Preservation

Nearly 90% of the land is held in common ownership in its natural state and is managed by the homeowners' association.

Process of Design and Approvals

The primary goal of the homeowner covenants with respect to design is to ensure harmony with the natural landscape. All structures, including fences and accessory structures, and alterations are subject to review and approval by the association. Proposals must specify the nature, kind, shape, height, materials, and location of the new structure or alteration. The overriding guide is in harmony with the external design and location in relation to surrounding structures and topography. Membership in the homeowners' association is mandatory.

The covenants also include the following significant provisions:

- In order to preserve the natural landscape, gardening shall be confined within patio walls, except that shrubs and plants may be planted adjacent to the exterior walls of the premises. No trees shall be planted outside patio areas without approval.
- Native growth may not be removed or altered, except as is necessary in the construction of residences.
- All electrical service and telephone lines shall be underground.

A member of the Architectural Committee reports that recent conflict occurred over their denial of a request to plant an apple tree—a non-native species—in one homeowner's yard. This serves to illustrate the dedication of the homeowners in preserving the native landscape.

Market Review

Initially, lots sold very slowly because there was little development pressure in the county, and the project was not economically successful. As development activity has increased in the county, the subdivision has enjoyed increasing popularity, with four to five new homes recently constructed.

Western Rural Development Pattern Language

A number of significant historical western development patterns may be distilled from the Santa Cruz County/Casas Arroyo de Sonoita case study. Moreover, the project teaches some important lessons and suggests additional patterns that respond to modern land use planning and environmental concerns and objectives. Both of these historical and contemporary lessons are summarized and categorized below with explanatory comments provided as appropriate.

Dispersed Rural Settlement

Environmental

- *Locate buildings at the toes of slopes and edges of meadows in a manner that allows for natural windbreaks and creates a feeling of shelter.*
- *Where natural vegetation or topography do not allow for "hiding" development, locate structures such that they are subordinate to the surrounding landforms and any significant viewsheds.*
- *Nestle structures below ridges and within the folds of hills.*
- *Where vegetation of the contextual natural landscape is sparse, severely limit additional landscape plantings, except for native plants in limited, carefully selected areas.*
- *In sparsely vegetated contexts, avoid any kind of fencing altogether, thereby allowing the landscape to flow uninterrupted* (Figure 3-30).

All homes in the development are carefully tucked off of ridges and out of meadows, maintaining the sweeping views and natural character of the land. Fencing has been kept to a minimum throughout the development, including at the entryway.

- *Protect wildlife habitat and enhance movement corridors in a manner that allows for continued*

3-30 Meadows at the entryway have been preserved, and fencing is restricted throughout the development.

Source: Chris Duerksen

free movement of the broadest possible variety of species.

By maintaining large, contiguous blocks of open space—almost 90% of the development—and restricting the use of fences, the development maintains excellent habitat for wildlife as well as corridors that facilitate their movement.

- *Construct the narrowest rural roads possible, without undue impacts on public safety, in order to minimize adverse affects on vegetation, natural drainage patterns, and the natural terrain. Place roadways in a manner that minimizes "cut and fill."*

The narrow gravel roads of the development blend in well with the landscape and terrain. For the most part, they follow the natural terrain and are unobtrusive. However, some traverse steep slopes, and there is some evidence of erosion in those places.

Architecture/Design

Form

- *Design building profiles that mimic the profiles of the natural landscape: in steep, mountainous areas,*

steeply pitched rooflines are appropriate; in areas that are flat or rolling, a lower profile is fitting.

Color and Materials

- *Use natural materials in a manner that reflects an organic integrity and harmony with the natural surroundings. Stone and wood are often appropriate as the primary construction material.*

- *Avoid the use of a multiplicity of building materials, colors, and architectural styles. Doing so also serves to produce a commonality of architectural style.*

- *As a first choice, use natural, earth-tone colors; however, do not do so exclusively. With an appropriate building profile, bright historical colors such as red, green, or ochre may serve as a beautiful counterpoint to the natural landscape.*

Building colors must very strictly conform to the local, natural, earth-tone colors. In this case, brighter colors are avoided and would not be appropriate, given the context of the natural and cultural landscape. Wood, stone, and stucco are the predominant building materials. The overall effect is one of compatibility and respect for the landscape and rolling hills.

CONTACTS

Santa Cruz County Planning
Brian Friedman
(520) 761-7800
www.governet.net/AZ/CO/SAC

Lee Nellis, A.I.C.P.
(520) 290-0828
www.sonoran.org/si

SOURCE

Interview with Lee Nellis, Santa Cruz County planning consultant, 2000.

CASE STUDY 7

City of Claremont, California

A CENTURY OF THOUGHTFUL PLANNING

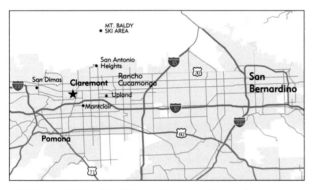

Distinguishing itself from the vast, blurred conglomeration of towns and cities that make up much of greater Los Angeles, this town of 35,000 successfully maintains and enhances its architectural treasures and the historic land use fabric, with a sensitivity to its natural setting. Its success is based on a century of open government; citizen participation; and thoughtful, balanced land use regulation.

Geographical, Climatic, and Social Setting

Situated between 1,000 and 3,000 feet above sea level on the extreme eastern edge of Los Angeles County, the City of Claremont enjoys an average annual temperature of 63 degrees F and an annual average rainfall of 17.3 inches.[11] Median household income in 2000 was $78,389 for a predominantly white population with sizable Asian and Hispanic minorities. Of the adult population over age 25, 28% hold advanced professional degrees.[12] A college town now boasting eight higher educational institutions, Claremont began as a speculative town site along the Santa Fe Railroad in 1887. The citrus industry dominated the economy for many decades until the last packinghouse closed in 1971.[13]

Claremont's early citizens, New England congregationalists, imprinted their values of commitment to freedom, to learning, and to high standards of citizenship on the town, resulting in an open style of government still evident today. They established Pomona College in 1887.[14] The success and growth of Pomona College ultimately led to the creation of a group of institutions divided into small "Oxford-style" colleges rather than a single university. Among these are the nationally recognized Pomona College, Harvey Mudd College, Claremont McKenna College, Pitzer College, and Claremont Graduate University.

Regulatory Standards and Planning Processes

Introductory Overview

Unlike the project-specific contemporary studies of this book, this case study encompasses a town in its entirety and is therefore organized somewhat differently. Significantly, the analysis goes beyond regulations and practices governing "bricks and mortar" to review the historical and cultural context giving rise to citizen-driven planning.

Important regulatory standards, practices, and planning processes are reviewed and illustrated with contemporary examples, as applicable, including the following:

1. Historical Claremont District (Land Use & Development Code)

2. Claremont Village District & Overlay (Land Use & Development Code) and Village Design Plan

3. Rural Residential District (Land Use & Development Code)

4. Incidental Outdoor Uses (Land Use & Development Code)

5. Hillside District (Land Use & Development Code)

6. Claremont Village Expansion Area Specific Plan

7. Street tree program

History of Regulations and Process

The Early Years

Conscientious planning by citizens in Claremont occurred far in advance of professional planning involvement. With few exceptions, many patterns established early on have been repeated and maintained over the years through programs, regulations, and practices, producing a remarkable organic unity of form.

Claremont was created by the Pacific Land Improvement Company as a speculative town site on 365 acres in 1887 along the then-new Santa Fe railway line. To create as many separate land holdings as possible, lots in the proposed business section were only 20 by 100 feet in size (Figure 3-31). A pleasant, unintended consequence of this action was multiple narrow storefronts, contributing to the vitality of a pedestrian-oriented village core. The city continues to encourage this pattern, which is reflected in the Claremont Village Expansion Area Specific Plan. Lots in the residential section were 50 by 150 feet. To lure prospective buyers, the land company cleared brush, constructed a few homes and built the Claremont

Hotel. Fast-growing eucalyptus trees were first planted in 1890 by early residents.[18]

In the same year as the establishment of the town site, the congregationalists of Los Angeles established Pomona College as a Christian college in the tradition of earlier colleges they had established (Yale and Harvard).

Until formal incorporation in 1907, town citizens practiced the town meeting form of government using committees, volunteer work, and voluntary financial contributions to govern. In advance of formal regulations governing architectural style, lot size, and building setbacks, citizens demonstrated concern about the visual appearance of the town. Recorded in the minutes of a 1903 Town Meeting was the following:

> *Mr. (Henry) Kingman brought to the attention of the town the need of putting houses and barns back from the street for the better appearance of the town. After discussion it was voted that as a town we request builders to place barns and other buildings well back from the street in as far as the exigencies of the situation will permit.[15]*

This concern is demonstrated today in the Claremont Village Expansion Area Specific Plan provisions for reducing impacts of garages with the use of rear alleys, and in the Land Use & Development Code requirements limiting the size, height, and location of secondary structures.

The town demonstrated early on its commitment to a well-planned community at the time of incorporation in 1907 with an "artistic" city plan prepared by the Board of Trade (predecessor to the chamber of commerce), and the establishment of the first Planning Commission in 1924 by the chamber of commerce to "investigate matters of civic improvements, especially a civic center." [16]

The ingenuity and resourcefulness of the community were demonstrated in a 1909 city ordinance requiring the use of round, granite boulders in street curb construction, a resource in abundant

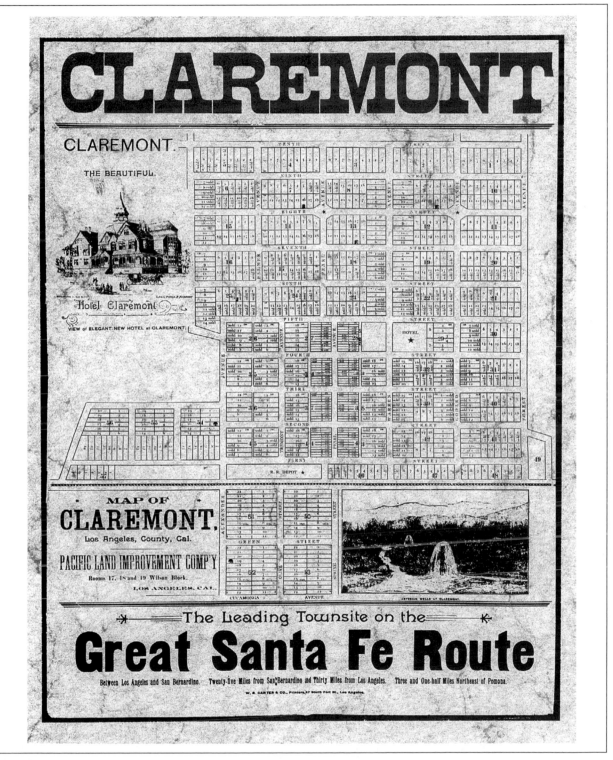

3-31   Town site map showing street and lot layout from a promotional poster of April 7, 1887.

Source: Judy Wright

3-32   Split-face granite stone curb. Today's Claremont residents refer to these as "elephant toes."

Source: James van Hemert

supply. The stones are split to show a clean face. Types and sizes were specified by the city. The stones were arranged in rows and the gaps filled with concrete mortar from the bottom to 1½ inches over the top of the stones (Figure 3-32).

The 1925 Sanborn Fire Map reveals several patterns, influenced by the early land speculators and subsequent builders (Figure 3-33).

Most streets have a 60-foot right-of-way. College and 5th Avenues were surveyed with 80-foot rights-of-way. Harvard Avenue was clearly intended as the primary commercial street by virtue of its narrow lots, although it had a narrower 60-foot right-of-way. A 1930s Public Works Administration project widened this street, cutting off all the storefronts on the western side.[17]

Several blocks in the town core have alleys, which are given a 20-foot right-of-way. However,

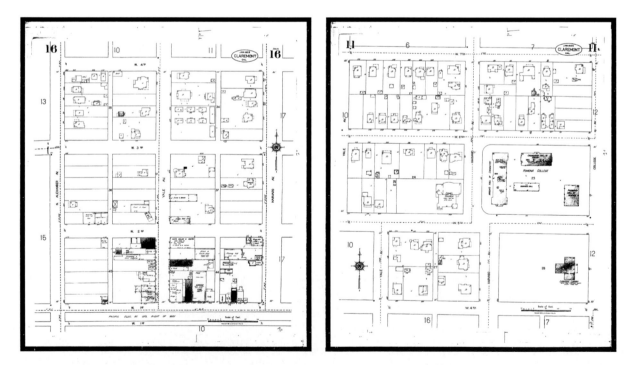

3-33   1925 Sanborn Fire Maps.

whether or not an alley is in place, in accordance with early Town Meeting direction, all accessory structures such as garages are placed to the rear of lots.

Virtually all commercial structures are constructed to the street right-of-way. Residential structures, such as those along 6th and 7th Avenues, vary in their street setbacks between 20 and 40 feet. The 1925 Sanborn Fire Maps reveal larger corner houses with wrap-around porches at 6th and Harvard Avenues, and 3rd and Yale Avenues.

First Planning Committee and Comprehensive Plans

The chamber of commerce took the lead in town planning by creating the Postwar Planning Committee in 1944. Dubbed the "Committee of One Hundred" (although it never exceeded 77 members), its purpose was to "foster the aid of local organizations and individuals in cooperating with city council and the planning commission in matters for civic good."[18] The committee worked for a year laying the groundwork for significant planning decisions in subsequent decades on numerous issues, including the business district, finance, zoning ordinances, school district planning, street trees, and park planning. Local historian Judy Wright observes that the early work of the Planning Commission and this committee placed the city in a strong offensive position during the postwar development boom in the 1950s to accept the kind of growth it wanted and reject the kind that might seriously damage the character of the community.

During the period of post-World War II development pressure, new residents believed that without a group of citizens actively involved in guiding its development, a city is likely to find that major decisions would be made by subdividers or city staff. This view was apparently supported by Lewis Mumford, the renowned urban historian, who wrote the following in response to a member of the Core Study Group in 1967 requesting advice:

None of the current modes of design can be applied to a town like Claremont without destroying its scale and texture: all the popular patterns, whether derived from the suburb, the supermarket, or from La Ville Radizuse would empty the city of such vitality as Claremont and Scripps originally gave it . . . planning decisions should be established before a planner is called: otherwise he will be tempted to use the stale fashionable cliches.[19]

The second community plan, the Official Plan of 1956, focused on development of raw land; its successor, approved in 1980, focused on a much wider range of policy issues, such as housing diversity, traffic management, and historic preservation, reflecting a maintenance—rather than growth-oriented—community.

Development Codes and the Architectural Control Commission

The Claremont Land Use & Development Code was first adopted in 1958. The city was a pioneer in establishing one of the earliest design review boards in the form of the Architectural Control Commission in 1963. The Land Use & Development Code requires architectural review of all new development. The Architectural Control Commission generally reviews all nonsingle-family development, significant modifications to properties in the Historical Claremont District, and new tract development. The commission is aided in its review with a set of general review criteria from the Land Use & Development Code, and a set of design guidelines entitled the "Village Design Plan" and the "Rural Claremont Architectural and Landscape Standards" adopted in 1987, as well as design guidelines in several specific plans. These standards and guidelines incorporate important, recognized historic patterns, further discussed in subsequent sections.

In 1970, the Historical Claremont District was added as a specific zone district of the Land Use &

Development Code and was applied to the town's earliest residential area. The district's standards were revised in 1976, and "downzoned" the area from multifamily to preserve the single-family character of the neighborhood.

In 1980, the city adopted a Register of Sites of Historic or Architectural Merit. Over 1,000 buildings, many outside the Historical Claremont District, were placed under a 90-day demolition delay and review under the California Environmental Quality Act. Claremont Heritage, an influential volunteer organization, played a major role in surveying and nominating structures to this register.

The city adopted the Hillside Plan and ordinance in 1981 for the foothills and steep slopes of the San Gabriel Mountains. The plan reduced the planned density of much of the area from mostly one to three dwelling units per acre throughout the approximately 3,000-acre hillside area to approximately 525 units for the entire area. A total of 125 units were approved as part of the 125-acre Claremont Hills Specific Plan. There is still potential for an additional 40 homes within the planning area (which includes land both inside and outside the city boundary).

In 1991, the city annexed 2.4 square miles of the hillside that included much of what is now the city's 1,200-acre Claremont Hillside Wilderness Park. The development credits were removed from the 1,200 acres and transferred to the 125-acre Claremont Hills Specific Plan project area.

Recognizing the value of outdoor incidental uses such as outdoor seating, the city established in 1994 an Incidental Outdoor Uses ordinance to encourage and properly manage outdoor activities, particularly in the downtown village.

The city established the Claremont Village Expansion Area Specific Plan in 2001 in order to foster and control additional commercial and residential growth in an historically industrial area. This 35-acre area lies adjacent to the west side of the village downtown.

Desired Goals of the Standards

The 1981 General Plan's reflection of an overall vision for the community is "To uphold Claremont's distinctive character and livability." Specific regulatory documents, processes, and practices conscientiously reflect the community's consensus in how the details of development and redevelopment must be worked out on a day-to-day basis. In all cases, the regulations are the result of extensive community participation. The Claremont Village Expansion Area Specific Plan approved in 2001, for example, required three years and 30 public meetings. Detail on the intent of specific regulations is covered separately in their respective subsections.

Support and Implementation of Legislation

The Claremont General Plan, upon which land use-oriented legislative ordinances are based, is authorized and required by California Government Code Section 65302(a). The Land Use & Development Code is authorized under Sections 65800 to 65912 of the California Government Code. The Specific Plan follows those requirements and policies identified in the Claremont General Plan, Land Use Plan, and the State of California requirements for specific plans in accordance with Section 65450 et seq. of the state code.

Contemporary Illustrations of Development Regulations

1. *Historical Claremont District*

Introduction

Established in 1970, this zone district covers the early residential neighborhood of Claremont, built from the turn of the 19th century to the 1940s. It comprises a variety of architectural styles, including Victorian, Spanish Colonial Revival, and Craftsman. The structures exhibit a quality of workmanship and character not often found in current times. The houses vary in size and are set back amidst tall trees on streets laid in a grid pattern, featuring parkways planted with street trees (Figure 3-34).

Large houses are mixed with smaller homes, which predominate, and corner houses tend to be larger and more dominant, serving as anchors for the rest of the block (Figure 3-35). Garages are frequently accessed from or located to the rear of properties.[20]

3-34   Indian Hills Boulevard at Harrison Avenue. The extensive landscaping, complete with flowering jacaranda trees, is part of a comprehensive street tree and landscaping program.

Source: James van Hemert

3-35   Claremont "corner house" in "The Village."

Source: James van Hemert

Intent

The district seeks to preserve and protect the single-family residential character, and the historic and architectural integrity of the neighborhood, while allowing for sensitive and compatible alternations, additions, and in-fill development. Its implementation is viewed as a locally controlled alternative to the establishment of a national historic district.

Key Features of District Standards

Land use is restricted primarily to single-family dwellings and secondary units that meet stringent bulk requirements, in keeping with the historical character of the neighborhood. Accessory structures are permitted up to a maximum of 300 square feet, excluding parking structures. Conditional use permits may be granted for secondary dwelling units not exceeding 700 square feet. The height of secondary units is restricted to no greater than one story, or 15 feet, and in no case higher than the primary structure.

Illustrations

To maintain the historical relationship between lot and structure size, the maximum size of any new structure is 1,500 square feet plus 25% of the lot size. New homes must be consistent in scale and articulation, but not necessarily restricted to a particular architecture style. Design of all additions or alterations must be compatible with existing architecture (Figures 3-36 and 3-37).

Process of Design and Approvals

Applications for exterior modifications, additions, and new construction are accepted and reviewed by city staff. With a few exceptions, the Architectural Control Commission subsequently reviews all applications. Review includes all exterior structural details, and changes in site features including parking areas, landscaping, walls, and outside

3-36 New two-story home on 8th Avenue. This home meets the regulatory front yard setback of 20 feet, but this is less than that of the adjacent home, built at a more generous setback.

Source: James van Hemert

3-37 A second-story addition on 8th Avenue matches existing materials, color, and roof pitch.

Source: James van Hemert

lighting. The commission has final authority on granting approvals. Claremont Heritage provides referral comments on all applications. This relationship enables Claremont Heritage to effectively achieve many of their objectives for the Historical Claremont District through this process.

2. *Claremont Village District & Overlay and Village Design Plan*

The Claremont Village District, covering the historic village commercial core, is intended to provide for a broad range of uses, typical of a downtown area. The intent is to maintain pedestrian scale, enhance storefront design, and to promote a "walkable" place. The Claremont Village Overlay District is intended to preserve economic stability and health of the retail commercial core. Accordingly, it encourages retail uses in pedestrian arcades and on the first floor of buildings that attract pedestrian traffic (Figure 3-38).

All new construction, additions, and alterations and use changes must be reviewed by the Architectural Control Commission in accordance with the Village Design Plan, a detailed set of design guidelines. This document recognizes that the village is more than simply a collection of buildings and streets, and is an organic whole that through street and building patterns, rhythm, scale, and their relationship to one another, a quality of life has emerged with a place where people can meet, mingle, and engage in the discourse of public life. Economically, the village "downtown" core is apparently thriving: vacant space is scarce, restaurants are full, and new construction is evident.

Key Features

• *Building Height and Street Relationship*

The district restricts all buildings to no higher than three stories, or 40 feet, in order to maintain the historic, pedestrian-oriented pattern. No street setbacks are required, encouraging maintenance of the historic street wall. Companion guidelines con-

3-38 Early morning discussion over coffee on Harvard Avenue.

Source: James van Hemert

tained in the Village Design Plan discourage breaking from the established street wall enclosure.

• *Pedestrian Orientation*

The Claremont Village Overlay District specifically addresses the preservation and use of display windows. For commercial spaces with existing ground-level display windows, only retail uses and similar uses that attract pedestrians and frequent customer visits are permitted (Figure 3-39).

Canopies and awnings are encouraged and specific suggestions provided as to their construction. Cloth awnings for first- and second-floor windows are recommended because they add quality and color to the street scene. To encourage nightlife, parking requirements for operations after 5:30 PM may be reduced up to 100%.

Illustrations

• *Civic Center Example: City Hall*

City Hall, the public library, and the U.S. post office are located at the junction of Harvard and 2nd Streets, downtown, forming a central civic core (Figure 3-40). In 1999, the city undertook a

3-39 Narrow shop frontages and large display windows on Harvard Avenue.

Source: James van Hemert

3-40 Claremont's renovated Spanish Colonial Revival City Hall.

Source: James van Hemert

3-41   Spanish Colonial Revival train depot.
Source: James van Hemert

major renovation of City Hall to enhance its functioning and bring the facility in line with contemporary building codes. Despite the considerable cost, the community chose to preserve and expand the historical Spanish Colonial Revival structure rather than build a new structure in a new location outside the downtown civic core, as many other communities have done when faced with the same dilemma.

• *Community Focal Point: Train Depot*

The historic train depot, almost lost to demolition, has been beautifully restored. It not only serves as part of the contemporary greater Los Angeles commuter rail system, but its outdoor public

space is used for a variety of community events (Figure 3-41).

• *Commercial Development on Bonita Avenue*

Located on a former gasoline station site, a new retail commercial development in the village incorporates many critical components of the Claremont Village District and the Village Design Plan (Figure 3-42).

Viewed as a success by residents, this building enhances the experience for pedestrians passing by with its use of large display windows, awnings, and an inviting corner entryway. Although its design is contemporary, it fits comfortably in the historic village because it respects the "street wall," is consistent with the scale of the other buildings, and makes use of natural materials. Note the use of river rock—a building material used in many of Claremont's finest historical buildings—and the wood window frames.

Located one block away on another former gasoline station site, another recent commercial retail development fails to satisfy. Although this Spanish Colonial Revival-style building meets the land use district standards, was carefully reviewed and approved by the Architectural Control Commission, and borrows heavily on historical architectural themes, it lacks the pedestrian appeal so prevalent in the village (Figure 3-43). The minimal presence of display windows, lack of awnings or canopies, and scarcity of shade trees may be a significant part of the problem. Additionally, the lack of protective street parking, serving as a buffer for pedestrians from traffic, contributes to its low appeal.

3. *Rural Residential District* *(Land Use & Development Code)*

Introduction and Intent

This district, located primarily in the northeast section of town, is intended to provide for single-family homes and agricultural uses with a density range of one to 1¼ dwelling units per gross

3-42   New retail commercial building at the northwest corner of Yale and Bonita Avenues. Successful implementation of design standards.

Source: James van Hemert

acre. New development must be in harmony with the rural character of the area, which is defined by the presence of agricultural features such as citrus groves, barns, rock walls, pump houses built of rock, and other characteristics such as mountain vistas; minimal outdoor artificial lighting; narrow streets accompanied by equestrian, pedestrian, and bike trails; and native landscaping. The lack of such urban features such as curb and gutters, streetlights, and sidewalks also contribute greatly to the rural character of this area.

Key Features

Minimum setbacks are related to the size of the primary residential structure—the larger the

structure (beyond 4,000 square feet), the greater the setback. The size of the main structure is limited according to the size of the lot: the maximum floor area must not exceed 1,500 square feet plus 25% of the lot area. This standard is similar to that applied in all other single-family residential districts and serves to establish a comfortable ratio between structures and lot size. In no case may total lot coverage, including carports, cover patios and decks over 3 feet above grade, exceed 20%. All primary structures are limited to a height of two stories and 25 feet.

All exterior lighting must conform to the outdoor lighting and glare standards set forth in the Rural Claremont Architectural and Landscape Standards, and additionally must not exceed 60

3-43 Restaurant at Indian Hills Boulevard and Bonita Avenue. Building and its relationship to the street fail to provide a satisfying pedestrian environment.

Source: James van Hemert

watts, must be directed downward into the interior of the lot, and shall not be greater than 14 feet above grade level, except for fixtures illuminating second-story entryways.[21]

Illustrations

• *Rural Residential*

A new residential development of ¾-acre lots on Mills Avenue illustrates the Rural Residential Standards. Buildings are set back a minimum of 40 feet. Local river rock is generously used in community landscaping features, notably the entry wall (Figure 3-44). To maximize the preservation of a dark night sky, street lighting is restricted to shielded lamps on 12-foot poles. The poles are wooden to further enhance the rural character. The city requires river rock swales along roads for

3-44 "Creekside," a Rural Residential development on Mills Avenue. Note the generous use of local river rock within the entryway landscaping.

Source: James van Hemert

drainage, using a locally available resource, and to further enhance rural character (Figure 3-45). The river rocks, abundantly in supply everywhere in the local earth, are affectionately referred to as "Claremont Potatoes."

4. *Incidental Outdoor Uses*
(Land Use & Development Code)

Claremont's mild and sunny climate is conducive to outdoor dining and shopping. It is the intent of the Incidental Outdoor Uses section of the Land Use & Development Code to encourage outdoor displays, sidewalk sales, and outdoor seating. Clear standards are established in the context of encouraging creativity in the design of outdoor uses.

Key Features

The code provides an incentive for the use of public sidewalks for outdoor seating by exempting the additional seats from parking requirements, subject to certain conditions. Minimum standards include the following:

- maintenance of a minimum 5-foot-wide continuous path
- vertical clearance of a minimum 8 feet above the path
- maintenance of a minimum 2-foot clear space adjacent to edge of street curb or parking area
- sturdy construction of tables and chairs, made of quality materials, and designed to complement the character of the streetscape

The 10- to 12-foot width of most sidewalks in the village area is adequate to provide a single row of tables and chairs adjacent to commercial establishments (Figure 3-46).

5. *Hillside District*
(Land Use & Development Code)

The Hillside District, covering several square miles of hilly terrain in the northern portion of the town, is intended to restrict development from

3-45 Rural streetlight with wooden pole and shielded fixture. Note the river rock drainage swale used in all rural areas of the city.

Source: James van Hemert

environmentally unsuitable areas and to provide for limited development in areas that are flatter and in proximity to available infrastructure (Figure 3-47).

The Hillside District achieves several important objectives, namely that it:

- ensures that 2,600 of the 3,000 acres of hillsides between Webb Canyon and the San Bernardino County line will be preserved as permanent open space;
- discourages construction of homes dotted all over the hillsides and encourages the preservation of large tracts of open space;

3-46   Outdoor seating in front of Heroes on Yale Avenue. Comfortable chairs, building canopies, and shady street trees combine to create a comfortable outdoor living room.

Source: James van Hemert

3-47   View of pre-hillside ordinance development from Indian Hills Boulevard.

Source: James van Hemert

- focuses development in areas that are best suited for development; and
- protects the right of owners of all parcels to receive some economic benefit from their land because the development credits can be transferred.

Key Features

A notable feature of the regulations is the slope density standards that correlate intensity of development to the steepness of the terrain. Maximum residential densities range from 1-20 acres per unit, depending on the district classification and the slope density calculation. (Refer to Appendix B for the Slope Density Tables.)

The Hillside Plan, a component of the General Plan, identifies 3,000 acres of hillside area of which 2,600 acres are considered undevelopable and 400 acres developable, based upon proximity to services, steepness of terrain, and an attempt to give as many property owners as possible a piece of developable cluster areas.

A transfer of development credits program has been established to allow for transfer of entitlements based upon the units calculated with the slope density standards, from undevelopable areas to developable areas. Developable lands are subject to design criteria that include preservation of outstanding natural features, including highest crests of hill ranges, canyons, natural rock outcroppings—particularly desirable vegetation—and natural watercourses.

Illustration

The protection of land from development in designated undevelopable areas is a significant measure of success. The development credits associated with 1,200 acres of undevelopable land have been transferred to a developable area known as Specific Plan 6/Claremont Hills. This developable cluster will accommodate 125 residential units on 125 acres. A Specific Plan for the area has been approved; construction is yet to begin. The transaction enabled the city to purchase at a reasonable cost a 1,200-acre wilderness park within the undevelopable area of the plan, thereby achieving almost 50% of the desired 2,600 acres of permanent open space.

Process

The Architectural Control Commission must review all development proposals of five lots or more. Any development proposal of 6+ acres must receive approval as a Residential Unit Development and requires approval of a Conditional Use Permit by the Planning Commission. The provisions of the Residential Unit Development allow greater flexibility in design and encourage creation of common amenities, and the preservation and enhancement of valuable natural areas and vistas such as those in the Hillside District. The process for obtaining a Conditional Use Permit requires: (1) submission of a preliminary development plan for review by staff; (2) review of the preliminary development plan by the Architectural Control Commission for comment; and (3) formal application for a Conditional Use Permit, to be acted upon for approval by the Planning Commission.

Any transfer of development credits is authorized concurrently with a Residential Unit Development's Conditional Use Permit. Both the donor and receiver parcels must be part of the same application. The number of transferred development credits may not exceed the number determined for the donor parcel through applying established slope-density standards.

6. *Claremont Village Expansion Area Specific Plan*

The Specific Plan establishes a bridge between the city's General Plan and the development of individual properties within the Village Expansion Area. The vision is to expand the village by adding new retail, commercial, and housing opportu-

nities while at the same time preserving the economic viability of the village. The existing village patterns form the basis for comprehensive regulatory standards that are incorporated into the city's Land Use & Development Code. This plan successfully pulls together the various historic and contemporary development patterns into a cohesive whole, exemplifying a collaborative approach to codifying time-tested patterns for future development.

History

The decline and demise of the citrus industry and associated industrial uses provided the town with an opportunity to expand the downtown village core. The plan, adopted in January 2001, represents a collaborative effort of the business community, residents, Planning Commission, Architectural Control Commission, and city staff over three years and involving 30 public meetings.

The Plan

The plan covers a 35-acre area immediately to the west of the existing downtown village area, including one-half block of the existing village east of Indian Hill Boulevard, the primary division between the village and the village expansion area. At one time, four citrus packing plants operated in this area and vicinity, the last one closing in 1971. A significant portion of the plan area—40%—is city owned. The plan specifies allowed uses (e.g., excluding banks and beauty salons) consistent with the city's interest in expanding its pedestrian-oriented retail base (Figure 3-48).

Process

The plan was reviewed through an extensive public input and review process over several years, involving a variety of committees, including the Architectural Control Commission and the Planning Commission. Final approval was granted by city council.

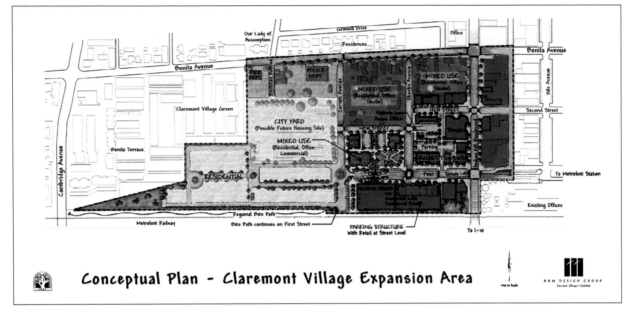

3-48   The Circulation Plan clearly illustrates the manner in which Claremont Village Expansion Area Specific Plan thoughtfully ties into the existing pedestrian-oriented development pattern.

Source: Claremont Community Development Department

Summary of Planning Principles and Standards

• *Principles*

— pedestrian orientation
— evening uses
— ground-floor commercial
— buildings to street edge
— adaptive reuse for former citrus packing plant
— small business ownership
— street parking
— mix of timeless (historic) architectural styles

• *Standards*

— general
— split-face granite curbs
— no meandering sidewalks
— residential
— 50-foot minimum lot width
— 10- to 12-foot street setbacks
— maximum 25-foot height

— maximum primary building area of 1,500 feet, plus 25% of lot area
— minimum front porch size of 75 square feet
— commercial
— 25-foot minimum lot widths
— 0- to 20-foot minimum street widths
— 35-foot maximum building height
— awnings and canopies encouraged

7. Street Tree Program

While not part of any development standards or regulatory program, Claremont's street tree program is noteworthy. The city maintains 23,000 trees along its streets and within its parks, and has won the National Arborists Tree City Award for 15 consecutive years. Street tree planting began in the early years with volunteers planting and handwatering trees. The trees serve to moderate temperatures, provide shade, and create a pleasing, unifying aesthetic to the entire town (Figure 3-49).

3-49 Large trees, generous parkways, and modest houses characterize much of Claremont. View of 7th Avenue.

Source: James van Hemert

CONCLUDING COMMENTS

The success of Claremont as a vibrant, livable community should be attributed to more than simply a collection of thoughtful regulatory documents, although they played a dominant role. First, the historical, social, and cultural environment of citizen leadership and involvement contributed to the quality and relevancy of the documents beyond and in advance of the technical expertise of professionals.

Lewis Mumford advised the city in the 1960s of the need to establish planning principles in advance of professional advice. His key point was to advise citizens not to thoughtlessly apply current design and planning fads but to develop their own ideas and vision. Second, a critical review process, such as that of the Architectural Control Commission, provides a level of judgment and discernment that goes beyond anything that regulations can provide. None of this is meant to downplay the importance of appropriate regulatory documents, but is intended to underscore the importance of broadly based, long-term citizen involvement as a critical component of building

successful communities that reflect authentic development patterns over time.

Western Rural Development Pattern Language

A number of significant historical western development patterns may be distilled from the City of Claremont case study. Moreover, the project teaches some important lessons, and suggests additional patterns that respond to modern land use planning and environmental concerns and objectives. Both of these historical and contemporary lessons are summarized and categorized below with explanatory comments provided as appropriate.

Regional Development Patterns

- *In the face of development pressure, preserve existing country towns and villages and their development patterns.*

  Over the course of 100 years and in the context of the West's largest metropolitan area, Claremont has successfully retained its unique identity.

Town

Public Places

- *Concentrate community facilities around public "squares" at the intersection of community pathways or roadways.*

  Although there is no public square, Claremont's City Hall, public library, and post office are located at the same intersection within the village core.

- *Reserve sufficient space within the core of each neighborhood or town for at least several public community facilities; at least one should serve as a visibly prominent civic focal point.*

  The historic train depot, almost lost to demolition, has been beautifully restored. It serves as part of the contemporary greater Los Angeles commuter rail system, and its outdoor public space is used for a variety of community events.

Streets/Access

- *Establish a comprehensive street tree program to create shade canopies over sidewalks and public streets.*

Claremont's tree program provides generous shade canopies in both residential and commercial areas, creating a welcome respite from the sun.

- *Establish public transportation systems within and between towns.*

Claremont maintains a centrally located commuter rail link to the larger Los Angeles metropolitan area.

Public Realm

- *Ensure appropriately scaled, quasi-public space between public streets and residential structures.*

Streets in the historic neighborhoods, including those built in the 1960s and 1970s, maintain a pleasing relationship between public and private spaces with a 20- to 30-foot setback, serving as a quasi-public space. New rural development requires even greater setbacks.

- *In the central portion of towns, require that the majority of buildings be constructed immediately adjacent to the public right-of-way. When multiple buildings are constructed in this manner, a sense of enclosed urban space is created.*

The Claremont Village Design Plan consciously addresses the matter of maintaining and extending the "street wall" for renovations, additions, and new construction.

- *Encourage outdoor seating on sidewalks, courtyards, and within the quasi-public realm between street and private structures.*

Claremont provides regulatory incentives and clear guidelines to encourage the use of public sidewalks and private courtyards for public seating.

Environmental

- *Restrict development on steep slopes and in geologically hazardous areas.*

Claremont's Hillside ordinance restricts development on steep slopes. Dwelling unit credits, calculated according to a sliding scale, may be transferred to more appropriate sites.

- *Cluster development in a manner so as to maximize environmentally significant, unfragmented open space.*

The Hillside ordinance and Rural Residential Zone District together serve to cluster development in order to maximize contiguous open space and preserve significant natural features.

- *Restrict or shield lighting so as to minimize horizontal and vertical light trespass, thereby preserving the dark night sky.*

Standards for the Rural Residential District restrict both public and private lighting by limiting the height of light fixtures and requiring cut-off features.

Architecture/Design

Form

- *Limit the majority of buildings to four stories high. Taller buildings in small towns and rural areas should be exceptional and reserved for cultural or civic purposes.*

Buildings within the village are limited to 35 feet or three stories. All residential structures are limited to 25 feet or two stories.

- *Build arcades or canopies at the edge of buildings to provide shelter from sun and rain, and to ease the transition between public and private space.*

Arcades, canopies, and awnings are encouraged with specific design criteria established through the Village Design Plan and the recent Claremont Village Expansion Area Specific Plan.

- *Require pedestrian-oriented signs in commercial/civic districts.*

Signage at a pedestrian scale further enhances and reinforces the pedestrian character of Claremont's downtown.

- *In pedestrian-oriented areas, encourage narrow storefronts with large display windows.*

Claremont's standards require amply sized display windows and require that new uses in existing buildings be the type that maximizes the use of display windows.

- *Limit the size of residential buildings relative to lot size.*

In recognition of the historical patterns guiding residential development, Claremont restricts the size of additions and new construction relative to lot size. This further serves to limit the size of building footprints.

Color and Materials

- *Use natural materials in a manner that reflects an organic integrity and harmony with the natural surroundings. Stone and wood are often appropriate as the primary construction material.*

Only natural, handcrafted materials are permitted. River rock, an abundant historic building material, is encouraged in new construction.

- *Avoid the use of a multiplicity of building materials, colors, and architectural styles. Doing so also serves to produce a commonality of architectural style.*

Claremont's Village Design Plan restricts materials to two or three.

- *As a first choice, use natural, earth-tone colors; however, do not do so exclusively. With an appropriate building profile, brighter colors may serve as a beautiful counterpoint to the natural landscape.*

Bright colors and creative design are encouraged for cloth awnings.

Culture/Community

- *Reflect indigenous architectural patterns in contemporary construction as a way to connect with the region's cultural history.*

Claremont's design guidelines and codes recognize the value of maintaining historical patterns and using historical materials when feasible, without promoting thoughtless and clumsy mimicry.

- *Reflect indigenous architectural patterns in contemporary construction as a way to connect with the region's cultural history.*

Without resorting to copying past historical styles, Claremont's design guidelines encourage compatibility with historic architectural patterns.

Site Design

- *In towns, generously plant trees that are appropriate for the climate to maximize shade around buildings, parking lots, and gathering areas.*

Design standards and site plan review ensure adequate planting of appropriate tree types.

- *Minimize the size of building footprints.*

Claremont's residential standards limit building size according to lot size, therefore serving to limit the size of building footprints.

- *In towns, limit the size of secondary buildings, including garages, and require that they be placed at the rear of lots.*

Zoning standards ensure an appropriate balance of scale between building and lot size by limiting the height and square footage of both primary and secondary structures. Secondary buildings are limited in size and height in all residential districts. The placement of garages at the rear of lots maintains the pedestrian-oriented charm of residential streets in older areas. Garages, unfortunately, are not required to be set further back from the primary structure in new residential development outside of the historical and village districts.

- *Consider placing the largest and most architecturally significant homes on corner lots. Include wrap-around porches.*

This historic pattern has not been repeated in recent times; however, front porches—a significant feature of these larger homes—are encouraged in the village expansion area. Front porches must be a minimum 75 square feet in size.

Other Elements

- *Construct fences of historical materials that are unobtrusive. Use locally available natural materials.*

Historic walls of river rock have been replicated in rural density subdivisions as entry features.

CONTACTS

Anthony Witt
Community Development Director, City of Claremont
(909) 399-5341
e-mail: twitt@ci.claremont.ca.us
www.ci.claremont.ca.us

Ginger Elliott
Director, Claremont Heritage
(909) 621-0848

SOURCES

Interviews with Anthony Witt, City of Claremont's Director of Community Development, and Ginger Elliott, Director of Claremont Heritage, June 2002.

Claremont Land Use and Development Code.

Rural Claremont Architectural and Landscape Standards.

Claremont Village District and Village Design Plan.

Claremont General Plan.

Judy Wright, *Claremont: A Pictoral History*, Second Edition (Claremont, CA: Claremont Historic Resources, 1999).

NOTES

1. Theodore Roosevelt. American Museum of Natural History (www.amnh.org). Inscribed at the American Museum of Natural History rotunda.
2. U.S. Census. quickfacts.census.gov/qfd/states/08/08035.htm.
3. U.S. Census. quickfacts.census.gov/qfd/states/16/16043.htm.
4. U.S. Census. quickfacts.census.gov/qfd/states/35/35049.htm.
5. Santa Fe Board of County Commissioners, "The Santa Fe County Growth Management Plan" (October 1999), p. 13.
6. Santa Fe Board of County Commissioners, "The Santa Fe Community College District Plan" (October 2000), p. 1.
7. New Mexico Statutes Annotated 1978 in Chapter 3, Articles 19-21.
8. Teton County Planning Department/U.S. Census. quickfacts.census.gov/qfd/states/56/56039.htm.
9. U.S. Census. quickfacts.census.gov/qfd/states/08/08069.htm.
10. U.S. Census. quickfacts.census.gov/qfd/states/04/04023.htm.
11. City of Claremont Community Development Department.
12. U.S. Census. quickfacts.census.gov/hunits/states/06000.htm.
13. Interview with Anthony Witt, Director of Community Development, City of Claremont, June 18, 2002.

14. Judy Wright, *Claremont: A Pictorial History,* Second Edition (Claremont, CA: Claremont Historic Resources, 1999), pp. 125-131.

15. *Ibid.,* p. 162.

16. *Ibid.,* p. 243.

17. Interview with Ginger Elliott, Director of Claremont Heritage, June 18, 2002.

18. Judy Wright, *Claremont: A Pictorial History,* Second Edition (Claremont, CA: Claremont Historic Resources, 1999), p. 335.

19. *Ibid.,* p. 377.

20. Claremont Land Use & Development Code, Chapter 1, Part 5, Historical Claremont District, 150 Intent.

21. Rural Claremont Architectural and Landscape Standards.

CHAPTER

4

Focused Case Studies

*A thing is right
when it tends to preserve
the integrity, stability,
and beauty of the biotic community.
It is wrong when it tends otherwise*[1]

—ALDO LEOPOLD, *A SAND COUNTY ALMANAC: WITH ESSAYS ON CONSERVATION*

To complement the longer, detailed case studies in Chapter 3, we undertook a number of targeted case studies that highlight a particularly noteworthy development or regulatory process and that has resulted in projects that fit well in the western landscape. Several of these are private development initiatives; others involve an innovative piece of government legislation. Some protect open space; others are particularly sensitive to ridgeline protection or scenic views.

All have a common, unifying theme of respecting historical precedents and maintaining a *True West* sense of place. Many suggest additional patterns that echo the historical precedents, and respond to modern land use planning and environmental concerns and objectives. Both of these historical and contemporary lessons are summarized and categorized with explanatory comments as was done with the major case studies. As with the major case studies, these focused case studies are based on interviews, site visits, or review of site plans or regulations.

1. NATURAL AREA AND OPEN SPACE PRESERVATION

Jefferson County, Colorado

Guiding Patterns

The Rural Cluster Process was created to encourage the clustering of residential dwellings in order to preserve natural areas and open space. Specifically, objectives may include maintenance of rural character, preservation of common open areas, protection of wildlife habitat, protection of critical or unique environmental areas and resources, preservation of agricultural lands suitable for farming or ranching operations, and preservation of historical or cultural buildings and sites (Figure 4-1).

Project Description

The Helker Rural Cluster comprises 140 acres with eight building parcels on 5-acre sites, with the remaining 100 acres preserved with a perpetual conservation easement. Forested land, rock outcroppings, and ridgelines characterize the open space (Figure 4-2). Additionally, the State Division of Wildlife assisted in protecting an elk calving area located on the property and described within a local area plan. Alternatively, the land could have been divided into four 35-acre parcels with minimal county review and no guarantees for the preservation of sensitive lands, ridgeline protection, and contiguous open space.

The Rural Cluster Process provides for an exchange of four additional building sites for 100 acres of significant, natural-area open space that is

4-1 Helker Rural Cluster development provides an understated entry and rural cross-section road.

Source: James van Hemert

preserved in perpetuity. In this particular case, the land is zoned Agricultural-Two, which requires a minimum lot size of 10 acres. The Rural Cluster Process overrides the existing zoning and allows a minimum lot size of 5 acres per building site.

This project significantly achieved the objectives of the county as embodied in the Rural Cluster Process, according to county staff. However, the relatively remote location of the project required cutting an emergency access road across a long, steep slope.

History and Process

In January 1999, Jefferson County implemented the Rural Cluster in response to state legislation enacted in 1996 concerning water well permits in counties with a Rural Land Use Process (H.B. 96-

1364). Colorado Revised Standards 30-28-401 authorizes counties to establish a Rural Land Use Process that offers a development option to allow for the division of land, whether or not previously platted, which creates parcels less of than 35 acres each for single-family residential purposes, as long as at least two-thirds of the total area of the tract is reserved as open area. The resulting parcel is allowed to have a water well without any special augmentation requirements.

Qualifying land must be a legal parcel of at least 70 acres in size, and a minimum two-thirds of the site preserved in perpetuity as open land. Land may be within any of the rural zoning categories. Applications may require formal public hearings before the Planning Commission and the Board of County Commissioners, who render a final deci-

4-2   Helker Rural Cluster. One of many rock outcroppings preserved via a conservation easement encompassing 100 acres.

Source: James van Hemert

sion. Neighborhood meetings are encouraged but not mandatory. For noncontroversial and compliant applications, where no concerns or issues have been raised by referral agencies or the public, hearings may be bypassed, and a written decision may be rendered by the Board of County Commissioners.

Western Rural Development Pattern Language

The Helker Rural Cluster example suggests additional western development pattern language that expands upon and complements the historical patterns discussed in earlier chapters.

Dispersed Rural Settlement

Environmental

- *Protect wildlife habitat and enhance wildlife movement corridors in a manner that allows for continued free movement of the broadest possible variety of species.*

  The design is sensitive to the protection of an elk calving area as identified by the Colorado Division of Wildlife.

- *Protect significant geological features such as rock outcroppings.*

  Home sites are carefully located to avoid destruction of rock outcroppings.

CONTACT

Jefferson County Planning Department
100 Jefferson County Parkway, Suite 3550,
Golden, CO 80419
(303) 271-8700
www.co.jefferson.co.us

SOURCES

Interview with Heather Scott, planner with the Jefferson County Planning Department, 2000.

Jefferson County Land Development Regulations, Rural Cluster Process.

2. NATURAL AREA AND OPEN SPACE PRESERVATION

Gallatin County, Montana

Guiding Patterns

Preservation of natural areas and open space guide the intent and provisions of the Planned Unit Development Overlay District of the Gallatin Canyon/Big Sky Zoning Regulation. Residential clustering provisions provide for mandatory open space standards characterized as described below.

Project Description

The Spanish Peaks Planned Unit Development comprises 5,020 acres consisting of a resort village with 345 dwelling units, 30 employee housing units and 100-room guest lodge, 273 low-density residential building sites, and 2,975 acres of common open space. Recent timber harvest areas and older harvest areas with regenerating timber stands characterize the mountainous property. Significant public amenities include the following:

- provision of public access and park land around Ousel Falls
- trail corridors providing east/west and north/south circulation
- open space blocks that protect large areas of wildlife habitats and view sheds
- a total open space system that includes approximately 74% (3,716 acres) of the total land area, of which 2,975 acres are common open space; applicant received a density bonus of 55 additional dwelling units in exchange for providing additional open space
- location of open space and trails in accordance with the County Wildlife Habitat and Trail Maps
- open space that may be used for passive and active recreation, wildlife habitat, and pro-

Table 4-1. Bonus Units

Amount of Open Space	Bonus Units
50%	10%
60%	15%
70%	20%
80%	25%

tection of scenic, unique, or important natural features

- condition that all open space shall be preserved in perpetuity

Additional "bonus" residential units may be awarded for minimum levels of open space protection as described in Table 4-1:

Western Rural Development Pattern Language

The Gallatin County case study suggests an additional western rural development pattern that expands upon and complements the historical patterns discussed in earlier chapters.

Dispersed Rural Settlement

Environmental

- *Cluster development in a manner so as to maximize environmentally significant, unfragmented open space.*

In the case of Gallatin County, modest density bonuses are offered in exchange for significant levels of open space preservation.

CONTACT

Gallatin County Planning Department
311 W. Main, Bozeman, MT 59715
(406) 582-3130
www.gallco.org

SOURCES

Interview with Randall Johnson, planner with the Gallatin County Planning Department, 2000.

Planned Unit Overlay District of the Gallatin Canyon/ Big Sky Zoning Overlay District.

3. SKYLINE AND RIDGELINE PROTECTION

Castle Rock, Colorado

Guiding Patterns

The protection of visually significant mesa and ridgeline landforms is a guiding principle behind the promulgation of Castle Rock's Skyline/Ridgeline Protection Overlay Zone District.

Project Description

The regulations are based upon computer simulation from 232 select locations, or "viewing platforms," to ascertain the relative impacts of development throughout the town's viewshed. A "skyline" is defined as that interface between land and sky. A structure is "skylined" if it interrupts this land/sky interface. Ridgelines may or may not be skylines depending on the vantage point. The Overlay Zone District distinguishes between major, moderate, and minor skyline areas as well as major and minor ridgelines. Major and minor ridgelines were determined on a more subjective level by a group field tour.

- *Major Skyline Areas* occur where a 28-foot high structure would be highly visible along the viewing platforms (determined by analysis to be where 28-foot structures skylined from 65 viewing platforms or more).

- *Moderate Skyline Areas* occur where a 28-foot high structure would be visible from several points along the viewing platforms (determined by analysis to be where 28-foot structures "skylined" from 17 to 64 viewing platforms).
- *Minor Skyline Areas* occur where a 28-foot high structure would not be visible, but a 35-foot high structure would be visible from several points (determined by analysis to be where 35-foot structures skylined from 17 to 64 viewing platforms).

Building Restrictions and Visual Impact Mitigation

- No primary or accessory structure may be constructed within major skyline or major ridgeline areas.
- No primary or accessory structures with a height of greater than 28 feet shall be constructed within Moderate Skyline Areas.
- Building heights are restricted to 35 feet within Minor Skyline Areas.
- Within all areas of the Overlay Zone District, all structures shall comply with measures to mitigate the visual impacts as follows:
  — Colors and roof materials shall repeat colors found most commonly in the land and vegetation around the building (earth tones).
  — Light reflective values shall not exceed 40.
- Reflective materials and bright colors that contrast dramatically with the colors of the land and vegetation around them shall not be used as dominant colors on any wall or roof surface.
- The area around each primary and accessory structure shall include at least one tree of a species with a mature height of at least 35

feet for each 2,500 square feet of lot or parcel area; however, this shall not exceed more than eight trees for a single-family residential lot.

- At least 50% of the trees required shall be located within 50 feet of the primary structure on the side facing the nearest viewing platform.
- Floodlighting shall not be used, and all lighting shall have cutoff light fixtures to avoid light emissions beyond property boundaries.

Western Rural Development Pattern Language

Review and observation of the Castle Rock example suggests additional western development pattern language that expands upon and complements the historical patterns discussed in earlier chapters.

Dispersed Rural Settlement

Visual

- *Avoid or mitigate ridgetop "skylining" that alters the natural land profiles with built structures.*
- *Where natural vegetation or topography do not allow for "hiding" development, locate structures such that they are subordinate to the horizon and any significant viewsheds.*

Castle Rock's standards provide for a variety of measures to reduce impacts on natural land profiles.

CONTACT

Castle Rock Planning Department
(720) 733-2202
www.castlerock.org

SOURCE

Town of Castle Rock's Skyline/Ridgeline Protection Overlay Zone District.

4. RANCH ARCHITECTURE AND PRESERVATION

City of Moab, Utah

Guiding Patterns

Historical ranch preservation and utilization of its key architectural elements in new construction guide the development of Moab Springs Ranch Planned Unit Development.

Project Description

In stark contrast with much of the banal, look-alike, tourist-oriented, strip commercial development in Moab, Utah, the approved Moab Springs Ranch recreational base camp reflects the character and heritage of the area (Figure 4-3). The 18-acre approved Planned Unit Development incorporates the remaining Victorian-style ranch home and several outbuildings into a recreational resort with 42 duplex/triplex units and a lodge.

4-3 Existing ranch outbuildings are constructed primarily of sandstone.

Source: McKay Edwards, AICP

WEST ELEVATION

4-4 Side elevation in stucco, stone, and board-and-batten.

Source: Thomas A. Buese, AIA, and Kenton A. Peters, Jr., AIA, Buese + Peters, Salt Lake City

The ranch dates back to the 1870s and was first settled by an African American prospector, and then occupied by a Mormon rancher. New construction will incorporate ranch-style architecture with simple, clean lines; stucco and board-and-batten siding and stone exterior materials; and tin roofing material.

History and Process

The land was previously zoned Highway Commercial, which would have permitted and promoted a style of development not necessarily suited to the character of the land and without any sensitivity to the historical context. The developer, McKay Edwards, AICP, rezoned the ground to Planned Unit Development with commitments to provide context-sensitive building styles and materials, and to preserve the existing ranch structures (Figure 4-4).

Western Rural Development Pattern Language

Review of the Moab example suggests additional western development pattern language that expands upon and complements the historical patterns discussed in earlier chapters.

Culture/Community

- *Integrate historical buildings in new development.*
- *Reflect indigenous architectural patterns in contemporary construction as a way to connect with the region's cultural history.*

The Moab Springs project illustrates how historical buildings can successfully be integrated in new development.

CONTACT

McKay Edwards, AICP
Club Utah Resort Group
(801) 588-0911

SOURCES

Interview with McKay Edwards, planner and project developer, 2000.

5. ARCHITECTURE: DESIGN, MATERIALS, COLOR

Summit County, Utah (The Promontory)

Guiding Patterns

The guiding pattern for development of The Promontory in Summit County, Utah, is that the natural landscape remains the dominant visual image. Building design, materials, color, and landscaping standards are based upon this premise.

Project Description

The Promontory is a 6,500-acre Planned Unit Development in Summit County, about 25 miles west of Salt Lake City. Significant portions of it are highly visible from Interstate 40 and Utah State Highway 248. Land disturbance, landscape, and architectural design standards are detailed in a manner so as to ensure that the natural landscape remains the dominant visual image.

Land Disturbance

- No more than 50% of site is to be disturbed, even if it means not using the entire building envelope.
- Fines of $2,500 will be charged for removing vegetation without approval.

Landscaping

- Driveways must use colored, exposed aggregate concrete pavers, bomonite, or other pattern and texture methods. No uncolored concrete or asphalt is permitted.
- Fences may not be used to arbitrarily delineate the building envelope. Fence design emulating old Utah ranch lands is strongly encouraged.

- Landscaping in transitional areas shall be a series of concentric planting zones.
- The first zone, with the most formal planting, must be situated adjacent to the residence, or an accent border within 6 feet of either side of the entry drive or parking apron.
- The second is a transitional zone with a soft edge.
- The final zone is the building envelope itself; no planting may be outside of this.

Architectural Design Standards

- The goal is to create the highest quality home within the smallest possible volume consistent with the satisfaction of the owner's need for space.

Height and Massing of Structures

- Home sites with frontage on two roads can have no portion of a structure exceeding a true vertical height of 22 feet above original natural grade directly below the point of measurement.
- All other home sites shall be 32 feet.
- Roof forms for homes on sloping sites step down with the grade to integrate with the natural setting.
- All residences must have pitched roofs with a minimum pitch of 5:12 and a maximum pitch of 12:12.
- No building wall may extend more than 20 feet in height without an offset in the vertical plane of at least 2 feet.
- No single-story building wall may extend more than 30 feet in length without an offset of at least 2 feet. No two-story building wall may extend more than 20 feet in length without an offset of at least 2 feet.

Exterior Materials

- Predominant exterior materials will consist of wood or native stone, including shingles, beveled or tongue-in-groove board siding, board-on-board, board-and-batten, and native stone.

- Stucco, metal siding, fiberglass, and vinyl siding are prohibited.

Roofs

- The overall profile and articulation of the roof should be sufficiently irregular to break up anything that would otherwise appear too boxy or discordant with the landscape or neighboring structures. Expansive roof structures shall be articulated by way of gable or shed dormers. Overhangs shall be provided at all roof edges exceeding 3 feet.
- The roofs of all two-story homes should include single-story elements. The higher masses should generally occur toward the center, with the lower profiles occurring toward the outer portions of the house. At no time can the highest point of a house be at any of the outside walls.
- Roof materials permitted include patinaed corten steel, copper wood shakes, architectural-grade fiberglass shingles, flat concrete tiles, and other low-reflectivity tiles.

Entrances

- Entrances proportioned to convey a sense of human scale are appropriate. Entries that are too ornate, monumental, or imposing will not be approved. Trellised entries can be used as a welcoming transition between indoor and outdoor spaces.

Exterior Colors

- Exterior colors shall be generally subdued to blend with natural landscape. Earth tones are recommended; accent colors must be used judiciously and with restraint.
- In no case will colors approaching the primary range be permitted, nor will drastic contrasts in value be allowed. White may only be used as an accent or trim color.

Light-gray siding stains, which approach white or off-white in appearance, will not be allowed.

- All colors must be within a Light Reflectance Value (LRV) range of 15-35.

Garages

- Garage doors shall not dominate the residence when viewed from the street.
- All residences must incorporate the design of low-flow toilets, with 1.5 gallons per flush or less.

Western Rural Development Pattern Language

A number of significant historical western patterns may be distilled from the Promontory Planned Development case study. Moreover, the project teaches some important lessons and suggests additional patterns that respond to modern land use planning and environmental concerns and objections. Both historical and contemporary lessons are summarized below with explanatory comments provided as appropriate.

Dispersed Rural Settlement

Visual

- *Less is more: minimize exotic landscaping, the size of building footprints, and the amount of impervious surface devoted to roadways. Allow the natural landscape to dominate.*
- *Where natural vegetation or topography do not allow for "hiding" development, locate structures such that they are subordinate to the surrounding landforms and any significant view sheds.*

Architecture/Design

Form

- *Avoid building large, monolithic structures. Buildings should comprise a complex of smaller buildings or parts that manifest their own internal social realities.*

Height restrictions and required articulation produce the desired effect of quality within the smallest possible space.

- *Arrange roofs so that each distinct roof corresponds to an identifiable social entity in the building. Place the largest roofs—those that are highest and have the largest span—over the largest and most important and most communal spaces; build the lesser roofs off these largest and highest roofs. Allow for and expect additions to be made over time.*

The Promontory design standards produce this effect by virtue of requiring single-story elements in all two-story structures.

Color and Materials

- *Use natural materials in a manner that reflects an organic integrity and harmony with the natural surroundings. Stone and wood are often appropriate as the primary construction material.*

Exterior materials exclude most manufactured composite materials.

- *As a first choice, use natural, earth-tone colors; however, do not do so exclusively. With an appropriate building profile, bright historical colors such as red, green, or ochre may serve as a beautiful counterpoint to the natural landscape.*

All colors are restricted in accordance with an established LRV range, allowing some room for judicious use of accent colors.

CONTACTS

Summit County Planning Department
Kerwin Jenson, Planning Director
(456) 336-3131
www.co.summit.ut.us

Pivotal Group
Rick Sauntag
(602) 956-7200
www.pivotalgroup.com

SOURCES

Interviews with Kerwin Jenson, Summit County Planning Director; and Rick Sauntag, project developer, 2000.

6. AGRICULTURAL LAND AND WATER RESOURCE PROTECTION AND ENHANCEMENT

Rio Arriba County, New Mexico

Guiding Patterns[2]

The protection of irrigated agricultural farmland threatened by inappropriate development is the guiding principle for Rio Arriba County's Agricultural Protection and Enhancement ordinance. The basis for this ordinance goes beyond merely preserving farmland and open space; however, irrigated farmland in this part of New Mexico is a central feature of the "Acequia System," a physical and political method of distributing water. The acequia tradition remains a central community structure in Rio Arriba County and is viewed as a necessary support to the sustainability of local traditional communities.

Project Description

The physical structure of the acequia can be described as trenches or excavated ditches along a watercourse, such as Rio Chama or the Rio Grande, that move or divert water through gravity flow. In political terms, acequias are political subdivisions of the State of New Mexico. Both as a political body and as a physical structure, their function is to allocate and distribute water for irrigation of fields for supporting crops, livestock water, or other beneficial uses.

The history of diverting water from a source (e.g., a river) goes back to the original inhabitants of the Americas, but the current system and practice go back to 1600 AD. The Spanish settlers realized the potential and value of the lands that could be irrigated, and constructed the acequias in the valleys; they instituted the "mayordomo," "La Comission," and the "Parciantes" as the structure of the acequia system. This system formed the basis for the priority system (law of appropriation), referred to as "first in time, first in line." This form of regulation originated from the Spanish colonial government via the "Laws of the Indies."

Individual deeds within a community were established separating the irrigated parcels of land. The administration of the acequia was to ensure that water resources were distributed equitably to all community members. Today, the acequia tradition is a strong community structure in Rio Arriba County and is seen as important in maintaining the sustainability of local traditional communities.

A typical acequia plot of land is characterized as a 5-acre narrow strip bifurcated by an irrigation acequia, with a home, well, and septic system on the dry land portion and productive orchards and other agricultural crops on the irrigated side.

This sustainable rural pattern is threatened by pressure to develop agricultural land for residential purposes. Market values for irrigated land are rising to ranges between $20,000 and $55,000 per acre. Further exacerbating the threat are increased valuation of water rights concurrent with residential development, recreational facilities (golf courses), and increased urbanization and commercial uses in Santa Fe and Española.

The conversion of agricultural land to other uses has affected the ability of acequias to determine the future of water rights along an acequia as well as the maintenance of the acequia itself. Increasingly, acequia parcels are converted to residential uses; the remaining "parciantes" (owners) along an acequia are required to maintain the system with fewer resources. Typical residential conversions split an acequia parcel into equal-sized residential lots as small as ¾ acre, each with their own septic system and well. The agricultural land is put out of production, groundwater contamination becomes a threat, and former agricultural

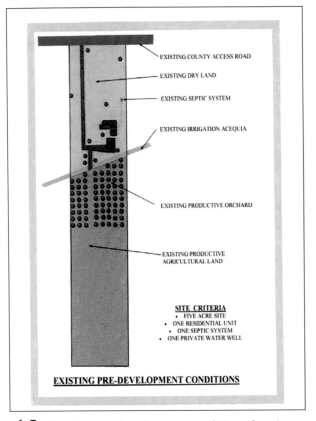

EXISTING COUNTY ACCESS ROAD

EXISTING DRY LAND

EXISTING SEPTIC SYSTEM

EXISTING IRRIGATION ACEQUIA

EXISTING PRODUCTIVE ORCHARD

EXISTING PRODUCTIVE AGRICULTURAL LAND

SITE CRITERIA
- FIVE ACRE SITE
- ONE RESIDENTIAL UNIT
- ONE SEPTIC SYSTEM
- ONE PRIVATE WATER WELL

EXISTING PRE-DEVELOPMENT CONDITIONS

4-5 Existing pre-development conditions drawing.
Source: Rio Arriba County Planning Department

land becomes a maintenance problem for new owners (Figure 4-5).

To preserve the traditional acequia agricultural way of life and landscape, Rio Arriba County has enacted the Agricultural Protection and Enhancement ordinance, which encourages a "clustered" approach to residential development and simultaneously preserves the irrigated agricultural lands. Under this scenario, a 5-acre acequia parcel could be developed with a shared well and shared advanced wastewater treatment system as a means of ensuring water quality. Development is concentrated on approximately 1½ acres of dry land, retaining the remaining 3½ irrigated acres for agricultural uses (Figure 4-6).

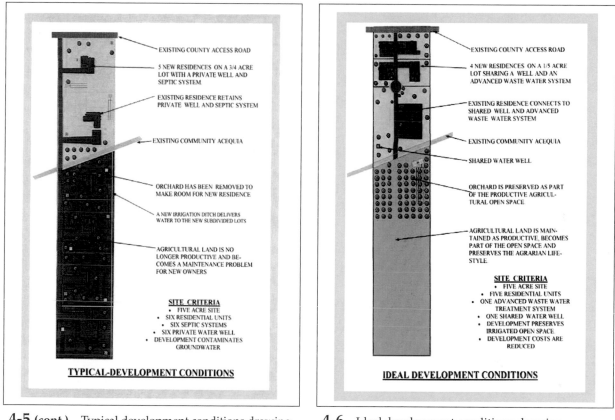

4-5 (cont.)   Typical development conditions drawing.

Source: Rio Arriba County Planning Department

4-6   Ideal development conditions drawing.

Source: Rio Arriba County Planning Department

Western Rural Development Pattern Language

Several historical western development patterns may be distilled from the Rio Arriba example. These are summarized and categorized below with explanatory comments provided as appropriate. Moreover, modern ordinances suggest a pattern that responds to current land use planning and environmental concerns and objectives.

Regional Development Patterns

- *Sustain traditional community practices that support agriculture, cultural practices, and the resultant physical landscape.*

The Arriba County ordinance is unique in its thoughtful approach to sustaining traditional community practices.

Dispersed Rural Settlement

Cultural

- *Preserve irrigated agricultural lands.*

Environmental

- *Cluster development in a manner so as to maximize visually and environmentally significant unfragmented open space.*

CONTACT

Rio Arriba County Planning Department
Patricio Garcia, Planning and Zoning Director
(505) 753-7774

SOURCES

Interview with Patricio Garcia, Rio Arriba County
Planning Department, 2000.

Arriba County's Agricultural Protection and
Enhancement ordinance.

7. VISUAL RESOURCE AND AGRICULTURAL LAND PRESERVATION

Routt County, Colorado

Guiding Patterns

The primary guiding pattern illustrated by the Priest Creek Ranch project in Routt County is visual resources protection. Open rural views along State Highway 40 are preserved, ridgelines are protected from "skylined" development, and an important visual resource for the southern gateway of Steamboat Springs is preserved. Additionally, agricultural land and operational resources are preserved as part of a larger ranching operation.

Project Description

*Land Preservation Subdivision
Exemption/Priest Creek Ranch*

The 366-acre Priest Creek Ranch parcel lies just to the south of Steamboat Springs. Two creeks, meandering through relatively flat hay meadows on the south and giving way to wetland areas to the north, traverse the land. The creek bottoms include dense stands of cottonwoods and riparian habitat. A pair of terraces rise above the creek to the east and transition to a steep hillside at the northeast corner. The hillsides and terraces are covered with oak brush and some aspen. A steep ridge defines the north boundary at the west end

of the parcel. Elk winter concentration areas are located on the east side of the property toward the north end. Walton Creek offers habitat to numerous species.

Attached to the parcel, across RCR 24, to the south is 1.8 acres of land that include barns, sheds, and corrals to be used and restored as common facilities. An irrigation ditch serving the existing hay meadows enters on the east side of the tract, and traverses the base of the hillside as it heads north and west.

Under the standards of the Land Preservation Subdivision (LPS) Exemption, 12 single-family lots (averaging 4 acres each), along with one primary and one agricultural employee unit, are created. The "remainder parcels" total 318 acres, of which 143 acres is subject to a potential annexation and rezoning by the Town of Steamboat Springs for a golf course.

If divided into 35-acre parcels, the property could accommodate 10 parcels. Under the LPS, the 360-acre tract is entitled to 13 single-family dwelling units based on over 300 acres being set aside in remainder parcel(s), allowing the property three "bonus" parcels. Three units are located on the westerly access road located above Walton Creek; 10 units are located to the east on a terrace overlooking the property. All of the lots include building envelopes that avoid sensitive and hazardous lands as well as maintain visual quality.

Visual Resources

The ridge on the northeastern part of the property is the most visible portion of the land from surrounding public roads and neighborhoods. This is also very important elk habitat connecting Walton Creek and the surrounding meadows with the forested hillsides and public land to the east. As part of the remainder parcel, there will be no development on this ridge as proposed. The building envelopes placed on the lots will prevent any structures to be "skylined" from State Highway 40. The enclosing ridges to the north and east further prevent skylining. The lots are located on terraces with ridges rising behind these building envelopes.

The petition reserves the area between State Highway 40 and Walton Creek as open space. This land represents an important visual resource for the entry into Steamboat Springs. The tall cottonwoods lining Walton Creek form a visual barrier and screen direct views of the building envelopes. The easterly building envelopes form a residential cluster that will be visible from State Highway 40 as well as other parts of the valley. This clustering of buildings is encouraged by the LPS regulations.

Agricultural Land

All of the lots are located so as to avoid the most productive agricultural land. Grazing land, hay meadows, and the irrigation ditch will be maintained as part of a ranching operation. An agricultural employee is needed to perform this work, including running ranch operations on the remaining 1,270 acres owned by Alpine Lands. The proposal accommodates an agricultural employee unit on a 30-acre remainder parcel at the southeast corner of the project. This unit will not count toward the parcel's density limit, because the unit is located on a remainder tract and will be associated with a primary unit on the lot. The agricultural employee living in this unit must work at least 20 hours per week on the agricultural operation.

Land Preservation Subdivision Exemption Criteria

Eligible land for an LPS exemption must meet the following four criteria:
- All of the land subject to the application is within the Agriculture/Forestry (A/F) Zone District.
- All of the land is contiguous.
- The land is at least 70 acres in size.
- The owner is willing to execute an agreement restricting further development and subdivision of the subject property.

Additionally, the location of building envelopes and the configuration of the proposed lots are acceptable under a set of design criteria that includes visual resources, agricultural land preservation, lakes/rivers/riparian area protection, minimization of infrastructure, and preservation of wildlife habitat.

Bonus buildable lots are granted for each 100 acres of land placed on a "remainder parcel" that remains free from buildings.

Western Rural Development Pattern Language

The Routt County example exemplifies several of the historical western development patterns discussed in earlier chapters.

Dispersed Rural Settlement

Environmental

- *Protect wildlife habitat and enhance wildlife movement corridors in a manner that allows for continued free movement of the broadest possible variety of species.*

Cultural

- *Preserve irrigated agricultural lands.*
- *Preserve and integrate historic ranching operations.*

Visual

- *Nestle structures below ridgelines and within the folds of hills.*
- *Preserve and protect significant foreground views along significant "viewing platforms or passageways" such as public gathering places and major roadways.*

CONTACT

Routt County Planning Department
www.co.routt.co.us

SOURCES

Interview with Allison Willets, Routt County Planning Department, 2000.

Land Preservation Subdivision ordinance, Routt County.

8. SLOPE PROTECTION

Salt Lake County, Utah

Guiding Patterns

The guiding development pattern featured is preserving the natural character of the foothills and canyons within the unincorporated portions of Salt Lake County, which are experiencing severe development pressure. Some of these canyons are important watersheds for Salt Lake City's water supply. Specifically, development is encouraged that fits the natural slope of the land in order to minimize the scarring and erosion effects of cutting, filling, and grading related to construction on hillsides, ridgelines, and steep slopes (Figure 4-7).

Project Description

The Foothills and Canyons Overlay Zone chapter of the Salt Lake County Development Code is featured without any specific application. The Overlay District encourages clustering of development with a 25% bonus. Clustering, compared to a more traditional site development plan, better provides open space, preserves existing trees and vegetation coverage, and preserves sensitive environmental areas such as stream corridors, slide areas, wetlands, and steep slopes.

Slope Protection Standards

- No development or site disturbance may occur on slopes greater than 30%. All lands with slopes greater than 30% shall remain in natural private or public open space.

- No development may intrude on identified and designated ridgeline protection areas as designated by the county. Ridgeline protection areas consist of prominent ridgelines that are highly visible from public rights-of-way or trails, and shall include the crest of any designated hill or slope, plus the land

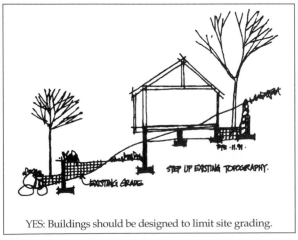

YES: Buildings should be designed to limit site grading.

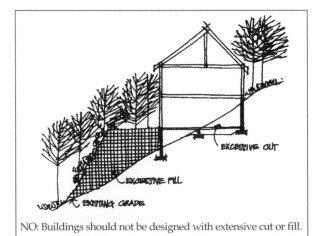

NO: Buildings should not be designed with extensive cut or fill.

4-7   Buildings on a slope.

Source: Salt Lake County Zoning Code

located within 100 feet horizontally on either side of the crest.

Grading Standards

- Grading and excavation report/plans must be reviewed and approved in advance of any disturbance for buildings, utilities, or services.
- Cutting and grading to create benches or pads for additional or larger building sites must be avoided to the maximum extent possible.
- The original, natural grade of a lot shall not be raised or lowered more than 4 feet at any point for construction of any structure or improvement. This may be raised to 6 feet when appropriate retaining walls are used or for driveways with retaining walls.
- Separate building pads for accessory buildings and structures other than garages (e.g., tennis courts, swimming pools, outbuildings, and similar facilities) are discouraged except where the natural slope is 20% or less.
- Cut man-made slopes shall not exceed a slope of 50%.
- All cut, filled, and graded slopes shall be recontoured to the natural, varied contour of the surrounding terrain.
- Retaining walls may not exceed 6 feet.
- Terracing shall be limited to two tiers. The width of the terrace between any two 4-foot vertical retaining walls shall be at least 3 feet.

Driveways

- Driveways longer than 50 feet in length shall not be allowed to cross slopes between 30% and 50%. However, when no alternatives are available, a short run of no more than 100 feet or 10% of the driveway's entire length, whichever is greater, is allowed subject to strict guidelines.
- No driveways shall cross slopes greater than 50%.

- Driveways shall to the maximum extent feasible follow natural contour lines.

Western Rural Development Pattern Language

The Salt Lake County example illustrates some of the historic western development patterns discussed in earlier chapters, as well as other patterns that are complementary and address contemporary planning and environmental objectives.

Dispersed Rural Settlement

Visual

- *Nestle structures below ridges and within the folds of hills.*

Environmental

- *Locate buildings at the toes of slopes and edges of meadows in a manner that allows for natural windbreaks and creates a feeling of shelter.*
- *Design buildings on hillsides to follow the natural terrain in a manner that minimizes earth disturbance.*
- *Construct the narrowest rural roads possible, without undue negative impacts on public safety, in order to minimize impacts on vegetation, natural drainage patterns, and the natural terrain. In placing roadways, do so in a manner that minimizes the need for "cut and fill."*
- *Restrict development on steep slopes and in hazard areas.*

CONTACT

Salt Lake County Planning and Development Services
(801) 468-2000
www.co.slc.ut.us

SOURCES

Salt Lake County Development Code, Foothills and Canyons Overlay Zone.

9. RURAL SCENIC CORRIDOR PROTECTION

Santa Fe County, New Mexico

Guiding Patterns

A desire to protect the scenic quality of Interstate 25 and New Mexico State Highway 599 served as a catalyst in creating the Santa Fe Metro Area Highway Corridor Plan. In addition to functional transportation and land use goals, a major goal was to protect the scenic vistas and natural landscape of the Santa Fe areas viewed from the highways.

Project Description

The scenic corridor design standards establish the following criteria for new development:
- minimum setbacks from highway right-of-way
- maximum building heights
- maximum lot coverage
- landscaping standards
- outdoor lighting standards
- architectural standards

The standards provide clarity in the high degree of specificity, and provide flexibility by establishing both critical (required) and desired (negotiated) standards. The higher negotiated standards may be achieved through TDR, conservation easements, trades, density bonus incentives, acquisitions, and other means.

The two levels of standards are well illustrated with respect to minimum setbacks from highway right-of-way and the relationship to ridgetops (Figure 4-8).

An additional measure worthy of mention is lighting. The minimization of outdoor lighting is critical in maintaining the quality of rural nighttime darkness. Standards implemented through the development review process include the following (Figure 4-9):
- Outdoor lighting shall be minimized in the scenic corridor. No overhead utilities, including streetlights, are allowed within the required setback area.
- Light design and installation shall emphasize low-level uniform lighting to avoid the nuisance and hazardous conditions caused by abrupt changes from bright lights to darkness.
- All lighting, including signs, shall be fully shielded and directed downward.
- A maximum of 0.5 average horizontal foot-candles shall be permitted for all uses.
- Parking and security lights shall not be taller than buildings (maximum of 17 feet).
- Landscape lighting shall be low-level lighting only (maximum 4 feet; no pole lights).
- No façade lighting will be permitted.
- Streetlights are prohibited except where necessary for vehicle and pedestrian safety at busy intersections. At intersections, safety lighting shall consist of approach lighting only, set back far enough from the intersection to give motorists at least two seconds of warning of the coming intersection and consisting of a series of uniform lights.
- All streetlights shall be designed and installed to meet residential or rural freeway lighting levels (0.4 to 0.6 average horizontal foot-candles). No streetlights may exceed 24 feet in height.

Western Rural Development Pattern Language

The Santa Fe Metro Area Highway Corridor planning effort suggests additional western development pattern language that expands upon and complements the historical patterns discussed in earlier chapters.

Dispersed Rural Settlement

Visual

- *Nestle structures below ridgelines and within the folds of hills.*

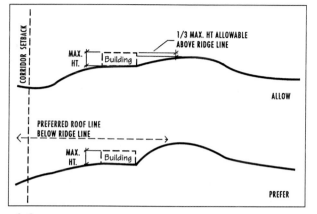

4-8 Two-thirds of a structure's height should be sited below a ridgetop whenever possible. The preferred standard restricts the height below the ridgeline, as shown above.

Source: Santa Fe Metro Area Highway Corridor Plan, 1999

- *Minimize visual clutter within scenic corridors.*
- *Restrict or shield lighting so as to limit horizontal and vertical light trespass, thereby preserving the dark night sky.*

CONTACT

Santa Fe County
Jack Kolkmeyer102 Grant Ave., P.O. Box 276, Santa Fe, NM 87504
(800) 894-7078

SOURCE

Santa Fe Metro Area Highway Corridor Plan.

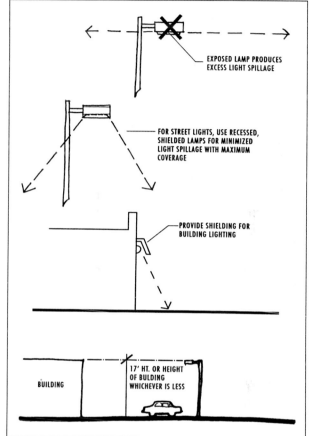

4-9 Lighting standards.

Source: Santa Fe Metro Area Highway Corridor Plan, 1999

4-10   DC Ranch home.

Source: Dino Tonn Photography

10. ECOLOGICAL AND
HIGH DESERT PRESERVATION

Scottsdale, Arizona (DC Ranch)

Guiding Patterns

Guiding patterns for the development of the 8,300-acre DC Ranch include a desert color palette and preservation of the unique desert landscape, including special natural features preservation, ridgeline protection, and native plant salvage.

Project Description

Located on the outskirts of Scottsdale, Arizona, DC Ranch preserves 4,500 acres of desert in a private land trust. The City of Scottsdale contributed financially in the creation of this trust and in the preservation of the land. The developed portion will comprise 3,700 acres of commercial and residential land uses. Grassland, riparian corridors, and desert characterize the land. Significant visual features include saguaro cactus, ridgelines viewed from a distance, and unique rock outcroppings.

Major ridgelines were protected even though the developer had the "right" to develop them. Desert wash protection beyond that required by the city ensures that, from both an ecological and aesthetic perspective, key elements of the desert are preserved within the context of development. Additionally, significant wildlife habitat and movement corridors are preserved. Native plants located in the path of development have been salvaged and replanted (Figure 4-10).

A professional colorist was brought on board to establish proper color control for distant views, while expanding the palette for character and diversity at the street-scene level. Architectural themes are keyed to historically relevant architectural styles of the southwest, including vernacular ranch design.

Western Rural Development Pattern Language

The DC Ranch example suggests additional western development pattern language that expands upon and complements the historical patterns discussed in earlier chapters.

Dispersed Rural Settlement

Environmental

- *Create a program for salvage and replant native plants that lie in the path of development.*

- *Protect significant geological features such as rock outcroppings.*

- *Restrict development on steep slopes and in geologically hazardous areas.*

- *Cluster development in a manner so as to maximize environmentally unfragmented open space.*

Architecture/Design

Color and Materials

- *Establish a color palette for buildings within distant views that reflects the surrounding landscape: expand the range of colors to reflect the character and diversity at the street-scene level.*

- *Expand the typical range of exterior wall and roof colors to reflect the character and diversity at street level.*

- *Create authentically based architectural design character, and control colors and materials that reflect the design heritage of the area and complement the native environmental context.*

CONTACTS

Scottsdale Community Development and Planning
(480) 312-2500
www.ci.scottsdale.az.us

Dale Gardon Design, LLC
8160 N. Hayden Rd., Suite J108, Scottsdale, AZ 85255
(480) 948-9666
e-mail: dale@dalegardondesign.com

DC Ranch Information Center
(877) 345-2425

Brent Herrington, DMB
7600 E. Doubletree Ranch Rd., Suite 300,
Scottsdale, AZ 85255
(480) 367-7000

SOURCE

Interview with Dale Gordon, architect, 2000.

11. LIGHTING

Dark Sky Ordinance—Tempe, Arizona

Guiding Patterns

The guiding pattern for the Dark Sky ordinance of Tempe, Arizona, is to restrict the undesirable effects of outdoor lighting that may have a detrimental effect on astronomical observations. It might be added that this principle would be appropriate on a broader scale to protect the enjoyment of the night sky by those living in the West.

Regulation Description and Analysis

The lighting standards apply to all outdoor, artificial illuminating devices tied to buildings, recreational areas, parking lots, landscapes, streets, and outdoor advertising lighting. Mitigation measures include shielding and light filtering for a variety of fixture lamp types. The preferred light source is low-pressure sodium. Table 4-3 identifies requirements for shielding and filtering by fixture lamp type.

Table 4-3. Requirements for Shielding and Filtering

FIXTURE LAMP TYPE	SHIELDED	FILTERED
Low-pressure sodium[1]	None	None
High-pressure sodium	Fully	None
Metal halide[2]	Fully	Yes
Fluorescent	Fully[4]	Yes[5]
Quartz[3]	Fully	None
Incandescent greater than 160W	Fully	None
Incandescent 100W or less	None	None
Mercury vapor	Not permitted (Sec. 25-138(d))	
Glass tubes filled with neon, argon, krypton	None	None
Other sources	As approved by Sect. 25-133	

(1) This is the preferred light source to minimize undesirable light into the night sky affecting astronomical observations.
(2) Metal halide lamps shall be in enclosed luminaries.
(3) For the purposes of this table, quartz lamps shall not be considered an incandescent light source.
(4) Outdoor advertising signs of the type constructed of translucent materials and wholly illuminated from within do not require shielding.
(5) Warm white natural lamps are preferred to minimize detrimental effects.

Western Rural Development Pattern Language

The Tempe Dark Sky ordinance, one of many enacted by Arizona communities, suggests additional western development pattern language that expands upon and complements the historical patterns discussed in earlier chapters.

Dispersed Rural Settlement

Visual

- *Restrict or shield lighting so as to limit light trespass, thereby preserving the dark night sky.*

CONTACT

Tempe Planning Department
(480) 350-8331
www.tempe.gov/tdsi/planning

SOURCE

Tempe Dark Sky ordinance.

12. CLIMATIC AND ECOLOGICALLY SENSITIVE BUILDING

Civano—Tucson, Arizona

Guiding Patterns

Harnessing the sun's energy for power, warmth, and light defines Civano—a new high-desert community on the edge of Tucson, Arizona. Complementary hallmarks include water-harvesting strategies, recycled building materials, and highly insulating materials for building construction.

Project Description

Located in the desert outskirts of Tucson, the Federal National Mortgage Association (Fannie Mae) is financing a 1,145-acre community that will ultimately contain 2,500 homes and preserve a portion of the Sonoran desert. The community is a unique blend of New Urbanist, mixed-use, small-town ideals with high ecological standards.[3]

Solar energy is harnessed both passively and actively for electricity with the use of photovoltaic cells (Figure 4-11). Homes are oriented on an east/west axis to minimize exposure from the hot afternoon sun. South-facing entrances are buffered with covered "loggias." A stated community objective is to reduce overall home energy consumption by 50% beyond the 1995 Model Energy Code.[4]

Durable and energy-efficient building materials include straw-bale construction (Figure 4-12), "thermal-mass materials" that share qualities with traditional adobe, and RASTRA—panels made of 85% recycled polystyrene foam punched with holes for concrete pouring.

Low water consumption is a primary goal for Tucson. In Civano, water is harvested in rain barrels from roof drain spouts and recycled effluent for landscape watering. All homes have a pair of silver and purple water meters (i.e., silver for potable water and purple for recycled).[5] The project anticipates a 65% reduction in overall potable water consumption.[6]

Western Rural Development Pattern Language

Civano embodies a number of historical western development patterns. These patterns are summarized and categorized below with explanatory comments provided as needed.

Architecture/Design

Form

- *Use biodegradable, low energy-consuming materials, which are easy to cut and modify on site. For bulk materials, use earth-based materials such as earth, brick, and tile.*

4-11   Solar energy home in Civano.

Source: Bill Webber, MD, and Solarbuilt

- *Harvest water through simple and ingenious methods, and incorporate them into the design of buildings and communities.*

Site Design

- *Orient buildings and groups of buildings to take advantage of the sun for winter warmth and mitigation of summer heat. Place buildings to the north of outdoor spaces and keep outdoor spaces to the south, with opportunities for dappled shade from trees or trellises.*

CONTACTS

Tucson Planning Department
(520) 791-4505
www.ci.tucson.az.us

The Community of Civano
Lee Rayburn, Managing Partner
(520) 298-8900
www.civano.com

4-12   An age-old technique—straw-bale construction, as seen in this model home—works well and reuses material that would otherwise be wasted. The thick bales provide for pleasingly deep sills and door jambs.

Source: C. Alan Nichols, PE

13. CULTURAL AND OPEN SPACE PRESERVATION

Lewis & Clark County, Montana

Guiding Patterns

Ranching as a way of life is rapidly disappearing in many parts of the intermountain West. Preserving this important aspect of American western culture goes beyond merely preserving the physical artifacts of the ranch, namely its buildings, fences, pastures, and overall scenic qualities and vast open spaces. Conservation easements uniquely tailored to the land, and the individuals who work and live on the land, offer a viable alternative to rural subdivision and development and allow ranching as a way of life to continue.

Project Description

In 1995, the 1,000-acre Rocking Z Ranch, owned by Zack and Patty Wirth, was in financial distress, yet the owners did not want to subdivide as is commonly done. A conservation easement, drafted by Lane Coulston of American Conservation Real Estate and held by the Montana Land Reliance, allows for the sale of a 20-acre "homestead" parcel and the development of three small guest cabins at the ranch headquarters. The buyer of the homestead parcel gains recreational access to the rest of the ranch. The Wirths retain agricultural use rights to 18 of the 20 acres sold. Except for this 2-acre building envelope, the new homestead will not be fenced off from the rest of the ranch. The Wirths identified a site they referred to as "the wild hay field," which is located near a creek with a view of a hay meadow and the mountains beyond. They required that any building on the property be rustic in appearance.[7]

A conservation easement offers three distinct advantages for landowners in the Wirths' position: (1) they receive an immediate income tax deduction based on the difference between the property's fair market value before and after an Internal Revenue Service-qualified easement is established; (2) the value of the taxable estate is reduced; and (3) the landowners know that the deeded land will continue to be used as specified in the agreement in perpetuity.

Western Rural Development Pattern Language

The Rocking Z Ranch case study illustrates additional western development pattern language that expands upon and complements the historical patterns discussed in earlier chapters.

Dispersed Rural Settlement

Cultural

- *Preserve and integrate historic ranching operations.*

    Integration of historic ranching operations provides a critical link with the past while preserving a cultural way of life unique to the American West. It further serves to maintain a distinct feature of the landscape.

CONTACT

Lane Coulston
(406) 443-7085
www.conservationrealestate.com

SOURCE

Interview with Lane Coulston, 2000.

14. WILDLIFE-FRIENDLY FENCING

Colorado Division of Wildlife

Guiding Patterns

Ensuring injury-free movement for wildlife is the guiding principle behind the Colorado Division of Wildlife's guidelines for wildlife-friendly fencing.[8] These guidelines have been proven in practice to allow for effective livestock fencing as well as safe movement of wildlife, and cost no more than standard fencing (Table 4-4).

Table 4-4. Wildlife-Friendly Fencing

	Fence Type		
	Four-wire	**Three-wire**	**Solid**
Heights	16, 22, 28, and 40 inches	16, 26, and 38 inches	Minimum 40 inches for top rail; 22 inches for bottom. For fences over 50 inches, deer and elk crossings with lower height should be incorporated.
Materials	Smooth wire on top, barbed permissible for center two wires	Smooth wire on top, barbed permissible for center wire	Typically wood

Project Description

Cattle fencing dominates land enclosure in the West. Colorado's Department of Wildlife has promulgated fencing guidelines that help ensure that wildlife can move about freely and safely. Both electrical and standard fencing that follows the guidelines will accommodate a variety of wildlife.

Antelope usually cross below or through the wires of a fence; 16 inches minimum clearance will give them enough clearance to pass under the fence without damage. A maximum 40-inch top wire permits deer and elk to easily cross the top (Figures 4-13 and 4-14).

A minimum of 12 inches between the top and the second wire is important to prevent deer or elk from entangling their rear legs in the fence as they jumps across. For areas with frequent crossings by deer or elk, flagging the top wire will reduce the frequency of damage to the top wire. White is the most effective flagging color. Pipe or lumber may also be used instead of a top wire.

Western Rural Development Pattern Language

The Colorado Division of Wildlife fencing guidelines offer additional western development pattern language that builds on the historical patterns discussed in earlier chapters.

Other Elements

- *Construct fences that are wildlife-friendly.*

CONTACT

Colorado Division of Wildlife
Andrew Hough
(303) 297-1192
www.dnr.state.co.us/edo/wildlife

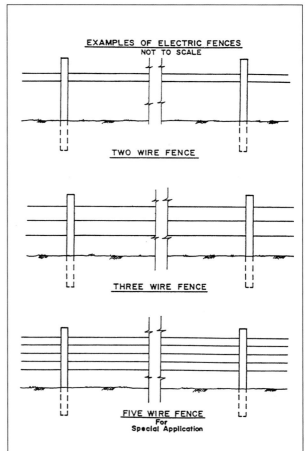

4-14 Wildlife-friendly fences.

Source: Colorado Division of Wildlife and the Sangre de Cristo Habitat Partnership Committee, *Fences for Man and Beast* (Westcliffe, CO: Crestone Graphics, undated).

4-13 White men can't jump? Neither can antelope.

Source: Chris Duerksen

15. SINGLE-RESIDENCE SITE DESIGN

Boulder, Colorado

Guiding Patterns

Boulder's single-residence Site Plan Review (SPR) focuses on sensitive utilization of a site's natural terrain while minimizing the impacts on the environment, including wildlife habitat. Critical factors include building profile, color, and appropriate siting on challenging terrain.

Project Description

Robb Residence—Mountain Landscape

This proposal added approximately 2,000 square feet to an existing house built in 1966 by adding a garage, a new living area, and a new roofline. A significant feature of this proposal is the structure's low profile and design, which settle the house into the topography. The resulting low profile is particularly important on this site due to the lack of significant tree coverage for screening and the fairly prominent location high on a ridge. This low profile further serves to safely accommodate the high winds experienced in the western Rocky Mountain foothills. Natural colors and the preservation of evergreens also help this house blend with its surroundings. Primary house materials include stucco, rock, and concrete with a composite roof (tar and rock) (Figure 4-15).

Criteria for approval include, among others, sensitivity to wildlife movement corridors and habitat, appropriate materials and color, sensitivity to ridgelines, and preservation of significant environmental features of the land.

Wildfire safety is addressed with a 30-foot defensible space perimeter. The defensible space minimizes fuel loading and does not necessarily preclude all landscaping. The home is also designed to take full advantage of Colorado's sunshine with a passive solar design.

4-15   The unpretentious home blends in well with the surrounding landscape.

Source: James van Hemert

History and Process

Boulder County reviews site plans for new, single-family residences and for additions over 1,000 square feet in rural parts of the county. The SPR, Section 4-800 of the Boulder County Land Use Code, was first adopted in 1993 in response to increased development in the mountains. Soon thereafter, the SPR was applied to the plains as well.

In the mountains, the lots upon which construction hasn't already taken place often have poor access and steep slopes, which lead to erosion problems and/or wildfire hazards. In the plains, new development has a direct impact on agricultural lands and the rural character of open areas. In both areas, the impact of development on natural resources and existing character of the surrounding neighborhood is an issue raised by Boulder County citizens experiencing the impact of new development.

Western Rural Development Pattern Language

The Boulder case study illustrates several historical western development patterns.

Architecture/Design

Form

• *Design building profiles that mimic the profiles of the natural landscape: in steep, mountainous areas, steeply pitched rooflines are appropriate; in areas that are flat or rolling, a lower profile is fitting.*

Color and Materials

• *As a first choice, use natural, earth-tone colors; however, do not do so exclusively. With an appropriate building profile, bright historical colors such as red, green, or ochre may serve as a beautiful counterpoint to the natural landscape.*

In this particular setting, contrasting brighter colors are not appropriate.

• *Use natural materials in a manner that reflects an organic integrity and harmony with the natural surroundings. Stone and wood are often appropriate as the primary construction material.*

Site Design

• *Orient buildings and groups of buildings to take advantage of the sun for winter warmth and mitigation of summer heat. Place buildings to the north of outdoor spaces and keep outdoor spaces to the south, with opportunities for dappled shade from trees or trellises.*

Additionally, we may note the consideration given to defensible space for wildfires. An appropriate pattern for most Rocky Mountain communities may be further recommended.

Dispersed Rural Settlement

Environmental

• *Site homes and arrange landscaping in a manner so as to maximize wildfire defensible space.*

CONTACT

Boulder County Land Use Department
(303) 441-3930
www.co.boulder.co.us

16. COMMUNITY FOCAL POINT AND CLIMATE MODERATING URBAN FOREST

Walla Walla, Washington

Guiding Patterns

President Theodore Roosevelt praised Walla Walla as making "the pleasantest impression upon my mind of any city I visited while in the Northwest."[9] Although Walla Walla's downtown experienced a downturn in the 1970s and 1980s, this town of 30,000 is now recognized as one of the best places to live in the West, according to *Sunset* magazine.[10] A partnership of private land and business owners, nonprofit volunteer organizations, and local government contribute to the success of downtown.

The city also prides itself in its mature urban forest. Contemporary tree standards for Walla Walla serve to preserve and enhance the town's urban forest, "a valued component of the urban infrastructure," according to the city's Comprehensive Plan. City tree standards cover tree retention, tree health, protection during construction, and tree planting standards for new development.

Project Descriptions

Community Focal Point: Downtown

Walla Walla has been piling up the awards for its successful downtown improvement and historic preservation efforts. In 2001, Walla Walla was one of five award winners of the "Great American Main Street Award" by the National Trust for Historic Preservation. In 2002, the National Trust named the city as one of its 12 Distinctive Destinations due to its overall historic character and activity.[11] It also received the 2002 "Municipal Achievement Award" by the Association of Washington Cities for its downtown revitalization efforts.

However, in the early 1980s, downtown Walla Walla was in a serious state of decline. Two malls opened on the outskirts of the city, Sears and J.C. Penney left town, and the business district vacancy rate neared 30%.[12] The nonprofit Downtown Walla Walla Foundation was founded in 1984 by concerned business and property owners to address the situation, and continues to play a key role in fostering ongoing revitalization efforts. Its mission is to "strengthen the economic and cultural vitality of downtown while enhancing and preserving its historic character and beauty." [13]

The city has no designated historic district and receives no state or federal funding for its downtown revitalization efforts. The rehabilitation projects facilitated by the foundation have resulted in $25 million of private-sector investment and $15 million by the public sector. Aggressive business recruitment efforts and building restorations have reduced the downtown vacancy rate to just 4% today. Eight hundred new jobs have been created and 125 new businesses have opened or expanded downtown since the revitalization efforts began. Aggressive historic preservation efforts have encouraged 249 downtown property rehabilitation projects.[14]

In its commentary on the 2001 "Great American Main Street Award," the National Trust for Historic Preservation observed that the most important change in the last 16 years has been the dramatic shift in the public's perception of downtown. While few people seemed to care about Walla Walla years ago, it is now a symbol of community pride.[15]

The city's role in downtown revitalization is one that plays gently on regulations and more heavily on business self-interest: promoting attractive buildings as an important business resource, not as an end in itself. In the past 10 years, business owners have recognized the benefits of removing the now-unattractive slipcovers off the buildings and revealing the beautiful red bricks.[16]

The independent, nonprofit Downtown Walla Walla Foundation uses an incentive-based approach to encourage good design. New construction and building additions and alterations must be reviewed by the foundation's Design Review Committee in order for business owners and landowners to take advantage of modest grants and low-interest loans for building improvements. The city contributes modest sums to this endeavor and also has a seat on the Design Review Committee. In this way, city planning staff are able to work "hand in glove" with the downtown foundation in design review.[17]

Because of the strong grassroots community support for downtown revitalization, the city has not adopted any special zoning overlay district with mandatory design standards. Walla Walla is very unusual in this respect, because experience in other communities has demonstrated that regulations are usually an essential element of a successful historic preservation program. The social pressure to "do the right thing" is worked out at the local coffee shop instead of at the public hearing room.

The city has consciously avoided promoting a particular design theme. Downtown's buildings reflect a range of styles, with the majority built between 1880 and 1920. New buildings or additions must focus on compatibility, not inauthentic mimicry.[18] Figure 4-16 illustrates this principle with the new Waterbrook Winery building.

The only standards being considered for downtown cover "big picture" community living room patterns such as ensuring that street walls are maintained by establishing "build-to" lines and minimum building heights.

Urban Forest

Large canopy trees, particularly deciduous trees, play a significant role in moderating the harsh sunshine and extreme summer heat of the West. Trees lower air temperature through shade and evapotranspiration. Shade-tree canopies can lower

4-16 Waterbrook Winery: compatible architecture.

Source: Robert C. Martin, AICP, Plan First Consulting, LLC

teers during community planting bees. The city now boasts a significant number of champion trees—those in the largest 1% of its species nation-wide—some of which were selected and placed by Frederick Law Olmstead in his design for Pioneer Park.[20] Figures 4-17 and 4-18 illustrate the growth of trees planted in Pioneer Park in 1902. Today, the trees are 6 to 7 feet in diameter.

The foresight of early settlers and the continued planting maintenance of trees by subsequent gen-erations have provided the city with a tree canopy that would otherwise be absent in the arid envi-ronment. Figure 4-19 views Main Street and the mature tree canopy beyond.

The city's tree ordinances, while not particu-larly demanding with respect to the size and num-ber of trees required, is comprehensive and serves to extend the legacy of the urban forest.[21] Key fea-tures include the following:

- There is a restriction of the removal of trees from private property in connection with new development.

- On-site tree planting for new, multifamily residential, commercial, and industrial development[22] must achieve a range of between 18 and 24 inches total caliper per gross acre, excluding parking lot landscap-ing. For example, a 21,000-square-foot lot multifamily project would require on site a total of 12 caliper inches, or six trees of 2-inch caliper in size.

- Parking lot landscaping must cover a mini-mum 5% of interior space and include decid-uous trees that provide shade for at least 20% of the vehicle accommodation area, and no parking space may be further than 50 feet from a landscaped area.[23]

- The density of street tree planting must pro-vide 100% canopy coverage of the parking strip and adjacent sidewalk at tree maturity.

Street design accommodates tree plantings. All streets must have minimum 6-foot-wide planting strips and 6-foot-wide sidewalks. With typical,

air temperature by several degrees[19] and signifi-cantly reduce the effects of urban heat sinks. The shade provides relief from the bright sunshine during the summer months. During the winter months, deciduous trees allow sunshine to shine through windows and to outdoor living spaces.

Walla Walla's mature urban forest is testimony to the efforts of early residents to create a shaded town amidst the rolling plains of eastern Washing-ton. Early city settlers raised money to purchase train carloads of hardwood tree seedlings from New England. The trees were planted by volun-

4-17 Trees planted in 1902 in Pioneer Park.

Source: Whitman College archives, Walla Walla, Washington

4-18 The same trees in Pioneer Park 100 years later, in 2002. Period costume worn by woman in photo.

Source: Robert C. Martin, AICP, Plan First Consulting, LLC

4-19 Main Street trees planted in 1992 as part of a streetscape local improvement district. Mature tree canopy is seen in the background.

Source: Robert C. Martin, AICP, Plan First Consulting, LLC

local residential streets at a 50-foot right-of-way, these standards have the effect of also narrowing the curb-to-curb roadway. The city is willing to sacrifice on-street parking in order to protect the ability to provide planting strips and sidewalks. In some cases, when there is insufficient right-of-way to accommodate the full design template, street trees may be required on private property.[24]

Tree standards are applied administratively by planning staff through the development review process for individual site plans. The City Parks and Recreation Department provides primary advice with regard to trees.[25]

The city manages a heritage tree program in order to provide reasonable assurance that its rich tree heritage will continue. Any individual may nominate an exceptional tree—rare or unusual species, exceptional aesthetic quality, or large size—for registration as a heritage tree. Participation in the program is voluntary and may include trees on both private and public property. Decisions on registration are made by the city's Urban Forestry Committee, relying on advice from the city arborist.[26]

Western Rural Development Pattern Language

The City of Walla Walla case study suggests additional western development patterns that expand upon and complement the historical patterns discussed in earlier chapters. Additional comments are provided as appropriate.

Town

Streets/Access

- *Establish a comprehensive street tree program to create shade canopies over sidewalks and public streets.*

Architecture/Design

Form

- *Within the existing urban fabric, new buildings, additions, and alterations should be compatible without resorting to inauthentic mimicry of older styles.*

Walla Walla's approach to maintaining the health of its downtown is practical and successful, representing a natural, organic growth.

Culture/Community

- *Preserve significant historic buildings.*
- *Integrate historic buildings in new development.*

Site Design

- *In towns, generously plant trees that are appropriate for the climate to maximize shade around buildings, parking lots, and gathering areas.*

CONTACTS

City of Walla Walla
Development Services
Linda Kastning
(509) 527-4535
e-mail: lkastning@ci.walla-walla.wa.us

Bob Martin, Plan First LLC
(509) 527-4537
e-mail: rmartin@ci.walla-walla.wa.us

SOURCES

Interviews with Linda Kastning, City of Walla Walla Development Services; and Bob Martin, planning consultant, July 2002.

City of Walla Walla ordinance.

17. TOWN AND COUNTRY SEPARATION

Deschute County and the City of Bend, Oregon

Guiding Patterns

In Oregon, more than any other western state, towns in rural areas have distinct boundaries, and houses and businesses do not ooze out into the countryside. The result is better preservation of agricultural lands, open space, and wildlife habitat, and more efficient delivery of government services. This clear delineation between town and country is a direct result of the state's ambitious growth management legislation.

The statewide growth management statutes, which establish mandatory goals, objectives, and procedures for local governments, were adopted by the state legislature in 1973 and are supervised by Oregon's Land Conservation and Development Commission—a seven-member body appointed

by the governor and confirmed by the Senate.[27] Program Goal 14, "Urbanization," requires each community to adopt an Urban Growth Boundary. Factors in determining the extent of the urban growth area include both need and locational factors.[28] Nineteen state goals include detailed policies on housing, coastal resources, and a wide range of other land use topics.[29] Three that have a direct impact on rural town and regional settlement patterns involve urban growth boundaries, agricultural lands, and forest lands (Figure 4-20).

- *Urban Growth Boundary Goal:* To provide for an orderly and efficient transition from rural to urban land use.

Urban growth boundaries shall be established to identify and separate urbanizable land from rural land. Establishment and change of the boundaries shall be based upon long-range urban population growth; housing and employment opportunities; provision of public facilities; maximum efficiency of land uses within and on the fringe of existing urban areas; environmental, energy, economic and social consequences; and compatibility with and retention of agricultural land.[30]

4-20 Towns in rural Oregon have distinct boundaries.

Source: 1000 Friends of Oregon

- *Agricultural Land Goal:* To preserve and maintain agricultural lands.

The policies establish minimum parcel sizes of 80 acres for agricultural lands and 160 for rangeland. Nonfarm uses must have minimum impacts on agricultural productivity. Preservation priority is given to high-value farmlands.[31]

- *Forest Land Goal:* To conserve forest lands by maintaining the forest land base; to protect the state's forest economy by making possible economically efficient forest practices, which ensure the continuous growing and harvesting of forest tree species as the leading use on forest land consistent with sound management of soil, air, water, and fish and wildlife resources; and to provide for recreational opportunities and agriculture.[32]

  Non-forestry-related parcels are limited to 80 acres, and their uses must be limited to those supporting forest operations; conserving soil, water, and air quality; providing for fish and wildlife resources, agriculture, and recreational opportunities appropriate in a forest environment.[33]

The most significant feature of the Oregon statewide growth management legislation, compared with that of most other western states, is that the goals are mandatory and implemented through a series of detailed regulations promulgated by the state. Local plans and regulations must conform.

How have the goals and regulations played out on the ground? Deschutes County and the City of Bend (located in central Oregon on the dry east side of the Cascade Mountains) provide a good illustration of how these three state growth management policies have made their imprint on regional settlement patterns.

The complicating factor is that Deschutes County is dotted with over 16,000 unserviceable "sagebrush" lots of ½-1 acre that were platted in the 1970s. The proliferation of these substandard lots in Deschutes County and elsewhere in Oregon

helped fuel some of the flames that led to the creation of a statewide planning program.

As noted above, state planning guidelines established in 1973 required urban growth boundaries and restricted the creation of additional lots in rural and forested areas. Because of the huge inventory of lots and the generous size of early urban growth boundaries, the impact of the state regulations has been somewhat slow; however, it is beginning to emerge.

Detailed Geographic Information System (GIS) mapping by Deschutes County of existing, future, and the composite total potential development paints a clear picture of the benefits that will flow from the state goals: directing growth to established towns and limiting development in rural areas that are rich in farming and forestry resources. George Read, Planning Director, points out that only now are they beginning to see the benefits of the state guidelines. Today, Deschutes County has only a 15-year supply of rural lots for development—the first county in the state to see the end of rural land supply based on state guidelines for growth. The GIS mapping, therefore, paints a realistic picture of the final regional development pattern.

Existing, Future, and Total Potential Growth to 2020 for Southern Deschutes County and the City of Bend

The future and total potential development maps are based on coordinated population forecasts provided by the state's Office of Economic Analysis. This population was then allocated by the county for planning purposes, and adopted into the comprehensive plans of the county and the City of Bend. The maps reviewed identify anticipated change over the course of 18 years.

The Existing Development map of the southern portion of the county (Figure 4-21) reveals almost 5,000 rural residential parcels and 18,600 residential units in the City of Bend. Actual developed residential parcels are shown for the county, and

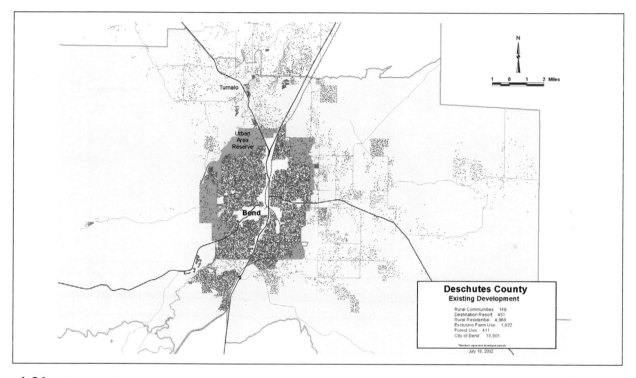

4-21 Existing Development map.

Source: Deschutes County Planning Department

residential units are "averaged" for the City of Bend. Of total units, existing rural residential development represents 19% and urban development within the City of Bend represents 73%. The remaining 8% comprises units categorized as rural community, destination resorts, exclusive farm use, and forest use.

The Future Development map identifies additional growth between now and 2020 within the existing Urban Growth Boundary, and shows a dwindling supply of rural residential lots available for development (Figure 4-22). Approximately 90% of the rural growth will occur on land already subdivided, much of it platted prior to state growth guidelines. This map identifies 13,275 additional units for Bend and 1,400 rural residential units. Thus, the amount of future development that will take place in rural areas

will be greatly reduced as a percentage of the total growth from the area—9% versus 19% today—clearly revealing the impact that the Urban Growth Boundary policies will have in directing growth to the town rather than the countryside, thus preserving agricultural lands, open space, and wildlife habitat.

The Total Potential Development map combines Existing with Future Development (Figure 4-23). Under current state guidelines, this map represents the "end state" of development for the rural part of the county. Under this scenario, 77% of all residential development lies within the City of Bend and 15% in rural residential areas. George Read states that this is the first county to see the end of residential growth in rural areas on scattered lots,[34] and that the coming years will test the extent to which the Oregon planning system

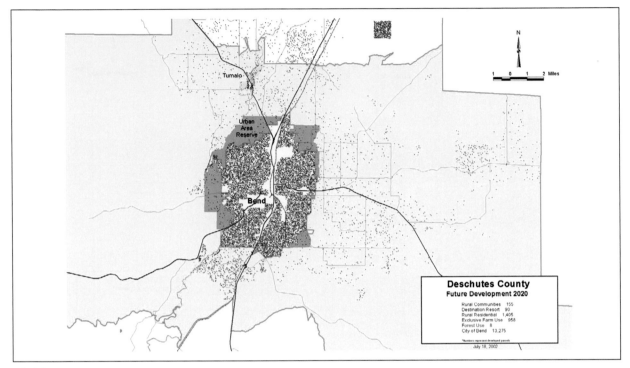

4-22   Future Development map.

Source: Deschutes County Planning Department

works and citizens have the political will to continue to focus developments in towns and cities rather than the countryside. Importantly, a safety valve does exist; additional development beyond that identified today could occur in the Urban Area Reserve around Bend. Residential development is currently not allowed in the Urban Area Reserve, which acts like a holding zone.

Western Rural Development Pattern Language

A number of significant historical western development patterns may be distilled from the Deschutes case study. Moreover, additional patterns are suggested that respond to modern land use planning and environmental concerns and objectives. Both historical and contemporary lessons

are summarized below with explanatory comments as appropriate.

Regional Development Patterns

- *In the face of development pressure, preserve existing country towns and villages and their development patterns.*

- *Concentrate development in a compact manner within towns.*

The Oregon statewide growth management goals are perhaps the most ambitious attempt in the West to preserve existing towns by focusing development there instead of in rural areas and surrounding countryside. While unincorporated rural communities are given some leeway to growth and existing legally subdivided rural lots may be built upon, over time most

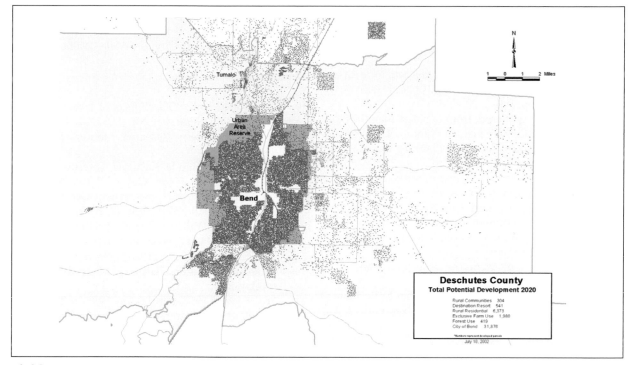

4-23   Total Potential Development map.

Source: Deschutes County Planning Department

growth will take place in and adjacent to existing communities.

Town

Environmental

- *Maintain agricultural land in close proximity to town dwellers.*

  The statewide growth management system preserves agricultural land very close to towns as well as open space and wildlife habitat.

Dispersed Rural Settlement

Environmental

- *Protect wildlife habitat and enhance wildlife movement corridors.*

By focusing development in towns, the statewide regulations ease development pressures in rural areas and help maintain large contiguous blocks of open space.

CONTACTS

George Read, Planning Director,
Deschutes County, Oregon
(541) 388-6575
e-mail: George_Read@co.deschutes.or.us
www.co.deschutes.or.us

James Lewis, Planning Manager, Bend, Oregon
(541) 330-4017
www.ci.bend.or.us

SOURCES

Interview with George Read, Deschutes County Planning Director, July 2002.

State of Oregon's Land Conservatiom and Development Commission.

NOTES

1. Aldo Leopold, *A Sand County Almanac: With Essays on Conservation* (New York: Oxford University Press, 1949), p. 190.

2. Information gathered from written materials co-authored by Patricio Garcia, Planning Director and Moises Gonzales, Assistant Planning Director, Rio Arriba County.

3. www.civano.com/aboutcivano/index.shtml.
    As this book went to press, the project has run into financial troubles, and Fannie Mae has assumed control. Reportedly, some of the environmental features added to construction costs and made marketing more difficult.

4. www.terrain.org/Archives/Issue_5/Civano/civano.htm.

5. Barbara Flannagan, "Building the New Hometown," *This Old House* (January/February 2000), pp. 101-105.

6. www.terrain.org/Archives/Issue_5/Civano/civano.htm.

7. John Covert and Sarah B. Van de Wetering, "Saving the Ranch, Saving the Land," *Chronicle of Community* 2 (3): 17-20.

8. Colorado Division of Wildlife and Sangre de Cristo Habitat Partnership Committee, *Fences for Man and Beast* (Westcliffe, CO: Crestone Graphics, undated).

9. Lawrence Cheek, "Best Main Street: Wall Walla, Washington: Coming Together Downtown," *Sunset* (March 3, 2002), pp. 90-91. www.sunset.com.

10. *Ibid.*

11. www.nthp.org.

12. www.mainstreet.org/Awards/GAMSA/2001/WA_WallaWalla.htm.

13. www.downtownwallawalla.com.

14. *Ibid.*

15. *Ibid.*

16. Interview with Bob Martin, former Development Services Manager, City of Walla Walla, July 29, 2002.

17. *Ibid.*

18. *Ibid.*

19. David J. Norwalk, "The Effects of Urban Trees on Air Quality" (Syracuse, NY: U.S.D.A. Forest Service, Northeastern Research Station, December 1995), p. 3.

20. Interview with Linda Kastning, Interim Development Services Manager, City of Walla Walla; and Bob Martin, former Development Services Manager, City of Walla Walla, July 17, 2002.

21. City of Walla Walla Ordinance, Section 20.106.120, "Preservation and Protection of Trees."

22. City of Walla Walla Ordinance, Section 20.106.035, "Table of Minimum Planting Standards for New Development."

23. City of Walla Walla Ordinance, Section 20.106.100, "Required Landscaping of Parking Areas."

24. Interview with Linda Kastning, Interim Development Services Manager, City of Walla Walla, July 17, 2002.

25. *Ibid.,* July 25, 2002.

26. City of Walla Walla Ordinance, Section 212.50, "Heritage Trees."

27. www.lcd.state.or.us/fastpdfs/fastfacts.pdf.

28. www.lcd.state.or.us.

29. www.lcd.state.or.us/goalhtml/goals.htm.

30. *Ibid.*

31. *Ibid.*

32. *Ibid.*

33. *Ibid.*

34. Interview with George Read, Planning Director, Deschutes County, July 29, 2002.

5

True West Implementation: Effective Development Code Standards

To plan is heavenly,
To implement, divine.

—ANONYMOUS

1. INTRODUCTION

As the case studies so amply illustrate, it will take a variety of tools for local governments to implement effective, context-sensitive small town and rural development strategies. Acquisition of open space will often be a key component. Capital investment policy—where roads, streets, and utilities are constructed—will have a profound impact in directing growth. Development codes—zoning and subdivision ordinances—will also play an integral role.

One of the enduring modern myths in some western jurisdictions is that an effective growth management strategy that ensures compatible, "True West" development can be crafted without land use regulations. While development codes are only one of the main tools that need to be used, they are an essential one. They help establish a minimum code of conduct and a baseline from which development must work. As the old saying attributed to Teddy Roosevelt goes, "In the West, a smile and a six-shooter are more persuasive than a smile alone." Of course, a creative developer willing to work closely with local planners can be the key to success.

This chapter looks at a number of key site design elements (such as landscaping and fencing, roads, open space, view protection, and lighting) that help shape a development and determine whether it fits in a particular locale. In each section, we examine a variety of land use regulatory regimes, ranging from straightforward

165

and simple to more detailed and sophisticated. The appropriate approach will often differ for each jurisdiction depending on variables such as community goals, staff resources, and political will.

For example, a mountain community in Colorado was recently considering new stream and wetland protection regulations. The draft that emerged from a citizen-based effort, drawing on ordinances in other communities, was long and complex, covering almost every conceivable aspect of development impacts and procedures. It called for detailed plan submissions and multiple public hearings before the Planning Commission and elected officials. While the political will was present, the community's only planner quaked at the notion of making such a complex system work. It was more tailored for a city or county with a full-time environmental planner.

For that reason, we have shied away from promoting "model" regulations, because one size rarely fits all. They must be tailored carefully to each locality. We also discuss incentives that should be considered as complements to regulations.

Thus, this section suggests different approaches that can be explored rather than being a comprehensive discussion of specific regulations. For rural and small-town jurisdictions, simple will often be more effective in the long run than complex. We offer a menu of approaches and examples. Whatever tools are chosen, legal counsel should be consulted. While most western states grant local governments broad land use regulatory authority, powers differ from state to state; therefore, the local governments should check to see if they have the authority, for example, to enact landscaping and vegetation protection regulations. Each section ends with a list of other resources that can be tapped to assist in drafting specific regulations.

2. LANDSCAPING, VEGETATION PROTECTION, AND FENCING/BUFFERING

Most communities in the West, particularly in urban areas, have adopted landscaping regulations that require developers, at a minimum, to plant trees in and around parking lots and as buffering around the building site. They often regulate the location, placement, and look of fencing. For example, Henderson, Nevada, is fairly typical in requiring that sites be buffered with trees according to a specified number per lineal foot of site perimeter and that 10% of a parking lot's surface area be devoted to trees. Brighton, Colorado, requires builders to place at least one tree in the yard of each residential lot in a subdivision.

Increasingly, small towns and rural areas are enacting similar requirements. The Community College District regulations in Santa Fe County, New Mexico (discussed in Chapter 3) also require planting of street trees in each development (Figure 5-1). This first-generation approach—straightforward and quantitative—-has become the bare minimum and should be a starting point in any jurisdiction, large or small. It is easy to understand and administer, and is something important to both government planners and developers who often just want to know what the rules are.

Landscaping

A growing number of communities are recognizing that more is needed. Issues such as what types of vegetation can be planted, of what size, and how they will be maintained must be addressed. Thus, many jurisdictions now maintain permitted plant lists that recommend native plants, which are particularly suited to dry, harsh western climates. Exotic, nonnative species are prohibited.

Acceptable tree/shrub sizes, based on specifications from state plant nursery associations, are common. Irrigation is often a requirement, and smart communities require a bond to be posted for several years to ensure that landscaping that dies

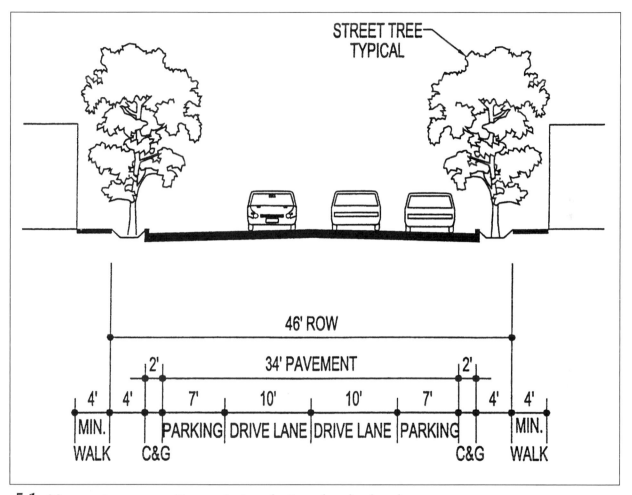

5-1 Many western communities require tree plantings along local roads.

Source: Santa Fe Community College District Regulation, Santa Fe County, New Mexico, December 2000

or is damaged a year or two after a project is completed is replaced. Some require special protection from wildlife—elk and deer seem to have an affinity for ornamental plantings.

The City of Fort Collins, Colorado, and the Town of Jackson, Wyoming, have good examples of more comprehensive landscaping ordinances and what might be thought of as second-generation regulations. In addition to these standard provisions, the Town of Estes Park, Colorado, requires wildlife-protective fencing around ornamentals in commercial projects (Figure 5-2).

Mandatory xeriscaping (incorporating low water use vegetation and landscaping materials or, at the least, use of drought-tolerant plant species) is also gaining adherents in the West. For example, a new zoning code in Longmont, Colorado, requires xeriscaping on all publicly owned or maintained areas and encourages xeriscape practices on privately owned land.

Although incentive approaches to landscaping are uncommon, several jurisdictions have adopted bonuses for developers that bear examination. For example, Overland Park, Kansas, has a unique

5-2 Estes Park, Colorado, has adopted standards to protect landscape plantings from wildlife.

Source: Cara Snyder

5-3 The landscaping code in Oro Valley, Arizona, protects native plants.

Source: Matt Goebel

sliding-scale density system in residential zone districts. To attain the maximum density in a particular district, the developer has the option of providing additional landscaping and tree protection beyond that required in the ordinance. Many communities allow developers to count trees protected on a site toward any basic landscaping requirements. Similarly, some communities allow reduction of front and side setbacks if perimeter landscaping on a site is increased beyond a specified minimum.

Vegetation Protection

Possibly the most important and interesting development regarding landscaping is the trend toward requiring protection of existing vegetation on a site. Increasingly, local governments are asking developers to better understand the role existing vegetation plays in natural processes that are important to maintaining the character of a site and supporting wildlife. Native vegetation also gives many important clues as to how a site can and should be developed. Scanty vegetation on a steep slope probably means revegetation will be difficult. If trees do not occur in the natural landscaping, it may be a good tip that a forest will be difficult to establish and that existing sage and rabbit brush should be carefully preserved.

Communities in Arizona, particularly those with desert habitat, have been at the cutting edge of this movement. For example, Oro Valley, Arizona, has adopted "native plant preservation, salvage, and mitigation requirements" in its zoning code. Desert areas, riparian zones, rock outcroppings, and native vegetation are all targeted for protection. The code requires developers to submit a native plant preservation, salvage, and mitigation plan with any proposed subdivision or project. The plan must detail precautions that will be taken to avoid disturbing specified native plants as well as identification of native plants that will be transplanted (Figure 5-3).

Fencing

Fencing is a ubiquitous part of the western landscape, even in relatively remote areas. Barbed wire helped shape the West as much as any manmade implement. While almost all urban zoning codes address fencing issues—what types were appropriate (e.g., chain link or wood stockade), where a fence can be located (often not allowed in front yards), and how high it can be—few rural jurisdictions or small towns have paid much attention, at least until recently. Now, rural communities are realizing that fences can have tremendous aesthetic impacts as well as adverse consequences for wildlife if not designed and built properly.

While no one will argue that fencing is not essential for ranching and security purposes, there is increasing evidence that, if designed poorly, it can have serious adverse impacts on wildlife. For example, as discussed in Chapter 4, deer and elk can become entangled easily in fences that are higher than 42 inches, particularly if the top two strands are less than 12 inches apart (because they jump with their hind legs forward and can become easily ensnared).

The height of the bottom wire off the ground can be equally important. Small elk and deer may crawl under fencing, and pronghorn cannot jump at all, so they must crawl under that bottom strand as well. Fortunately, a number of state wildlife offices have published very useful guides for wildlife-friendly fencing. One of the best is *Fences For Man and Beast*, co-published by the Colorado Division of Wildlife, the U.S. Forest Service, and the U.S. Bureau of Land Management. The basics are relatively simple for barbed wire fencing:

- smooth bottom wire at least 16 inches above the ground
- at least 12 inches between the top two wires
- top wire 40 inches or lower (smooth wire preferred)
- stays to be used every 6-8 feet

The Colorado Division of Wildlife publication contains many other common-sense tips on building wildlife-friendly fencing, such as removal sections to allow migration, lay-down fencing for snow country, and adjustable fencing.

However, this doesn't end the inquiry about fencing and wildlife. There may be some instances where fencing needs to be carefully located outside wildlife migration corridors or nursing areas,

5-4 Summit County, Colorado, has one of the most progressive wildlife habitat protection programs in the nation.

Source: Mark Truckey, Summit County Long-Range Planning

for example. Increasingly, jurisdictions such as Summit County, Colorado (a mountain county home to Breckenridge and Copper Mountain ski resorts), are requiring developers to identify key wildlife habitat areas and then avoid fragmenting such areas with fencing (Figure 5-4).

Aesthetics are another major concern as towns sprawl into the countryside. More and more exotic fencing is being introduced that has no historical precedent in most areas of the West. (White three-rail, chain link, and solid stockade fencing are all common in the East and in larger cities, but stick out like sore thumbs in the western landscape.)

The solution? More rural jurisdictions and small towns are taking a cue from their city cousins and adopting regulations governing various aspects of fencing. Some restrict the type of materials that can be used to those that are indigenous, which may be barbed wire, log, native stone, masonry, stucco, or others, depending on the area. Chain link, cedar stockade, and other less attractive types are often prohibited outright in scenic areas or small towns.

SELECTED SOURCES

Abbey, Buck. *U.S. Landscape Ordinances: An Annotated Reference Handbook.* New York: John Wiley & Sons, Inc., 1998. A good general survey of landscaping ordinances across the United States, including western states, although many ordinances reviewed are outdated or have been revised.

Colorado Division of Wildlife, U.S. Forest Service, and U.S. Bureau of Land Management. *Fences for Man and Beast.* Westcliffe, CO: Crestone Graphics, undated.

Dorward, Sherry. *Design for Mountain Communities: A Landscaping and Architectural Guide.* New York: Van Nostrand Reinhold, 1990. The leading reference on development in mountain areas.

Duerksen, Chris and Suzanne Richman. *Tree Conservation Ordinances.* Chicago: American Planning Association, 1993. Examines the key elements of effective vegetation protection regulations with examples from around the United States.

Harper, Bonnie, ed. *Roadside Use of Native Plants.* Washington, DC: Federal Highway Administration, 2000.

Source Book on Natural Landscaping for Local Officials. Chicago: Northeastern Illinois Planning Commission, 1997. Excellent introductory handbook, although oriented to the Midwest.

USEFUL WEB SITES

Natural Landscapers
www.for-wild.org/landscap.htm

U.S. Environmental Protection Agency Green Acres Site
www.epa.gov/glnpo/greenacres/nativeplants

www.r1.fws.gov/jobs/orojitw/standard/fence-wldf

www.netcnct.net/community/oacd/fs10fenc.htm. Contains practical advice for fencing small acreages.

LOCAL GOVERNMENT CONTACTS

Community Development Director, Ft. Collins, Colorado: (970) 221-6287

Director of Planning, Henderson, Nevada: (702) 565-2372

Community Development Director, Estes Park, Colorado: (970) 577-3725

Planning Director, Jackson, Wyoming: (307) 733-0520

Director of Community Development, Brighton, Colorado: (303) 655-2021

Director of Planning and Zoning Division, Oro Valley, Arizona: (520) 797-9797

3. STREETS AND ROADS

Streets and roads shape developments and communities in profound, elemental ways. They are often the basic armature upon which a city is built. Consider how the City of Denver was shaped by its parkway and boulevard system during the City Beautiful movement. Commodious, tree-lined streets such as Speer Boulevard and Monaco Parkway add much to the city's ambiance and appeal, and enhance surrounding neighborhoods. It is hard to imagine the city without these place-defining thoroughfares.

As discussed in Chapter 2, most western cities were developed on the grid system. Sometimes these streets were narrow with buildings built tightly against them, and were common in the East. Often, particularly with main commercial streets, they were designed wide to accommodate wagons and teams of horses and oxen, and to take advantage of the sun (e.g., the broad main streets in Salt Lake City, Utah, and Cheyenne, Wyoming). These wide streets often provided great vistas of surrounding mountains and natural landmarks. Thus, there is no set street pattern that can be adopted slavishly for western communities. Like other site elements, local governments must take their cues from what exists and what will fit best on the landscape in a particular situation.

For example, if a town such as Salida, Colorado, was developed successfully on a grid system, it makes sense to extend that grid system as the community expands. However, as depicted in Figure 5-5, some communities permit the intro-

5-5 Salida, Colorado.

Source: Chris Duerksen

duction of different street patterns (such as cul-de-sacs) that are exotic imports from the East.

There has been a tendency in many communities to ratchet up street width standards to 40 or 50 feet or more in residential areas, despite the fact that standard widths in older neighborhoods in the same town rarely exceed 30 feet. According to the Congress for the New Urbanism, prior to World War II, the traditional neighborhood street was in the range of 28-30 feet with a corner radius of 5-10 feet. Since that time, the typical local street has grown to a width of 36 feet with a corner radius of 25 feet.

Why? First and foremost, the thinking has been that wider streets and a wider turning radius will move traffic more efficiently and quickly, despite adverse neighborhood impacts; also, pressure will be alleviated from fire departments, public

works, and other city agencies that want wide rights-of-way to accommodate equipment and utilities, arguing that wider is safer. Often, the mindset in some neighborhoods is that bigger must be better.

Interestingly, evidence is mounting that, at least in single-family residential neighborhoods, wider streets do not translate into safer streets. A report by Swift and Associates (based on a study of accidents and residential street typologies in Longmont, Colorado) found that narrower streets (less than 36 feet wide) are safer than wider ones.[1] However, aren't wider streets essential to accommodate modern fire trucks and emergency vehicles? The same study found that there were no more accidents or injuries due to fire in areas of town with narrow streets compared to neighborhoods with wide streets.

Because narrower streets in traditional residential neighborhoods have significant and well-documented advantages, many communities are re-examining their street standards and adopting dimensional regulations and other street design specifications much more attuned to historical development patterns. For example, the City of Phoenix, Arizona, has a 28-foot standard width for neighborhood streets with parking allowed on both sides. Fort Collins, Colorado, has adopted a 30-foot street width—again with parking allowed on both sides of the street. For areas of heavier traffic, the City of Boulder, Colorado, specifies a 32-foot standard width for roads supporting 100-2,500 average daily traffic volumes. All of these communities exemplify a simple, straightforward approach to street design and specifications.

Just how wide should streets be in residential areas? As explained in a recent publication by the Institute of Traffic Engineers, *Traditional Neighborhood Development: Street Design Guidelines*, local governments:

> . . . will not find a simple chart or table of how wide TND streets should be under different circumstances, here or elsewhere. As the width of a street increases, the more difficult it is for pedestrians to cross, the easier it is for motorists to traverse at higher speeds, and the more vehicular dominated the street becomes. A street should be no wider than the minimum width needed to accommodate the usual vehicular mix that street will serve.[2]

As a consequence of this and other important reports, many western cities are re-examining their often over-designed streets and accepting narrower streets in neighborhoods and commercial areas that do not generate high traffic volumes. For example, Portland, Oregon, was one of the earliest to adopt new, context-based standards for residential streets based on a comprehensive study by that city's transportation department, which looked carefully at safety and traffic issues

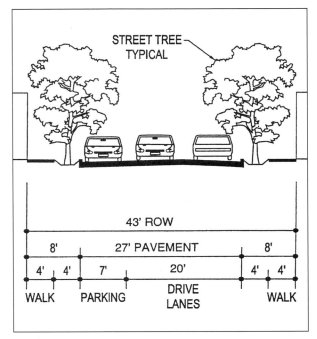

5-6 Santa Fe County allows narrower streets in its Community College District.

Source: Santa Fe Community College District Regulation, Santa Fe County, New Mexico, December 2000

before recommending that narrower streets were acceptable in certain situations. Local streets can be developed as narrow as 20 feet with parking on one side, and up to 32 feet with parking on both sides. In Santa Fe County's Community College District, neighborhood streets need only 20-foot drive lanes and 7 feet on one side for parking (Figure 5-6).

Again, however, there may be instances where wider is better. In the Denver Airport Gateway area around Denver International Airport, the city's plan for the area specifies wider east/west streets, especially in commercial areas, to take advantage of magnificent views of the Rocky Mountains.

What incentives can be offered to get developers to build narrower streets? Actually, in most cases, none are needed because narrow streets are far less costly to build and leave more land for development. It is typically other city agencies that view narrower streets with a skeptical eye because of access and service issues.

As communities gain more experience with access and streets in new subdivisions, they are moving beyond street design within new developments and focusing on how those developments relate to the rest of the town or city. Thus, connectivity of streets is another important issue on which progressive western communities are focusing. Driving through massive new developments and subdivisions such as Highlands Ranch in Douglas County, Colorado (just outside Denver), or Green Valley Ranch in Henderson, Nevada, can be an adventure without a road map. Curvilinear, loop-the-loop streets and ubiquitous cul-de-sacs make navigation all but impossible for a newcomer.

Many towns and cities are building subdivisions, not neighborhoods, because of the lack of any street connections between these new developments. Imposing cedar or masonry fences wall off the new developments, which often have only one or two major access points. However, the trend is for communities to discourage this type of site planning that turns its back on the community in a very uncivic way. For example, in Brighton, Colorado—a former small town now in Denver's growth orbit—new residential development standards require new local and collector streets to provide multiple, direct connections between the new residences and nearby parks, schools, and shopping. More specifically, the residential standards require:

- use of a "modified grid" pattern to lay out local and collector streets (i.e., both parallel and perpendicular streets in identifiable blocks, with the occasional diagonal or curvilinear street);
- all new subdivisions to provide future access to undeveloped, adjacent parcels at least every 660 feet along the shared boundary line;

- a maximum cul-de-sac length of 500 feet;
- a preferred maximum block length of 800 feet when the block fronts a local street, and a maximum block size of 6 acres;
- limits on the maximum arterial/collector street frontage that may be occupied by an opaque perimeter fence; and
- setback requirements for perimeter fences to provide for landscaping between the back of the sidewalk and fence.

Henderson, Nevada, has adopted similar standards for both streets and pedestrian connections, although they are less stringent.

While connectivity would seem to have many benefits and be amendable to some fairly straightforward approaches, cities and towns should not underestimate the potential opposition they will encounter from residents of some neighborhoods who see connectivity opening the door to through traffic, criminals, and all sorts of social horrors. Meetings with neighborhood representatives are a prerequisite to explain the purposes of fostering connectivity and benefits that will accrue (e.g., less driving because neighborhoods are connected to one another and parks, shops, and other activity centers; increased security because of easier access by police and fire services).

What of roads in rural areas? Again, a context-based approach has much to recommend. As the Casas de Sonoita development in Santa Cruz County, Arizona, illustrates so well in Figure 5-7, rural roads that respect and follow existing topography and contours of the landscape enable a project to fit the land much better than one that cuts indiscriminately across hills, steep slopes, ridges, and valleys.

Salt Lake County, Utah, has recently codified a minimum code of road-building conduct for sensitive canyons in its eastern reaches, as discussed in Chapter 4. A special Foothills and Canyons Overlay Zoning District in the zoning code addresses, among other things, the following key issues:

5-7   Santa Cruz County, Arizona.

Source: Chris Duerksen

1. To the maximum extent feasible, driveways and roads must follow the natural contour of a site.

2. Slopes steeper than 30% cannot be disturbed, except in unusual circumstances.

3. Access roads must avoid steep grades and sharp turning radii that can make access difficult in winter.

4. Roads and roadways that run perpendicular to the contours of a site are prohibited.

5. Shared driveways and parking areas are strongly encouraged to reduce maintenance and impacts on the environment.

6. Roads and driveways must be screened using existing landforms and vegetation, and any cuts and fills must be regarded to repeat adjacent landforms.

7. Long roadway tangents must be avoided in favor of curvilinear alignments reflecting existing topography.

Many jurisdictions have specific quantitative standards that prohibit cutting of roads across terrain that is in excess of a specified slope, or limit the length of any road segment on steep slopes.

One of the most helpful things localities can do to promote compatible roads in rural areas is to make certain that the road specification standards they adopt are not better suited to urban or suburban environments. Requiring wide rights-of-way, curb and guttering, and paving on a uniform basis is not only costly, but often inappropriate in a rural setting. While there may be instances where, for example, curbing is necessary to deal with drainage issues, rural jurisdictions should be careful to not require overengineering of country roads that are lightly used.

In this regard, one of the most encouraging developments regarding rural roads has been the recent emergence of alternative highway design standards that recognize the need to preserve the character of rural areas. This new trend in road construction—colorfully termed the "Asphalt Rebellion" by some planners and engineers—is actually an attempt to move away from the sterile requirements of road design proscribed for over 45 years in the official roadway standards (i.e., *Policy on Geometric Design of Highways and Streets*, or the so-called "Green Book," published by the American Association of State Highway and Transportation Officials).

The Green Book's standards for road construction are the result of transportation studies conducted by engineers whose overriding concern is to make roads safe for persons traveling at speeds considerably in excess of posted limits. To accommodate high speeds, the standards often require greater widths. The results often include two-lane country highways expanded to four lanes; streets that are wider than necessary platted in new urban neighborhoods; and historic, narrow bridges torn down in favor of new, wider steel structures. According to the Green Book, safety is the primary objective of road design; other concerns, including historic preservation and protection of aesthetic character, are secondary.

The Green Book has, until recently, enjoyed tremendous influence in road construction; indeed, until 1991, any road built with federal funding had to be built in accordance with Green Book standards. Today, though the book's standards are rarely legally mandatory, they nevertheless still constitute the unofficial "bible" of road design, and deviations are uncommon. For years, state departments of transportation have required local governments to comply with Green Book standards in order to receive funding assistance, oftentimes forcing communities to choose among fighting congestion, breaking the bank, or losing irreplaceable local treasures.

A 1995 situation in a rural Connecticut county just outside Redding illustrates the typical conflict. County officials sought funding from the Connecticut Department of Transportation to repair an attractive, historic, stone arch bridge on an infrequently traveled county road at Poverty Hollow. The state offered $350,000 in funding support, but only if the 17-foot bridge were torn down and a 28-foot steel and concrete bridge were erected in its place. Torn between accepting the money and saving an important part of their cultural and historic landscape, the county decided to decline state and federal assistance and repair the stone bridge themselves using money from the local coffers. Noted a local official: "It's a sad commentary on our system when historic preservation, neighborhood aesthetics, and common sense are displaced by cookie-cutter design requirements."

Similar incidents have occurred in other states where many communities are fighting to end the reign of the Green Book. Legislators in Vermont, for instance, have for years been proposing legislation to loosen the state's transportation design standards to allow more flexibility. In response, the state's Agency of Transportation recently drafted its own road standards and codified them. An overriding principle in the reform law is that roads should be designed for the safety of cars traveling at the posted speed limit, not 20 miles over it. Vermont's newly adopted legislation is considered one of the strongest highway design reform laws in the country so far.

Similarly, the incident at Poverty Hollow persuaded the Connecticut legislature to pass a law relaxing design standards on bridges. The state also has a new *Highway Design Manual* that encourages "context-sensitive highway design."[3] Importantly, the manual specifically instructs highway designers to develop solutions that meet operational and safety requirements, "while preserving the aesthetic, historic, or cultural resources of an area."[4]

In addition to highway and bridge standards, road design has become an issue in many urban neighborhoods. The Green Book's emphasis on wide streets runs counter to the trend in many communities that are encouraging neotraditional forms of development. In response, these communities are passing ordinances allowing more flexibility in road widths. Phoenix, for example, used to require that all new residential streets be at least 32 feet wide; in 1997, however, the city passed an ordinance offering developers the option of building narrower streets (with a minimum of 28 feet) in residential developments. Similarly, Eugene, Oregon, has reduced its minimum street width requirement from 28 to 20 feet.

The Federal Highway Administration (FHWA) has recognized that sometimes deviations from the sterile standards of the Green Book may be acceptable, especially in the design and maintenance of secondary roads. Indeed, Congress included language in two federal laws, making clear that good highway design should take into account the surrounding natural and built environment. The Intermodal Surface Transportation Efficiency Act, passed in 1991, notes that:

> *If a proposed [roadway] project . . . involves a historic facility or is located in an area of historic or scenic value, the Secretary may approve such project . . . if such project is designed to standards that allow for the preservation of such historic or scenic value and such project is designed with mitigation mea-*

sures to allow preservation of such value and ensure safe use of the facility.[5]

Similarly, the National Highway System Designation Act of 1995 states:

A design for new construction, reconstruction, resurfacing . . . restoration, or rehabilitation of a highway on the National Highway System (other than a highway also on the Interstate System) may take into account . . . [in addition to safety, durability, and economy of maintenance] the constructed and natural environment of the area; the environmental, scenic, historic, community, and preservation impacts of the activity; and access for other modes of transportation.[6]

In a recent publication, *Flexibility in Highway Design*, the FHWA discusses how to design highways that ensure both safety and efficiency, and also preserve and protect environmental and cultural values. While the book does not establish new design standards or criteria, it does promote innovative thinking by highway designers, and encourages consideration of the "aesthetic, scenic, historic, and cultural resources" that "help give a community its identity and sense of place." [7] The book highlights projects that demonstrate the flexibility of the Green Book, by working within designated parameters to obtain safety and mobility, while also preserving environmental and cultural resources. In sum, while the Green Book is still the nation's unofficial "bible" of road design, its usefulness seems to be evolving toward serving merely as suggested guidelines rather than being steadfast, inflexible "rules of the road."

SELECTED SOURCES

Flexibility in Highway Design. Washington, DC: U.S. Department of Transportation, Federal Highway Administration, undated. Revolutionary guide that encourages highway designers to go beyond standard "Green Book" thinking in designing roads

and streets that fit with the landscape and countryside.

Institute of Traffic Engineers. *Traditional Neighborhood Development: Street Design Guidelines.* Washington, DC: Planning Council Committee 5P-8, 1997. Excellent publication that discusses the principles of street design in traditional neighborhood developments.

New Standards for Residential Streets in Portland, Oregon. Portland, OR: City of Portland Bureau of Transportation Engineering, 1991. Ground-breaking background report establishing the basis for narrower street standards in Portland.

Policy on Geometric Design of Highways and Streets (the "Green Book"). Washington, DC: American Association of State Highway and Transportation Officials, 2001).

Residential Street Typology and Injury Accident Frequency. Longmont, CO: Swift and Associates, 1997.

USEFUL WEB SITES

Congress for the New Urbanism Narrow Streets Database
www.sonic.net/abcaia/narrow.htm

Federal Highway Administration
www.fhwa.dot.gov

Scenic America
www.scenic.org/roads.htm
(context-sensitive road design)

LOCAL GOVERNMENT CONTACTS

Senior Planner, Portland, Oregon: (503) 823-7198

Director of Planning, Henderson, Nevada: (702) 565-2372

Director of Planning, Boulder, Colorado: (303) 441-3291

Division Director, Planning and Zoning, Salt Lake County, Utah: (801) 468-2072

President, Scenic America, Washington, DC: (202) 543-6200

4. OPEN LANDS PRESERVATION

Preservation of open lands around small towns and rural areas in the West has not been a front-burner issue in many communities until recently. With thousands of acres of federal lands open to the public—often amounting to 70% or more of a jurisdiction's land area—other growth issues seemed more pressing.

All of that has changed, however, as the West has boomed. Often, private lands, such as hay meadows and stream corridors, provide the setting that makes a place special, offer access to public lands, and provide critical wildlife habitat, especially in the winter. In response, small towns and counties are beginning to focus on how to maintain the benefits that open space provides while providing their owners with a reasonable economic use of their property.

Communities can easily overlook a traditional tool—zoning—to preserve agricultural lands and open space (Figure 5-8). Large-lot zoning is an approach by which communities establish a large minimum lot size in certain districts. For example, some midwestern jurisdictions in Illinois, Michigan, Minnesota, and Wisconsin have required minimum lot sizes of 160 acres and more. In Weld County, Colorado (near Greeley), agricultural districts require minimum lot sizes of 80 acres per dwelling unit (Figure 5-9).

Large-lot zoning provisions may come in a variety of forms, including:

- *Quarter-quarter zoning:* Each landowner is entitled to one buildable lot per 40 acres of farmland. Once the allowable number of lots has been developed anywhere on the property, no more construction is allowed. This approach, which works best in rural areas with only moderate growth pressure and larger farms, is used extensively in the rural areas around Minneapolis/St. Paul, Minnesota.
- *Sliding-scale zoning:* This approach decreases the number of residences allowed per acre

5-8 Much so-called "rural" zoning in the West is nothing of the kind.

Source: Chris Duerksen

5-9 Weld County, Colorado, has employed large-lot zoning to protect agricultural lands.

Source: Lesli Ellis

as the parcel size increases (e.g., a 10-acre parcel may be allowed one residence; a 40 acre-parcel only two; and a 160-acre tract only three units). Sliding-scale zoning has shown to be effective in agricultural areas that are under development pressure. They do allow some development to occur, but in a limited fashion, thus preserving some farmland, particularly larger parcels. Adequate buffers must be established between agricultural and residential uses.

Large-lot zoning has some important advantages. It prevents the development of large tracts of open spaces and agricultural areas while reducing inflationary land speculation by reducing the prospects for easy conversions to higher intensity, nonagricultural uses. It is also a relatively simple tool to administer and involves little cost to government.

On the other hand, there are several pitfalls and drawbacks that local governments must consider. First, while the U.S. Constitution does not guarantee the "highest and best" use of a parcel, large-lot zoning must allow for some reasonable economic use of land, such as farming or ranching. Where no reasonable use is allowed, zoning may violate legal restraints against unconstitutional "takings" of private property. Generally, however, where the zoning regulation is reasonably related to a legitimate public welfare purpose, the regulation will be upheld unless it precludes all economic use of the property.

Second, large-lot zoning can diminish property values if prior zoning allows higher densities. Where such measures seek to preserve agricultural areas, lowered property values may create the opposite effect by depriving farmers of their collateral, thus rendering farming economically infeasible. In such cases, large-lot zoning measures can be combined with measures such as transferable development rights programs or tax incentives to ensure that the agricultural use remains viable.

Finally, regulatory authorities must be sensitive to whether any agricultural use in an area is feasible; if farming or ranching has become unprofitable in an area, unless other measures are undertaken in tandem, large-lot zoning provides little more than a short-term solution that cannot prevent conversions of farmlands to economically viable uses.

Large-lot zoning clearly will not be the right tool in all jurisdictions. Perhaps the simplest and most common approach to open space protection is that of requiring new residential subdivisions to set aside a specified percentage of their land in public open space. All western states provide authority for local governments to require dedication of public open space as part of the subdivision review process. In the 1970s and 1980s, local governments typically selected a number out of thin air—often 5-10% of the total land area of the subdivision—and required acreage to be dedicated for parks or trails. This basic approach still has much to recommend it, although modern practice requires a more rational approach.

Unfortunately, many rural counties have not enacted land dedication ordinances and thus get the worst of both worlds: they lose prime open space to development, and get no public open space in return to satisfy demands of new residents who move into the subdivision, which in turn puts more pressure on existing parks and recreational areas.

Thus, a first step is to enact a land dedication provision as part of local subdivision regulations. The next step is to ensure that the land dedication percentage bears some reasonable relationship to the demand created by the development. Accepted methodologies exist to calculate how much land a particular development should dedicate, typically based on a ratio of population/acres. For example, national standards recommended by the National Parks and Recreation Association suggest that for every 1,000 people (or fraction thereof) in a development, 10-20 acres of public open space should be dedicated. Land dedication standards might also take into account mitigation for sensitive wildlife habitat that is being developed, thus offsetting development impacts.

More sophisticated programs will give the local government some say about exactly which land should be dedicated. In Fort Collins, Colorado, for example, the city targets sensitive environmental areas and wildlife habitat for protection. Otherwise, the locality may end up getting lands that are not useful for either public recreation or habitat protection, or are fragmented throughout a development so as not to be usable.

Small towns and rural counties should also examine the use of in-lieu and impact fees. Most states allow local governments to accept money in lieu of land dedication—an option that many developers prefer. Of course, this means that a formula must be established to set an equivalent in-lieu fee, which should also cover the costs of administering such a program. An advantage from a public perspective is that the local government can accumulate funds and use them to purchase larger, strategically located blocks of open space. The downside is that such programs take more staff time and have transactional costs related to identifying and negotiating for the purchase of alternative property.

Impact fees are another step that an increasing number of western jurisdictions are embracing. While impact fee-enabling authority varies greatly from state to state, where it is available, impact fees offer a powerful tool to create a funding source for open space preservation. Again, studies must be done to establish a rationale for setting the fee at a particular level, but this can be done by consulting firms at a very reasonable cost (and the cost of the study can be folded into and recouped by the fee). Open space and recreational land impact fees have been adopted in a wide range of communities, including Greeley, Colorado; Park City, Utah; and Pitkin County, Colorado.

However, sophisticated jurisdictions are beginning to realize that a *private,* open space set-aside requirement is every bit, if not more, important than a public lands dedication standard or impact fees to preserve open lands. Public lands dedication can only be justified up to a certain point and will only amount to a small fraction of most sites. The beauty of a private, open space set-aside regulation is that it allows the developer to retain ownership of the property and take economic advantage of it while avoiding the need for main-

tenance by a public entity. The downside is that public access is not provided.

Here is how such a system typically works: A provision is inserted in the local zoning or subdivision ordinance requiring that a specified percentage of any site be maintained in an undeveloped state. Depending on the location of property, these percentages can range anywhere from 10-50% and more. Usually, the ordinance specifies which types of land should be given preference in selecting the set-aside—again, they will typically be environmentally sensitive lands (e.g., river corridors and wetlands) and scenic areas (e.g., meadows, stands of trees, and ridgelines).

The developer works with the local government to tailor the subdivision to the land. In some instances, the land set aside to meet such a provision must be subjected to an easement or other restriction permitting development and provisions made for long-term maintenance. In other instances, however, the set-aside may simply be a portion of a private lot.

To illustrate, in a development of 10-acre lots, the set-aside provision might require that the disturbed area on a site—including septic systems, roads, and the building site—not exceed 2 acres; the remaining 8 acres, or 80%, would remain open space. Fencing might be prohibited except around the 2 acres so that the remaining lands retain the appearance and functionality of open space.

While the legal basis for requiring both public land dedication and private, open space set-asides is clear and firm in most states, it may be less tenable from a political perspective. The idea of giving up private lands to the public in return for development approval somehow sticks in the craw of certain westerners.

Fortunately, there are some excellent examples of incentive and bonus programs that help take the sting out of such regulations. Many jurisdictions are providing a cluster or open-space subdivision option for developers. A developer is permitted to maintain the existing density allowed on a site by the underlying zoning, and reduce the minimum lot size so that the same number of units can be built on a smaller percentage of the site. In return, the developer must set aside a specified amount of open space—usually 50% or more. Thus, if a developer owned 100 acres zoned one unit per 10 acres, the developer could theoretically develop up to 10 units.

Under the cluster scenario, the regulations might allow the developer to reduce the minimum lot size to 3 acres, thus necessitating use of only 30 acres for the development and resulting in 70 acres being preserved. Because planning for a cluster subdivision is often more time-consuming than a typical cookie-cutter subdivision, many jurisdictions offer density bonuses as a carrot to foster use of this tool. Thus, in the hypothetical development above, the locality might grant a bonus of one unit per 20 acres of land preserved, or three units in this case.

While cluster development appears simple in theory, experienced jurisdictions know they must pay attention to knotty issues, such as who will maintain the open space (rural homeowner associations are notoriously dysfunctional), how to site the smaller lots to reduce their visual impact, and how to deal with potential opposition by neigh-

bors who have built on larger lots and fear the smaller cluster development will devalue their land. Fortunately, there is increasing positive experience with cluster developments around the United States and excellent references that can guide local governments in dealing with these questions. The case studies of Larimer County and Douglas County, Colorado (Chapter 4) are excellent examples of innovative cluster development programs that are showing positive results.

Just as cluster developments are gaining increasing popularity, so are transfer of development rights (TDR) and purchase of development rights (PDR) programs. Again, both are designed to take the sting out of land protection regulations and offer some "compensating" benefits. TDR programs involve the shifting of permissible development densities from unsuitable development areas to more appropriate sites. Where permissible densities are shifted off-site to other parcels, density transfer schemes are known as TDR programs, which encourage the maintenance of low-density land uses by establishing an off-site market for the sale of unused development rights.

Under this concept, a landowner in a "sending area" transfers development rights to another landowner in a "receiving area," who thus augments the property owner's development rights in that area in excess of their otherwise permissible limits. Under either of these types of programs, local governments can maintain low-density land uses in sensitive areas without depriving property owners of their development rights.

The TDR concept has also been applied in a number of jurisdictions. While the most successful TDR programs are in the East—Montgomery County, Maryland (Figure 5-10) and the Pinelands National Reserve in New Jersey—an increasing number of western jurisdictions are climbing on the bandwagon. In California, dozens of jurisdictions are utilizing TDR programs to protect open space, and several in Colorado have put together successful programs. Pitkin County (Aspen) and

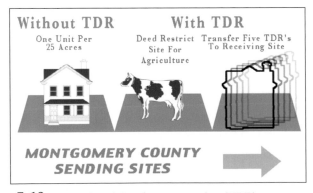

5-10 Transfer of development rights (TDR) programs are promising land preservation tools in the West as well as the East.

Source: Rick Pruetz

Boulder County, Colorado, are two good examples that are worth exploring for any jurisdictions interested in this tool.

TDR programs have some important strengths. They help alleviate pressures and incentives to subdivide or develop land by offering some means for landowners to recoup property values while maintaining low-density land uses. Moreover, where regulations impose low-density limitations on development rights, TDR programs restore the value of these rights to the landowners, thus providing a shield against constitutional taking of property claims and concomitant political objections.

Of course, as with any tool, TDR programs are not the only answer to a successful land development management program. Alone, they cannot ensure *quality* development and a number of conditions are essential to the success of TDR programs:

- Development pressures must be sufficient to make development rights valuable, in the sending area as well as in the receiving area.
- TDR programs rely upon appropriate market conditions and will not work where there are no buyers for the rights. While additional planning measures can influence such conditions, the TDR concept is generally most effective where strong development pressures place a high value on development rights.
- While TDR programs need not be overly complex, they do require some staff to administer, especially in the early years of an initiative.

PDR programs are also gaining increasing attention where funds are available for land purchase, but local governments want to "stretch" their acquisition dollars. In these programs, local governments pay landowners to forego exercising certain land development rights.

In the Seattle metropolitan area, King County, Washington, has administered a successful PDR program for the purpose of preserving agricul-

tural land in the face of metropolitan growth pressures. Drawing upon a $50 million bond issue, the program provided for the county's PDR for properties facing development pressures, with priority rankings determined in accordance with the intensity of such pressures. Participation in the program was voluntary for eligible landowners. Purchase prices were calculated as the difference between appraised highest and best uses and appraised values as farmland; upon purchasing development rights, the county recorded restrictive covenants on the property deeds, limiting development rights to 5% of the property's non-tillable area (Figure 5-11).

Other communities in the West, such as Gunnison County, Colorado, have stitched together a variety of funding sources, including grants from state lottery funds, to kick off PDR programs that bear watching.

Timing plays a key role in the success of a PDR program. Such programs are best administered when development pressures are not so strong as to inflate the values of development rights, and when the agricultural or other residual uses of the land remain profitable. Essentially, government should "buy low" so as to maximize its cost savings.

PDR programs have some distinct advantages. First and foremost, when the government acquires development rights, preservation is guaranteed. PDR programs also allow for continued private ownership; land remains on local tax rolls (although perhaps at a reduced value) and in productive use. Moreover, through PDR (as opposed to a fee simple purchase), the government avoids management and maintenance obligations and the property remains in productive use. Where planners can identify specific rights or uses to be reserved or prohibited, easement purchases provide an effective and relatively inexpensive tool for achieving specific restrictive or use objectives for land. Unless the property possesses resources or values that are so valuable or fragile as to require government stewardship, easement acqui-

5-11 King County, Washington, farm.

Source: King County Planning Department

sition provides a cost-effective alternative to fee simple acquisition.

Of course, PDR programs have some limits that need to be recognized. The cost of purchasing development rights may be cheaper than acquiring the entire property, but can still be high and may strain local government budgets. In addition, compared to purchase of fee simple interests, development rights purchases provide less control over the landowner's ultimate disposition or use of land; unforeseen conditions may arise that threaten the values associated with the land. Of course, there is an administrative burden that should not be discounted. If the local government owns development rights, it must police them; harmful acts prohibited by the purchase agreement, such as clearing woods along a stream, may occur without the knowledge of the local government.

All in all, local governments in the West have many creative and traditional tools to protect open space. Political will is, as with most things in land use management, often the essential element.

SELECTED SOURCES

Arendt, Randall et al. *Rural By Design: Maintaining Small Town Character.* Chicago: American Planning Association, 1994. While focusing on eastern small towns, this landmark publication has good design and land protection advice for western communities.

Duerksen, Christopher and Richard Roddewig. *Takings Law in Plain English.* Washington, DC: National Trust for Historic Preservation, 2003.

Pruetz, Rick. *Putting Transfer of Development Rights to Work in California.* Point Arena, CA: Solano Press Books, 1993.

Roddewig, Richard J. and Cheryl A. Inghram. *Transferable Development Rights Programs.* Chicago: American Planning Association, 1987.

Roddewig, Richard J. and Jared Shlaes. *Analyzing the Economic Feasibility of a Development Project: A Guide for Planners.* Chicago: American Planning Association, 1983.

Saving American Farmland: What Works. Washington, DC: American Farmland Trust, 1997. A comprehensive guidebook that presents the latest research on farmland protection tools.

USEFUL WEB SITES

American Farmland Trust
www.farmland.org

Colorado Department of Local Affairs
(growth management toolbox)
dlg.oem2.state.co.us/fs/toolspace.htm

Larimer County, Colorado
www.co.larimer.co.us

LOCAL GOVERNMENT CONTACTS

Director of Planning, Rural Land Use Center, Larimer County, Colorado: (970) 498-7683

Director of Community Development, Douglas County, Colorado: (303) 660-7460

Zoning Administrator, Douglas County, Colorado: (303) 660-7460

5. NIGHT LIGHTING

To visitors from the East, the brilliant night sky is one of the most memorable features of a trip out West. Thousands of stars vie for attention, constellations stand out, shooting stars are frequent, and the Milky Way seems to flow forever across the heavens—but the night sky, like the landscape, is changing.

Outside Fairplay, Colorado, in the spectacular and remote South Park Valley, the eerie glow of night lighting from Denver and Colorado Springs over 60 miles away washes out all but the brightest of stars on many evenings. Not surprisingly, citizens of Park County voiced their concern over this phenomenon during a recent comprehensive planning process, asking, "What can we do?"

Historically, a handful of western communities have been at the forefront in preserving the natural, dark night sky—notably those associated with observatories and astronomical research such as in Flagstaff, Arizona (Lowell Observatory). In other rural places, it did not matter as much—lack of growth was a rather effective tool to keeping the night sky dark. As the West has boomed over the past decade, however, residential and commercial growth has spilled out of the towns and into the countryside. Hillsides that only a few years ago were black apparitions on the night skyline are now often dotted with the glare of security lights from second homes. In the towns, super-bright commercial lighting for gas stations and chain stores is giving their big-city cousins a run for their money. Safety and security are often used as window dressing to justify what is really over-bright advertising by car dealers and similar uses. "Hey, look at me!" often seems to be the prevailing wisdom.

Though such visual antics may be effective in catching one's attention, this overlighting not only ruins the dark night sky—one of the most distinctive features of the West—but actually can create safety issues as it interferes with the night vision of drivers and is a slap in the face at energy conservation at a time when an increasing number of states are starving for electricity.

Lately, there are encouraging signs that people in the West have had enough. Many communities and states have "night sky" interest groups, such as the International Dark-Sky Association (IDSA), that are lobbying for more discrete lighting. There is a movement among lighting design professionals away from older, less energy-efficient and more obtrusive lamps, such as mercury vapor, to newer technology. Arizona and New Mexico have enacted statewide lighting control statutes; local governments have also been playing a role, adopting increasingly sophisticated standards for light-

5-12 San Juan Capistrano, California, has adopted sophisticated parking lot lighting controls.

Source: City of San Juan Capistrano

ing in their zoning and development codes. In Arizona, for example, 15 counties and 89 municipalities have passed lighting ordinances.

Actually, it is quite typical for most local zoning codes to have lighting control provisions. First-generation ordinances usually have a catchall section that forbids any spillover lighting or nuisance glare on adjacent properties. Take this example from one small western city: "All existing and/or new exterior lighting shall not cause light trespass and shall be such as to protect adjacent properties from glare and excessive lighting." The problem with these provisions is that they are either unrealistic (there will always be some spillover) or unenforceable (they are too vague).

Not surprisingly, local ordinances are becoming more sophisticated. Many now set standards based on specific, measurable limits in foot-candles or lumens. Typical is the ordinance from San Juan Capistrano, California, for parking lot lighting. Where such lots abut a residential area, lighting must be shielded so that "light measured five feet outside the property boundaries shall not

exceed 0.1 foot-candles." Others use limits on "average illuminance" on a site.

While such quantitative limits can be effective and are enforceable, they require a trained staff and well-calibrated equipment for enforcement. As explained by the IDSA, "Measuring average illuminance requires nighttime work, in areas often with automobile traffic, laying out a regular grid of points and taking illuminance measures at these points with a calibrated and carefully leveled meter."

For small towns and rural jurisdictions in the West, many of which have small or no professional planning staff, such measurement is unrealistic. As pointed out by the IDSA, "after-construction determination of compliance with any rule is a risky course, risking discovery of non-compliance after the money has been spent, the design finished, and the lighting literally set in concrete" (Figure 5-12).

In its *Outdoor Lighting Code Handbook*, the IDSA suggests a new approach that is not only simpler, but will probably be more effective and enforceable in the long run. In brief, it uses rigorous shielding standards that require all higher intensity lighting to be fully shielded (i.e., hoods are required so that all light is projected below the horizontal and not above). Such a provision is easy to enforce by simply having an applicant submit a photo of the proposed luminaire. Additionally, the code establishes a lumens-per-acre cap. This is, in effect, a light budget for each site based on the proposed use (more for commercial/industrial and less for residential) and its general location (rural vs. high-activity areas). This approach is easy to administer because each proposed light fixture has a lumens number associated with it. By adding these numbers, a plan reviewer can easily determine if the limit has been exceeded *before* construction takes place.

The model code also has special provisions for structures, including billboards (e.g., no upward-directed lighting allowed), sports facilities, outdoor display lots, service station canopies, and temporary uses. All of these sections help tailor the code to unique uses and circumstances.

Of particular interest is the modified approach for smaller residential lots, for which the lumens-per-acre cap is difficult to apply, and fully shielded fixtures can be difficult to purchase. Because the light pollution for such residences is minimal, the code specifies a maximum number of outdoor fixtures and maximum wattage that should permit ample outdoor lighting, while reducing light pollution and eliminating any significant enforcement burden.

An interesting aspect of the code is that it recommends against any blanket limit on light pole height—a common feature of many zoning codes. The rationale is that reducing pole height means that more lights will be required on a site, which may actually result in more light pollution. Additionally, more poles cost more to install and maintain, and may actually increase visual clutter during the day. As a consequence, the code suggests allowing poles up to 35 feet.

The key to using the model code and examples from other communities will be to tailor the lighting ordinance to local conditions. Some of the key issues that will usually need to be addressed include:

- *Type of lighting:* Increasingly, communities such as San Juan Capistrano, California are banning mercury vapor and incandescent lighting for industrial/commercial uses. For energy-conservation reasons and the quality of the lighting, metal halide and high- and low-pressure sodium are preferred.
- *Type of fixtures:* Many local governments have banned floodlighting of billboards and buildings. Cottonwood, Arizona (near Sedona), is a good example. Outdoor floodlighting by flood-light projection above the horizontal is prohibited.
- *Hours of illumination:* A common feature of most modern ordinances is a strict limit on

nighttime lighting, especially for nonresidential uses. Many have curfews on sports facilities and outdoor display lots. Douglas County, Colorado—one of the fastest growing jurisdictions in the nation—requires that "all lights, except those required for security as provided herein, must be extinguished within one hour after the end of business hours...." Stadium and exterior sports arena lights must be extinguished by 10 PM or immediately after conclusion of the final event of the day. Cottonwood, Arizona, requires all lights to be shut off by 10 PM unless the area is in active use.

- *Neon outlining/decorative building spotlighting:* Increasingly popular as an attention-getting device, outlining in neon or spotlighting buildings at night is becoming a favorite of commercial enterprises. Communities are responding by banning such illumination.
- *Retroactivity:* The issue of whether new lighting limits should be applied to existing fixtures can be controversial. Douglas County, Colorado, requires that all lights be retrofitted to meet strict new standards; other communities require replacement when lighting is changed or burns out.

SELECTED SOURCES

IES Lighting Handbook. New York: Illuminating Engineering Society of North America, 1993. This 1,000-page technical reference is a combination of two earlier volumes that separately addressed reference information and applications. Considered the "bible" of illumination engineering, the handbook provides broad coverage of all phases of lighting disciplines. The 34 chapters are organized into five general areas.

Lighting for Exterior Environments: An IESNA Recommended Practice. New York: Illuminating Engineering Society of North America, 1999. The leading handbook for lighting design professionals. Excellent discussion of specific uses and lighting types.

Outdoor Lighting Code Handbook. Tucson, AZ: International Dark-Sky Association, 2000. An excellent overall reference on outdoor lighting written in plain English. This handbook also contains a model lighting code with explanatory notes. Available on-line below.

USEFUL WEB SITES

International Dark-Sky Association
www.darksky.org

Reference center and on-line library source for the lighting industry
www.lightforum.com

U.S. Environmental Protection Agency Energy Star/ Green Lights Program
www.energystar.gov

Illuminating Engineering Society of North America
www.iesna.org

LOCAL GOVERNMENT CONTACTS

Director of Community Development, Douglas County, Colorado: (303) 660-7460

Zoning Administrator, Douglas County, Colorado: (303) 660-7460

Community Development Director, Cottonwood, Arizona: (928) 634-5505

6. PROTECTION OF VIEWS AND SENSITIVE NATURAL AREAS

As discussed in Chapters 2 and 3, a century ago when homes and ranches were nestled in valleys to take advantage of water and hunker down out of the wind, little development took place on ridges and other prominent venues. Commercial development was usually focused in a compact downtown, not stripped along the main road; however, times are changing. Unlike many other regions of the country where trees and topography can be used to hide development mistakes and bad design, in the West, the often sparse vegetation and sharp landscape features offer little relief.

Not surprisingly, the issue of view protection has roared to the forefront in many communities as new houses pop up on prominent ridges and hillsides and as insensitive commercial development sullies scenic roadways. Communities are tackling the challenging issue of view protection head on, often linking it with efforts to protect hillsides, steep slopes, and other sensitive natural areas.

In some, the approaches are quite simple and straightforward—new development must, for example, set back 100 feet off prominent ridgelines, and roofs must be painted or shingled to blend in with the surrounding landscapes. Other efforts are more sophisticated, such as in Denver, Colorado, where a mountain view protection ordinance limits the height of buildings according to a mathematical formula to preserve views of the Rocky Mountains from city parks (Figure 5-13).

Local view protection programs may be characterized in a variety of ways, depending upon their emphasis (i.e., the particular type of views and/or scenic resources afforded protection). One program, for example, might emphasize protecting views of a major river valley running through a community, while another may focus on protecting views of a locally prominent building. Some jurisdictions employ a multifaceted approach that emphasizes protecting more than one type of scenic or natural resource.

View protection programs typically fall into one of four categories: (1) viewshed protection; (2) view corridor protection; (3) programs linking view and environmental protection efforts; and (4) scenic roadway protection.

Preserving Viewsheds

Perhaps the most common category of view protection ordinance focuses on preserving viewsheds—those grand, scenic vistas that encompass a multitude of elements, both natural and man-made, and that give communities their special identity.

There are two common types of viewshed ordinances. The first allows new development subject to some type of design review. For example, some

5-13 Mountain view from Cranmer Park in Denver, Colorado.

Source: Chris Duerksen

jurisdictions have enacted ordinances that protect views of important local waterways by imposing height controls on new commercial buildings. Park City, Utah, has adopted height and building design controls, including regulations on the color of roofs and building materials, to ensure that development on the hills around the city does not mar the scenery (Figure 5-14).

A stricter type of viewshed ordinance sharply curtails the types of new development allowed in viewsheds in order to preserve the scenic areas in a relatively undisturbed state. These ordinances require sensitive siting or screening of any buildings allowed in the viewshed. Scottsdale, Arizona, has adopted this approach in protecting views of the rugged McDowell Mountains that frame that city.

View Corridors

A second category of view protection focuses on protecting view corridors—those openings in the urban fabric that allow either quick glimpses or more extended views of important man-made features (e.g., state capitols and historic buildings) or natural features (e.g., public parks and mountains). View corridor regulations can vary widely in form. They can be simple and straightforward, as is the case with ordinances that attempt to prevent shadows from falling onto important view corridors and public places. San Francisco, California, for instance, has adopted height controls on commercial buildings designed to prevent shadows on public plazas and parks at certain prescribed times. Denver also regulates the height of buildings on its 16th Street outdoor mall to ensure that maximum sunlight reaches sidewalks for pedestrians at lunchtime.

View corridor regulations may also be more complex, as is the case with the Denver and Austin programs that rely on mathematical formulas to calculate allowable building heights. Denver's mountain view ordinance (which withstood a court challenge) is a well-known example of this

5-14   Land use regulations in Park City, Utah, help new development fit in with the landscape.

Source: Miles Rademan

type of regulation. The Rocky Mountains have provided a stunning backdrop for Denver since the city's founding. To ensure that views of the mountains continue to exist from public places, the city enacted the mountain view ordinance to protect panoramic mountain views from parks and public places.

The city invokes both aesthetic and economic reasons to support the ordinance. The basic approach in Denver is to create a series of overlay zones with special restrictions tailored to each of the city's major parks. Thus, in Cranmer Park, no structure can be higher than 5,434 feet above sea level (the approximate height of the city) plus 1 foot for each 100 feet the structure lies from a reference point within the park. In practice, apartment buildings 300 feet from the reference point and at the same base elevation could be a maxi-

mum 30 feet high. In the Capitol/Civic Center District, the ordinance creates five zones, each with its own specific height limit, designed to protect the view of the Rocky Mountains from the state capitol and the view of the capitol itself.

The capitol view ordinance in Austin, Texas, is another oft-cited example of a view corridor protection scheme. Designed to protect views of the state capitol building from various vantage points around town, the Austin ordinance is similar in concept to the Denver mountain view ordinance. What distinguishes it from other efforts, however, is the amount of study and analysis that preceded its adoption. Furthermore, the ordinance contains a much more complex formula for determining acceptable building heights.

Adopted in August 1984, the Austin ordinance was introduced to serve aesthetic, educational, civic, and economic goals by protecting and reserving public views of the state capitol from selected points in the city such as parks, bridges, and major roads. The study that preceded adoption of the ordinance looked at the historical significance of the state capitol building (which is a facsimile of the U.S. Capitol, but only a few feet larger) and Austin's skyline. It paid particular attention to the policies of the city's comprehensive plan, which placed emphasis on maintaining the unique character of the community.

Sixty important view corridors were identified and broken down into four categories: (1) stationary parks; (2) thresholds along entryways to the city; (3) sustained views; and (4) dramatic glimpses. The study analyzed each view from the specific point identified (e.g., was the dome obscured?) and land uses within the corridor. The overall economic impact of the proposal was analyzed along with the economic impact within each corridor. All of this background work helped establish a strong framework for the ordinance and defused opposition to it, as opponents realized that adverse impacts were not as great as expected.

The final formula adopted establishes height allowances in each corridor defined by sightline elevations from the viewpoints to the base of the capitol dome. A grandfather clause governed projects already in the site plan review process. Local officials have been very pleased with the ordinance and have increased the number of designated corridors from the initial nine (designated in 1984) to 26 (as of 1998).

Linking Scenic and Sensitive Land Protection

A third type of view protection program aims to coordinate the protection of scenic resources with environmental protection efforts. Many communities are attempting to integrate relatively recent interests in regulating aesthetics with long-standing concerns for natural resource protection. One example is the increasing number of local tree and vegetation conservation ordinances discussed above. Such ordinances not only conserve important aesthetic resources—the greenery that contributes so much to community character—but also fulfill important environmental objectives by preventing soil erosion and enhancing air quality. Other view protection efforts may work in tandem with efforts to protect wetlands, floodplains, aquifers, watersheds, high-hazard slide areas, and wildlife habitat.[8]

Perhaps the best examples of a regulatory approach that focuses both on aesthetic and environmental protection are the hillside development ordinances, which are becoming increasingly popular, especially in mountain states. A 1993 survey found that 234 such ordinances had been adopted in 22 states, the majority in California (including the City of Claremont, as reviewed in Chapter 3).

The ordinances usually have at least two major objectives: (1) the protection of views; and (2) the protection of natural features associated with sensitive hillside ecosystems. Many hillside development ordinances also have a host of other goals, including fire prevention, the preservation of wildlife habitat, and the provision of adequate roadways to ensure quick access for public safety vehicles. The most common area of emphasis is the protection of scenic resources. Indeed, the survey found that 75% of all the examined ordinances listed "aesthetics" as a major purpose.

The ordinances vary widely in the approaches described. A jurisdiction might choose to encourage development while emphasizing public safety, thus requiring extensive mass grading and re-engineering of hillsides to provide high-quality roadways that allow quick access for public safety vehicles. A jurisdiction might also require selective grading and improvements of hillsides for safety concerns, while also imposing development standards (e.g., setbacks from ridgelines or restrictions on removal of native vegetation) to protect important natural features.

5-15 Development proposals on steep slopes spurred Salt Lake County, Utah, to adopt a "sensitive lands protection" ordinance.

Source: Chris Duerksen

A third approach could be to prohibit hillside development altogether. A combination approach might require grading and other engineering techniques in certain areas targeted for development, while prohibiting development altogether in other areas; the exact location and characteristics of these cluster developments (e.g., hilltops vs. valleys) could vary depending on local conditions.

Ordinances that do not prohibit hillside development altogether tend to vary widely in their areas of emphasis and scope of coverage. Increasingly, jurisdictions are adopting "sensitive lands protection" ordinances that include development standards in a number of different areas. Officials in Salt Lake County, Utah, for example, recently adopted a Foothills and Canyons Overlay Zoning District, which is intended, in part, to "preserve the visual and aesthetic qualities of the foothills and the canyons, including prominent ridgelines" (Figure 5-15).

The ordinance's wide-ranging scope is typical of many modern hillside development ordinances. Development standards address:

- lot and density requirements
- slope protection standards
- grading standards
- road and site access
- access to trails and public lands
- fencing
- tree and vegetation protection
- natural hazard protection
- stream corridor and wetlands protection
- wildlife habitat protection
- traffic

A key feature of the Salt Lake County overlay zone is that for every development subject to the ordinance, limits of disturbance must be established indicating the specific area(s) of the site in which construction and development activity must be contained. For single-family residential development, limits of disturbance include the area required for the principal structure, accessory structure(s), utilities, services, drainage facilities, and a septic tank. Area required for driveways and leach fields are not included. Limits of disturbance are designated individually for each development site, based on criteria such as minimization of visual impacts, erosion prevention and control, fire prevention and safety, and preservation of significant trees or vegetation.

Colorado Springs, Colorado, has also enacted a strong hillside protection program. This fast-growing city is facing intense development pressures in some of its spectacular hillside neighborhoods that back up onto Pike's Peak and the Front Range. Concerned about the potential destruction of its fragile foothills environment, Colorado Springs adopted a Hillside Overlay Zoning District that applies in addition to the base zoning districts. The purpose of the overlay district is to allow people to "develop and maintain hillside properties in an environmentally sensitive fashion," while also ensuring that visual impacts of development are mitigated to the maximum extent possible.

The city has adopted both mandatory zoning regulations and recommended design guidelines to help achieve its twin goals of aesthetic and environmental protection. Performance standards for hillside development are contained in the zoning code (regulating basic things such as setbacks, maximum height, lot coverage, drive grades, and access points). A separate manual supplements the code requirements with recommended design standards and guidelines.

The Colorado Springs review process for the development of hillside properties is typical of most local jurisdictions. The process encourages applicants to hold a preapplication conference with staff to review the proposed development and applicable local regulations. A separate session to discuss design review issues may supplement this conference. The formal application must include a site/lot grading plan for all proposed development, including an inventory of site features, an analysis of particular site constraints, and an evaluation of alternative development options. Building elevation drawings must also be submitted for all proposed structures. After review and evaluation, city staff approves or denies the application. The applicant may appeal to a local hearing officer. Follow-up inspections occur during the construction phase to determine compliance with the approved plans.

A partial list of the criteria for approval of the plans demonstrates the multiple objectives behind the Colorado Springs hillside development ordinance:

- Have applicable code development standards been met?
- Is terrain disturbance minimized?
- Have cuts and fills been minimized?
- Has the natural land form been retained?
- Have visually compatible stabilization measures been used for "cut and fill" slopes?

- Have visual impacts upon off-site areas been avoided or reasonably mitigated?
- Have natural features such as slopes and rock formations been incorporated into the site design?
- Has the structure been sited off from the ridgeline?

Given the multiple objectives behind modern hillside development ordinances, it is understandable that potential conflicts may sometimes occur among competing goals. Minimum road-width standards, for example, may run counter to provisions protecting native vegetation. The potential for such conflicts underscores the importance of laying a solid foundation for new ordinances of careful planning and extensive public participation, to ensure that any choices or tradeoffs made among competing objectives accurately reflect the community's stated goals and preferences.

Closely related to the hillside development ordinances are those ordinances limiting ridgeline development. Development atop ridgelines often may be seen from numerous locations throughout a community, and thus may even more dramatically infringe on special views than hillside development.

As discussed in Chapter 4, Castle Rock, Colorado, recently adopted one of the more progressive and sophisticated ridgeline protection ordinances in the country. The city's ordinance defines various "skyline areas" (i.e., any area in which all or part of a permanent structure would be visible along the skyline when viewed from one or more points on specially designated viewing platforms) and ridgeline areas (i.e., mapped areas having a major visual impact on the character of the town based on field observations). As part of the town's subdivision approval process, building envelopes must be defined to restrict the siting of improvements in these key areas. No primary or accessory structures may be constructed within the most sensitive skyline or ridgeline areas. Improvements that are allowed must mitigate their impacts on the visual landscape in several ways, including:

- *Color:* All primary and accessory structures must use predominant exterior wall colors that repeat the colors most commonly found in the land and vegetation around the building, and which have a light reflection value of no more than 40.
- *Vegetation:* The area around each primary and accessory structure must include at least one tree of a species with a mature height of at least 35 feet for each 2,500 square feet of a lot or parcel area (maximum of eight required trees).
- *Floodlights:* Floodlights shall not be used to light all or any portion of any primary or accessory structure façade; all outdoor lighting sources shall use full cutoff light fixtures.
- *Exposed basements:* On the side of each primary and accessory structure facing the nearest designated viewing platform, no basement wall shall be exposed for more than one-half of its height, unless a vegetated berm at least 3 feet in height is constructed as a visual buffer.

Recent Developments

The field of protecting sensitive views and natural areas is expanding as quickly as any of the topics addressed in this chapter. Increasingly, view protection is seen as an important aspect of rural preservation programs. Also, planners and legal experts are developing new tools, techniques, and programs at a rapid pace to assist communities in their efforts to identify and protect important scenic resources.

Jurisdictions are incorporating additional protections into their local development codes to protect features that contribute to rural character, such as undeveloped rolling hills, historic farmsteads, and other scenic features. Increasingly, the public is coming to believe that the protection of important viewsheds and view corridors is a nec-

essary component of efforts to protect and enhance rural and small-town character. As Randall Arendt points out in *Rural by Design: Maintaining Small Town Character,* "Public perception of community character is based largely on what can be seen from an automobile. . . . 'The view from the road' is more than a phrase—for most of us it comprises virtually everything we know about the natural and human-made features of our towns."[9]

Incentives have a particularly important role in protecting important views and sensitive natural areas. Communities may use density bonus and density transfer programs to reward developers who preserve sensitive lands, including view corridors. Similarly, an ordinance might provide an incentive in the form of allowing greater height of a structure on a sliding scale the further it sets back from a prominent ridge. Nonregulatory strategies should include pursuing an aggressive land acquisition program to purchase lands or development rights (either fee simple or through conservation easements) that have been prioritized based upon their environmental, scenic, and cultural values.

Again, it will be critical that these view and sensitive land protection strategies be tailored to local landscape and character. Moreover, given the potential for overlap and possible conflict between various goals, protection ordinances should have some administrative flexibility built into them. For example, an ordinance may require setbacks from a stream to protect views and riparian habitat, with the result that trees on an upland site may need to be removed to accommodate development. However, that same ordinance may have tree protection provisions that push development to riparian areas.

Some jurisdictions, such as Henderson, Nevada, grant the community development director authority to make minor adjustments in development standards up to 10-20% to work out these conflicts without the need for a public hearing, if there is no adverse environmental effect. These "safety valves" can help ensure the success of those important and ambitious initiatives.

SELECTED SOURCES

Arendt, Randall. *Rural by Design: Maintaining Small Town Character.* Chicago: American Planning Association, 1994. The classic work on the subject. While oriented to the eastern United States, it contains a wealth of good ideas and illustrations.

Bobrowski, Mark. "Scenic Landscape Protection Under the Police Power." 22 *Boston College Environmental Affairs Law Review* 697.

Duerksen, Christopher and Matthew Goebel. *Aesthetics, Community Character, and the Law.* Planning Advisory Service Report No. 489/90. Chicago: American Planning Association, 1999. Provides an overview of the policy and legal issues involved in design review, tree protection, sign regulation, and control of telecommunication facilities.

"Evaluating Scenic Resources." *Technical Information Series.* Volume 3, Number 1. Washington, DC: Scenic America, 1996. This is a good primer on techniques to identify and evaluate scenic resources in a community.

Olshansky, Robert B. *Planning for Hillside Development.* Planning Advisory Service Report No. 466. Chicago: American Planning Association, 1996. A good history of hillside protection ordinances and a survey of recent ordinances.

O, Say, Can You See: A Visual Awareness Tool Kit for Communities. Washington, DC: Scenic America, 1998. Developed jointly with the Landscape Architecture Department of the faculty of the State University of New York at Syracuse, this booklet features 16 tools for promoting and enhancing visual awareness at the local level.

USEFUL WEB SITES

Scenic America is the only national organization dedicated solely to protecting natural beauty and distinctive community character. www.scenic.org

The goal of this Great Plains site is to serve the people of the Great Plains—whether private citizens, business owners, elected or government officials, or scientists—in achieving long-term sustainability of the land and its natural resources. Their Web site features a useful Land Protection Options handbook for landowners. www.greatplains.org

LOCAL GOVERNMENT CONTACTS

Senior Planner, Park City, Utah: (435) 615-5066

Division Director, Planning and Zoning, Salt Lake County, Utah: (801) 468-2072

Director of Community Development, Castle Rock, Colorado: (303) 664-7460

Director of Planning, Colorado Springs, Colorado: (719) 520-6300

NOTES

1. *Residential Street Typology and Injury Accident Frequency.* Longmont, CO: Swift and Associates, 1997.

2. Institute of Traffic Engineers, *Traditional Neighborhood Development: Street Design Guidelines* (Washington, DC: Planning Council Committee 5P-8, 1997), p. 26.

3. Connecticut Department of Transportation, *Connecticut Highway Design Manual*, January 1999.

4. *Ibid.*

5. U.S.C. Title 49, Chapter 53.

6. *Ibid.*

7. *Flexibility in Highway Design.* Washington, DC: U.S. Department of Transportation, Federal Highway Administration, undated.

8. For additional examples, see Mark Bobrowski, "Scenic Landscape Protection Under the Police Power." 22 *Boston College Environmental Affairs Law Review* 697 at 713. Because there are a large number of detailed and excellent references on protection of sensitive natural areas and wildlife habitat, this publication does not address them, except in the context of view protection. These references include: Robert B. Olshansky, *Planning for Hillside Development*, Planning Advisory Service Report No. 466 (Chicago: American Planning Association, 1996); and Chris Duerksen et al., *Habitat Protection Planning: Where the Wild Things Are*, Planning Advisory Service Report No. 470/471 (Chicago: American Planning Association, 1997).

9. Randall Arendt, *Rural by Design: Maintaining Small Town Character* (Chicago: APA Planners Press, 1994), p. 192.

6

Western Rural and Small-Town Development Patterns

*And the Lord God took the man
and put him into the garden of Eden to dress it and keep it.
Look, Adam, he says, Look closely.
This is no jungle, this is a park.
It is not random, but shaped.
I have laid it out for you this year, but you are its Lord from now on.
The leaves will fall after the summer, and the bulbs will have to be split.
You may want to plant a hedge over there,
and you might think about a gazebo down by the river—
But do what you like; it's yours.
Only look at its real shape, love it for itself,
and lift it into the exchanges you and I shall have.
You will make a garden the envy of the angels.*[1]

—ROBERT FARRAR CAPON, *AN OFFERING OF UNCLES*

This study concludes with a complete compilation of the recommended western rural development patterns distilled from both the historical and contemporary case studies and research in earlier chapters. The patterns are organized in accordance with the categories set forth at the outset:

- regional development patterns
- town
- dispersed rural settlement
- architecture/design
- culture/community
- site design
- other elements

Some patterns do not fit neatly into any one category. All of the patterns will not be applicable to any given project, although it is hard to conceive of a successful development project in the West that would proceed without reflecting at least some of these patterns. The challenge is to carefully select the appropriate patterns in accordance with the local and regional cultural, physical, and environmental contexts.

We hope that using these patterns encourages local officials and developers to learn a new way of seeing that may transcend preconceived notions of what new development should look like and fit with the landscape. The patterns and lessons need to be applied in a methodical way throughout the entire land use planning and development process, and not just in reviewing new subdivisions or commercial projects. They can help in crafting comprehensive plans and in creating an authentic vision for a community's future. The patterns can assist in laying a solid foundation for zoning and subdivision regulations.

Perhaps the watchwords of this approach should be "Look Around." We believe there is much to learn from identifying and studying desirable existing and historical patterns in your local community:

- Where did the original homesteaders or Native Americans build?
- What architectural features are distinctive?
- What building materials were used?
- How wide are the streets in the center of town?
- What role did public spaces such as parks and squares play in focusing community life?
- What are the building setbacks and heights?
- How do these elements work together to form the character of your community?
- How does your town relate to the railway, the river, and the mountains?

The notes and sketchbooks developed by staff, planning commissioners, and elected officials can be translated into lists and pictures of development patterns that are appropriate for your area. We are not advocating a slavish devotion to the past, but a thoughtful, respectful reliance on the key principles and patterns that have served the West well.

To assist local planners and officials in this task, we have prepared a checklist that poses questions planning commissions, elected officials, and developers may find useful in assessing projects, working on a comprehensive community vision, or drafting development regulations. The checklist is followed by a compilation of all the *True West* rural development pattern language discussed in earlier chapters.

True West Plan and Development Proposal Assessment Checklist

Regional Development Patterns

- What are the obvious historical development patterns—compact towns? Open land between towns? Crossroad villages?
- Are there traditional land use patterns or uses that are key to maintaining the landscape? Irrigation/ditches? Ranching? Public land access?
- Are there significant views or features such as rock outcrops or ridgelines that help define the region?
- Are there sensitive natural areas or high hazard areas (e.g., wildfire prone) where development should be discouraged?

Town

- *Public places:* Are there gathering places such as public squares that can be emulated? Are civic buildings clustered in such places? Are public places within walking distance of citizens?
- *Streets/access:* How wide were streets historically? Were they oriented to maximize sunlight? Toward important vistas, such as mountains? What is the traditional street pattern? Grid? Modified grid? Connections?
- *Public realm:* What is the relationship between buildings and the street? How far are they set back? Do houses have large front yards? Do buildings face the street?

Are public spaces inviting to citizens? Do they have seating? Sun in winter? Shade in summer? Shelter from the wind?

- *Community:* Does the town have a variety of housing types (single family, multifamily, apartments)? Can people who work in town live there? Are there residential neighborhoods or subdivisions in and around town? What gives these neighborhoods a "sense of place"?

- *Environmental:* What is the town's optimal size based on character? Resource availability (e.g., water)? Physical constraints? Are there other towns in the region that are worthy models? Where does the town get its water? Is demand increasing? Is water reused? What kind of plants are native? Have trees been planted along streets? In parks?

Dispersed Rural Settlement

- *Environmental:* What is the native plant palette? Can native plants be salvaged and replanted? What kind of wildlife is in the area? Where is critical habitat located? Do road standards produce country roads that respect the landscape and minimize environmental impacts? Are wildfires a threat? Is development discouraged in those areas?

- *Cultural:* See Regional Development Patterns questions.

- *Visual:* Are there prominent ridgelines that help define the area's character? What was the development pattern of older ranches and homesteads? Where are rural buildings

typically located? In valleys? Toes of slopes? Edges of meadows?

Architecture/Design

- *Form:* Is there a traditional or indigenous architectural style? What defines that style (height, roof pitch, color, detailing, etc.)? What was the historic size of lots? Houses or buildings on those lots?

- *Color and materials:* Are there traditional building materials used in the region? Does your color palette reflect the natural landscape? Historical colors?

Culture/Community

- Are there historic buildings or groups of buildings worthy of protection? Can they be integrated into development?

- See Regional Development Patterns questions.

Site Design

- How are buildings oriented to take advantage of the sun? Shade?

- What is the relationship between main structures and accessory buildings on a site?

- Is there native vegetation on the site?

Other Elements

- What materials were used historically for fencing?

- Are residential lots in older neighborhoods fenced to provide privacy or security? Are front yards open or fenced?

- Are there crime/ security issues to justify bright night lighting?

True West Development Patterns— Comprehensive Summary

We have set forth below in detail a comprehensive list of the western rural development patterns that can guide development of your community in a *True West* fashion and help maintain its uniquely western character.

Regional Development Patterns

1. *In the face of development pressure, preserve existing country towns and villages and their development patterns.*

   Historical regional development patterns provide essential visual and cultural ties to a region's history. Their preservation reminds us of historic patterns that carry valuable lessons for contemporary development. Oregon's statewide planning guidelines concentrate development in existing communities, creating a distinct edge between town and country.

2. *Encourage the growth of new, self-contained towns in a dispersed manner across the countryside allowing ample open space between them. Concentrate development in a compact manner within the towns.*

   Historical Native American and Mormon settlements typify this pattern, maximizing the extent of regional countryside, preserving open lands and natural areas, and promoting the tight-knit geography of a cohesive culture. In Santa Fe County, New Mexico, the Growth Management Plan encourages the majority of new growth to occur in this fashion.

3. *Protect sacred sites to preserve people's spiritual roots and their connection to the past.*

   The centrality and pervasiveness of sacred sites within Native American settlements reflect their holistic approach to life and community building. Contemporary plan-ning should accord similar respect and attention to the important role of sacred sites. A recent example in Colorado is the Historic and Cultural Overlay Zone of the Highlands Ranch Open Space Conservation Area Plan, which respects the adjacent Tall Bull Memorial Grounds, a sacred site used by over 40 Native American tribal groups.

4. *Sustain traditional community practices that support agriculture, cultural practices, and the consequent physical landscape.*

   Land development patterns reflect and sustain regional culture. The historical northern New Mexico acequia irrigation practice is a physical and political method of distributing water. The acequia tradition remains a central community structure in Rio Arriba County and is viewed as a necessary support to the sustainability of local traditional communities. The system, protected through local ordinances, preserves critical agricultural lands and landscapes.

5. *Identify and preserve unique views.*

   Counties and towns are often defined by spectacular views or scenic areas. They are key elements of community character and identity. Many western jurisdictions (such as Park City, Utah) are protecting these vistas with a variety of tools such as ridgeline setbacks or controls on building materials and roof colors.

6. *Avoid development in wildfire-prone areas. Site homes and arrange landscaping in a manner so as to maximize wildfire defensible space.*

   Homes in mountainous areas and on steep slopes are particularly at risk from wildfire. Development in these areas should be limited by lowering allowable densities and requiring good access for emergency services. Boulder and Jefferson Counties in Colorado enforce wildfire safety with defensible space zones around homes. The defensible space minimizes fuel loading and does not necessarily preclude all landscaping.

Town

Public Places

7. *Provide and incorporate common areas within clusters of homes.*

    Family dwellings in Native American pueblos and cliff dwellings are centered on common areas fostering communal life. Common areas in Rancho Viejo in Santa Fe County, New Mexico, provide similar opportunity.

8. *Concentrate community facilities around public "squares" at the intersection of community pathways or streets.*

    Spanish colonial towns were designed with central public squares in accordance with the town ordinances of the "Laws of the Indies." The Spanish colonial City of Santa Fe, New Mexico, continues to enjoy this amenity and community focal point in the present day. Many other western communities, such as Aspen and Gunnison, Colorado, have centrally located squares and parks that serve as a focal point for community activities.

9. *Construct promenades within the heart of the community with main points of attraction at the ends and at other key midpoint locations.*

    Clearly defined pedestrian linkages between community attractions add vitality to the heart of a community. The porticos around the plaza of Santa Fe, New Mexico, provide protected pedestrian connections between important civic and commercial functions, notably the Governor's Palace, the church, and merchant shops. In

the late 19th century, western railway towns such as Cheyenne, Wyoming, provided a central commercial and entertainment "promenade" lined by numerous business and noteworthy clubs.

10. *Create public places appropriately sized for the community and within walking distance of all citizens.*

    The Spanish "Laws of the Indies" dictated that the town commons and plaza be sufficient in size for the anticipated population. The central location of these amenities facilitated pedestrian access for all citizens. The contemporary New Urbanist movement recognizes the importance of this core pattern.

11. *Reserve sufficient space within the core of each neighborhood or town for at least several public community facilities; at least one should serve as a visibly prominent civic focal point.*

    Prescott, Arizona, is one of the West's best examples of a town square and park with county offices that serve as a visual and civic focal point.

Streets/Access

12. *Orient streets in such a manner as to take advantage of the solar heat and light provided by the sun during winter months. Align streets in a northwest/southeast and northeast/southwest fashion to achieve the maximum effect.*

    The original plats of many towns along the Union Pacific Railway are laid out in a fashion to maximize the heat and light of the sun during the winter months. Cheyenne, Wyoming, provides an excellent example; unfortunately, subsequent plats ignored this pattern and resorted to straight north/south and east/west alignments.

13. *In places where the winters are long and cold, provide wide street rights-of-way for maximum*

sunlight penetration. In hotter climates, provide narrow street rights-of-way to maximize shade in public areas.

Early American towns in the northerly portions of the Rocky Mountain West were platted with wide streets ranging from 60-130 feet of right-of-way. Narrow streets providing shade to the public space characterize Spanish colonial towns, particularly in the warmer climate of New Mexico.

14. *Create wide streets or public rights-of-way to preserve distant views and to create a sense of spaciousness.*

Irrespective of climactic considerations, westerners value wide, open spaces and distant views, and often desire to preserve this sense of spaciousness within their towns. Wide streets characterized the initial platting in many railroad towns and in Mormon-influenced Utah.

15. *Establish a connected fabric of streets that respect topographical constraints without resorting to dead-ends.*

The design of many early American settlements, particularly those in the mountains, failed to respect topographical constraints in establishing their strict grid street layouts. The cul-de-sacs of many contemporary subdivisions may occasionally reflect topographical constraints; however, they more frequently serve only to isolate neighborhoods and fragment the community with the numerous dead-ends inherent in this pattern. The new Eagle Ranch development (adjacent to the Town of Eagle, Colorado) employs a grid system that integrates well into that town's existing streets. The central core of the Rancho Viejo villages in Santa Fe County reflects a modified grid pattern and connects with surrounding neighborhoods.

16. *Construct streets in such a manner so as to take advantage of distant views.*

Mountain views were historically taken into consideration in establishing the orientation and right-of-way widths of Denver's east/west streets. Denver's contemporary Gateway Area Plan requires a 40-foot building and parking setback from the right-of-way of east/west corridors aligned with designated public streets. These view corridors take advantage of views of the Rocky Mountains to the west. The primary street of entry for Belle Creek (a mixed-use development in Commerce City, Colorado) is angled to take advantage of views of Longs Peak, a "fourteener" (Colorado-speak for peaks over 14,000 feet in elevation) in Rocky Mountain National Park.

17. *Establish public transportation systems within and between towns.*

Sole dependence on the automobile is neither environmentally sustainable nor socially equitable. Publicly supported alternative transportation, such as bus or rail service, knits communities and regions together. Bus service in Santa Fe County, New Mexico, and in many mountain areas like the Roaring Fork Valley in western Colorado helps prevent traffic gridlock, provides affordable access to jobs and services, fights pollution, and reduces the need to obliterate more of the western landscape for roads and parking lots.

18. *Establish a comprehensive street tree program to create shade canopies over sidewalks and public streets.*

Walla Walla, Washington, and Claremont, California, both engage a vigorous tree planting and care program, resulting in a healthy urban forest that serves to moderate the climate through shade and evapotranspiration.

Public Realm

19. *Create an intimate relationship between buildings and the street by placing buildings close to the public right-of-way. In the central portion of towns, require that the majority of buildings be constructed immediately adjacent to the public right-of-way. When multiple buildings are constructed in this manner, a sense of enclosed and inviting space is created.*

    Almost without exception, historical Spanish colonial and American settlements reflect this pattern. This relationship provides a strong connection between private and public space.

    Enclosed communal urban space is effectively created in Claremont, California, and in the historic American settlement towns of Salida and Greeley, Colorado. These spaces create a community "living room" with immediate access to central civic, recreation, entertainment, commerce, and religious functions.

20. *Consider the orientation of buildings relative to public space to take advantage of the noontime sun.*

    This matter is particularly critical during winter months when the sun is low in the sky. Denver's downtown design review standards are geared to maximize sunlight penetration on the 16th Street Mall, a popular lunchtime gathering place. Within 50 feet of the 16th Street Mall, no building or portion of a building shall exceed 200 feet in height. Along the southwest side of the 16th Street Mall, the build-to zone is increased to 20 feet from the 10-foot norm for downtown.

21. *Ensure appropriately scaled, quasi-public space between public streets and residential structures.*

    Mature residential neighborhoods in places such as Greeley, Colorado, and Claremont, California, enjoy a comfortable balance and transition between public and private space. Standards for new, often more dense development must be cognizant of maintaining this balance by not reducing front yard setbacks too much and avoiding the use of unnecessarily wide street pavement.

22. *Encourage outdoor seating on sidewalks, courtyards, and within the quasi-public realm between street and private structures.*

    The Incidental Outdoor Use standards of Claremont, California, encourage outdoor seating. Eating or just lounging by a table outdoors in the community's "living room" is one of the most pleasurable public experiences. Provide shade in the summer and sun exposure in the winter.

Community

23. *Provide diverse housing opportunities including primary housing.*

    Sometimes referred to as "inclusionary housing," this concept is promoted as a conscious strategy in Santa Fe County and is evident in the Rancho Viejo development, consistent with the traditional New Mexico village model that features a variety of housing types geared for a range of incomes.

    The increasing scarcity of accessible and serviced land is dramatically driving the cost of housing upward in the West, particularly in tourist- and second-home-oriented economies. Appropriate design and programs that enhance housing affordability are critical for the future of functioning communities. Land development codes in Teton County, Wyoming, function effectively in the Melody Ranch Planned Unit Development to provide much-needed primary housing stock.

24. *Where possible, establish neighborhoods built on a foundation of common social or cultural interests.*

Common interests and values are reinforced by the geographic proximity of a neighborhood. Native American pueblos and Mormon settlements reflect their respective cultures in their design character. Contemporary implementation of this pattern suggests support for the development of neighborhoods based on a variety of cultural and social groups accommodated in a variety of housing types. Their diversity will contribute to unique neighborhood identities with a genuine "sense of place."

25. *Build neighborhoods, not just subdivisions.*

New developments are increasingly constructed on a subdivision-by-subdivision basis, often with no road or pedestrian connections with nearby developments or sharing of common open space. Many communities, such as Fort Collins and Brighton, Colorado, are requiring connections between new developments, and are limiting gated communities and tall fencing that contribute to a feeling of isolation.

Environmental

26. *Maintain agricultural land in close proximity to town dwellers.*

Compelling ecological, emotional, and physical health benefits are provided with the presence of agricultural land in close proximity to human settlement. Lambert Ranch RSP in Douglas County, Colorado;

Melody Ranch in Jackson, Wyoming; and Ludwick Farm in Larimer County, Colorado all provide for long-term agricultural land use. The Agricultural Protection and Enhancement ordinance in Rio Arriba County, New Mexico, provides for new settlements while maintaining valuable irrigated farmland in close proximity.

27. *Limit the population size and geographical extent of towns in a sustainable manner suggested by the natural and cultural geography of the region.*

The ecological concept of carrying capacity is reflected in this pattern. Mormon leader Joseph Smith's model town suggested an upper population limit of 15,000-20,000 for agrarian-based Mormon communities, reflecting both geographical and cultural (agrarian) constraints. Many contemporary communities, in seeking to retain an identity within a growing metropolis, desire to limit growth and create natural buffers surrounding their community. Eagle, Colorado, for example, based its comprehensive plan on a projected population buildout of about 5,000 people—a community size that compared favorably to other larger towns Eagle desired to emulate at full buildout.

28. *Collect and conserve water through simple and ingenious methods, and incorporate them into the design of buildings and communities.*

Reliable supplies of renewable water are increasingly scarce in the arid West. The Civano community in Arizona anticipates a 65% reduction in overall potable water consumption through water conservation. Water is collected from roof rainspouts and recycled landscape-watering effluent. This water is used to irrigate common areas.

29. *Plant native, drought-resistant trees to provide shade and to minimize water usage.*

Drought-tolerant trees are almost exclusively used for both public and private realms in the Civano community in Arizona and Rancho Viejo in New Mexico.

Dispersed Rural Settlement

Environmental

30. *Locate buildings at the toes of slopes and edges of meadows in a manner that allows for natural windbreaks and creates a feeling of shelter.*

    Lambert Ranch RSP in Douglas County, Colorado, places homes at the edge of a meadow and along the sides of hills in a manner that evokes a strong sense of shelter. The homes in Casas Arroyo de Sonoita in Santa Cruz County, Arizona, nestle within the folds of the rolling hills in an unpretentious manner.

31. *Protect wildlife habitat and enhance wildlife movement corridors in a manner that allows for continued free movement of the broadest possible variety of species.*

    As development increasingly encroaches on critical wildlife habitat and movement corridors, wildlife are either disappearing altogether from areas they once frequented or their numbers are seriously diminished. For many animal species, the American West is one of the last places with sufficient unfragmented habitat. Jacob's Island Park Ranch in Fremont County, Idaho, accommodates wildlife movement corridors and preserves significant habitat. Melody Ranch in Teton County, Wyoming, in accordance with county zoning standards, accommodates elk migratory movement and preserves a sufficiently significant portion of habitat to protect the regional integrity of the habitat.

    Douglas County and the Colorado Division of Wildlife have identified a broad area as a critical wildlife habitat movement corridor between the Front Range foothills and the plains to the east. The Lambert Ranch RSP preserves sufficiently wide swaths of open space in the most critical areas for wildlife movement. Most significantly, sufficient space is provided to protect the habitat of the federally listed threatened Preble's meadow jumping mouse, which lives primarily along creeks and rivers. The vast majority of Gambel oak, which provides the most critical cover for animals in this area, is preserved.

32. *Where fugitive dust is an air-quality health concern, pave rural roads.*

    Douglas County, Colorado, encourages the paving of rural roads. A paved road is not necessarily the rural visual characteristic evoked; however, in many western jurisdictions, the arid climate exacerbates the problems associated with fugitive dust. As traffic increases, paved roads are the most cost-effective and environmentally sound solution to minimizing this source of air pollution.

33. *Construct the narrowest rural roads possible, without undue negative impacts on public safety, in order to minimize impacts on vegetation, natural drainage patterns, and the natural terrain. In placing roadways, do so in a manner that minimizes the need for "cut and fill."*

    The relatively low density of the Jacob's Island Park Ranch development in Fremont County, Idaho, allows for narrow gravel roads that are characteristic of the existing ranch and the rural character of the area. The narrow gravel roads serve to minimize the amount of impervious surface. In Larimer County, Colorado, private rural road standards allow for roadways as narrow as 12 feet in particular circumstances.

It is often not enough, however, to focus on roadways. Long, rural driveways can have a significant impact on land disturbance. Utah's Salt Lake County Foothills and Canyons Overlay Zone restricts driveway "cut and fill" activity by designing driveways to follow natural contour lines and to avoid crossing slopes over 30%; except under strict guidelines when no alternatives are available, a short run across slopes of up to 50% is encouraged.

34. *Restrict development on steep slopes and in geologically hazardous areas.*

    Many jurisdictions still fail to prohibit development on steep slopes (e.g., greater than 25%) and within geologically hazardous areas. Engineered mitigation may be possible but is not necessarily appropriate. Salt Lake County's Foothills and Canyons Overlay Zone standards (Utah) and the sensitive lands protection standards in Gunnison County (Colorado) clearly restrict development from occurring within such areas in order to reduce the risk of erosion and avoid unsightly scars on the landscape.

35. *Salvage and replant native plants that lie in the path of development.*

    In many cases, it is not possible to avoid development in areas of significant native plant growth. A carefully crafted and implemented Saguaro cactus salvage operation was conducted as part of the development of DC Ranch in Scottsdale, Arizona. Other communities such as Fort Collins, Colorado, and Oro Valley, Arizona, require protection of native vegetation.

36. *Protect significant geological features such as rock outcroppings and desert washes.*

    In many areas of the Rocky Mountains and foothills, the integrity and beauty of the rock formations have been harmed by inappropriate development and outright destruction of significant geological features. The Helker Rural Cluster Process in Jefferson County, Colorado, protects from development significant rock outcroppings on land otherwise at risk from unregulated development on 35-acre tracts.

37. *Cluster development in a manner so as to maximize environmentally significant, unfragmented open space.*

    Satisfying a regulatory minimum percentage of open space preservation is not necessarily sufficient. Wyoming's Melody Ranch Planned Unit Development preserves an operating ranch as well as significant elk winter habitat within broad, uninterrupted areas. Conservation Subdivision Standards such as those in Routt County, Colorado, can effectively protect large tracts of land while allowing some development to proceed.

Cultural

38. *Preserve and integrate historic ranching operations.*

    Working ranches in the West are being sold for development at an alarming rate. The preservation and integration of historic ranching operations is critical in maintaining cherished western landscapes and associated social and cultural values.

    Although Lambert Ranch in Douglas County, Colorado, has ceased to function as an operating ranch, the central meadow, ranch homestead, and several outbuildings are preserved as the focal point of new development. Sensitive placement of homes has retained the historical visual character.

Integration of historic Jacob's Island Park Ranch operations provides a critical link with the past while preserving a cultural way of life unique to the American West. It further serves to maintain a distinct feature of the landscape. An added element that enhances the economic viability of the ranching operation are the tourist attractions programmed over the weekends.

Working ranches may also continue to operate under the financial benefits created with conservation easements. In exchange for a 20-acre homestead and recreational access, the 1,000-acre Rocking Z Ranch in Montana is restricted from any further development for perpetuity.

39. *Preserve irrigated agricultural lands.*

Irrigated agricultural land is a signature feature of many rural landscapes, even in the relatively arid West. From a visual and cultural perspective, Fremont County, Idaho, and Rio Arriba County, New Mexico, appropriately encourage preservation of irrigated lands through performance-oriented and overlay district zoning regulations.

40. *Ensure that new development respects and complements existing agricultural land use through the use of appropriate fencing, setbacks, and overall placement of structures.*

The management plan, fence controls, setbacks, and home clustering Ludwick Farm RLUP in Larimer County, Colorado, are intended to minimize future conflicts between rural residents and neighboring agricultural operations.

Visual

41. *Less is more: minimize exotic landscaping, the size of building footprints, and the amount of impervious surface devoted to roadways. Allow the natural landscape to dominate.*

The West's arid and sparsely vegetated landscape is particularly vulnerable to the visual impacts of the built environment. Minimizing the scale of infrastructure, buildings, and new landscaping best preserves the natural beauty that lures so many to live in the West. Jacob's Island Park Ranch in Fremont County, Idaho, provides a good example of this creed.

42. *Where vegetation of the contextual natural landscape is sparse, severely limit additional landscape plantings, except for native plants in limited, carefully selected areas.*

In some cases, no additional landscaping may be best. The unpretentious residential subdivision of Casas Arroyo de Sonoita in Santa Cruz County, Arizona, exemplifies this approach. Detailed landscape requirements of The Promontory in Summit County, Utah, establish concentric landscape transition zones surrounding home sites.

43. *Where natural vegetation or topography do not allow for "hiding" development, locate structures such that they are subordinate to the horizon and any significant viewsheds.*

In Ludwick Farm RLUP in Larimer County, Colorado, homes are clustered at the extreme far edge of the meadow, and they are not hidden by any existing or new plantings. This is consistent with the historical placement of ranch buildings; however, it bears singling out today as a new, additional pattern because its scale is likely to be broader, and existing ranches and farmsteads are associated with substantial mature vegetation introduced by the original settlers. Introducing substantial new vegetation is not necessarily appropriate.

44. *Cluster development in a manner so as to maximize visually significant, unfragmented open space.*

In Teton County, Wyoming, Land Development Regulations protect signature scenic vistas along major roadways. The Melody Ranch development implements this requirement by clustering homes adjacent to existing development and preserving a significant unfragmented foreground view along State Highway 191/89. In Larimer County, Colorado, Ludwick Farms RLUP homes are clustered at the extreme far edge of the meadow. They are not hidden by any existing or new plantings. This is consistent with the historical placement of ranch buildings.

45. *Nestle structures below ridgelines and within the folds of hills.*

In keeping with the theme of allowing the natural landscape to dominate, new rural development reviewed under Colorado's Routt and Douglas Counties rural site planning processes are subordinate to the profiles of ridges and hills.

46. *Avoid or mitigate ridgetop "skylining" that alters the natural land profiles with built structures.*

The ridgeline protection ordinance in Castle Rock, Colorado, clearly defines skylines, and articulates how development may or may not occur and under what circumstances. In this manner, signature ridge and hilltop profiles surrounding and within the town are preserved and maintain dominance.

47. *Minimize visual clutter within scenic corridors.*

The Rural Scenic Corridor Protection ordinance in Santa Fe County, New Mexico, provides clarity and flexibility in establishing critical and desired standards for development along major corridors. Strict outdoor lighting standards and maximum building heights reduce visual clutter for all times of the day. Park City, Utah, has defined key visual corridors in that town and restricted development that might block important views.

48. *Design buildings on hillsides to follow the natural terrain in a manner that minimizes earth disturbance.*

Well-designed plans may still go substantially awry without appropriate execution at the building construction stage. Salt Lake County's Foothills and Canyons Overlay Zone requires that buildings be designed to limit site grading.

49. *Preserve and protect significant foreground views along significant "viewing platforms or passageways" such as public gathering places and major roadways.*

In the West, a region's identity is often characterized by the landscape. Preserving the natural and historical cultural landscape is important in retaining an area's unique identity. The Priest Creek Ranch project in Routt County, Colorado, preserves a significant visual gateway into Steamboat Springs.

50. *In sparsely vegetated contexts, avoid any kind of fencing altogether, thereby allowing the landscape to flow uninterrupted.*

Fencing of any kind is clearly a cultural addition to the landscape. Even the most sensitive, minimalist design can detract from the natural landscape, particularly in a sparsely vegetated context. The minimalist approach to the design of Casas Arroyo de Sonoita in Santa Cruz County, Arizona, restricts all fencing, except for very limited privacy fencing immediately adjacent to homes.

Architecture/Design

Form

51. *Design buildings that mimic the profiles of the natural landscape: in steep, mountainous areas, steeply pitched rooflines are appropriate; in areas that are flat or rolling, a lower profile is fitting.*

The architectural roof profiles of historic barns in Montana's Gallatin County and of new housing construction in Wyoming's Teton County reflect the somewhat irregular and varied slopes of the mountain backdrops.

52. *Limit the majority of buildings to four stories high or less. Taller buildings in small towns and rural areas should be exceptional and reserved for cultural or civic purposes.*

Technology limited Native American pueblo and cliff settlements to a maximum height of four stories. The result was a human scale that is attractive even today. With the exception of important civic structures, buildings in small towns should not draw attention to themselves at the expense of the natural landscape or small-town scale.

53. *Avoid building large, monolithic structures. Buildings should comprise a complex of smaller buildings or parts that manifest their own internal social realities.*

As commercial and residential structures become larger, it becomes increasingly important to provide visual clues as to the functions of the parts in a manner consistent with historical patterns.

54. *Limit the size of residential buildings relative to lot size.*

The balance of lot-to-building size is threatened in many communities, particularly when older small- to moderate-sized homes are demolished to make way for large "stucco boxes" that fill the lot and loom over their neighbors. In Claremont, California, the size of homes is restricted relative to lot size in established neighborhoods.

55. *Arrange roofs so that each distinct roof corresponds to an identifiable social entity in the building. Place the largest roofs—those that are highest and have the largest span—over the largest, most important, and most communal spaces; build the lesser roofs off these largest and highest roofs. Allow for and expect additions to be made over time.*

Ranches and farmhouses across the West maintain a strong organic and human character in their lean-to and telescoping additions constructed over the years. Design guidelines for The Promontory in Summit County, Utah, reflect this pattern.

56. *Build arcades at the edge of buildings to provide shelter from sun and rain, and to ease the transition between public and private spaces.*

The Spanish town ordinances of the "Laws of the Indies" required portals (arcades) around the main plaza to protect merchants and shoppers from the elements. Contemporary Santa Fe, New Mexico, maintains these portals around its plaza today.

57. *Vary roof pitches, with shallower outer pitches.*

Traditional farm and ranch buildings exhibit this pattern, reflecting building additions constructed over time. This organic form of architecture is beautiful in its simplicity and is in harmony with most of the western landscape. The architectural guidelines of The Promontory of Summit County, Utah, require that the higher roof masses should generally occur toward the center, with lower profiles toward the outer edges of the homes.

58. *Expect that a building or complex of buildings is never complete, leaving room for organic future growth.*

    It is easy to review new structures and site plans as a fait accompli, yet growth and change are natural and should be expected. A structure's design and site plan should anticipate future additions and modifications.

59. *Require pedestrian-oriented signs in commercial/ civic districts.*

    Creative, pedestrian-scaled signs foster an intimate and comfortable environment for pedestrians. Claremont, California, provides clear standards for both pedestrian- and automobile-oriented signs in its downtown.

60. *In pedestrian-oriented areas, encourage narrow storefronts with large display windows.*

    A variety of storefront display windows provides an interesting pedestrian experience. Claremont, California, requires existing display windows to remain in use for retail or restaurant uses.

Color and Materials

61. *Use natural materials in a manner that reflects an organic integrity and harmony with the natural surroundings. Use stone and wood as the primary construction material.*

    Architectural guidelines for Wyoming's Melody Ranch and Utah's Promontory developments exemplify this approach in their requirements for almost exclusive reliance on natural materials.

62. *Use relatively thick, well-insulated exterior walls.*

    Thick exterior walls provide needed protection from the harsh elements of the western climate as well as a strong emo-tional sense of shelter. Adobe used in New Mexico, and more recent introductions of straw-bale construction such as at the Civano community of Arizona, are two examples using traditional and contemporary technology.

63. *Use biodegradable, low energy-consuming materials, which are easy to cut and modify on site. For bulk materials, use earth-based materials such as earth, brick, and tile.*

    The Native Americans and early American settlers had no choice but to use readily available, low energy-consuming materials. Today's plethora of manufactured composite materials overwhelm the simpler and often more appropriate choices available.

64. *Avoid the use of a multiplicity of building materials, colors, and architectural styles. Doing so also serves to produce a commonality of architectural style.*

    The beauty of Native American pueblos and Spanish colonial towns such as Santa Fe, New Mexico, is substantially because of the use of only one or two earth-based building materials. The Town Planning ordinances of the "Laws of the Indies" suggest that significant effort should be made to use a single type of building for the sake of beauty. While it is important to avoid monotony and allow creativity, identifying preferred materials, colors, and styles can help create an attractive streetscape.

65. *Establish a color palette that reflects the surrounding landscape; however, do not do so exclusively. With an appropriate building profile, bright historical colors such as red, green, or ochre may serve as a beautiful counterpoint to the natural landscape. Expand the typical range of exterior wall and roof colors to reflect*

1. LAWS OF THE INDIES

Selected Town Planning Ordinances

New Settlements

39

The site and position of the towns should be selected in places where water is nearby and where it would be possible to demolish neighboring towns and properties in order to take advantage of the materials that are essential for building; and, [these sites and positions should be suitable] also for farming, cultivation, and pasturation, so as to avoid excessive work and cost, since any of the above would be costly if they were far.

40

Do not select sites that are too high up because these are affected by winds, and access and service to these are difficult, nor in lowlands, which tend to be unhealthy; choose places of medium elevation that enjoy good winds, especially from the north and south ... and in case that there should be a need to build on the banks of a river, it should be on the eastern bank, so when the sun rises it strikes the town first, then the water.

42

Having selected the site for capital towns in each county, determine the areas that could be subjected and incorporated within the jurisdiction of the head town [English approximation: county seat] as farms, granges, and gardens without detriment to Indians or natives.

43

Having selected the area and having established existing opportunities for development, the governor should decide whether the site that is to be populated should be a city [cabecera], town [municipal], or village [pueblo].

89

The persons who were placed in charge of populating a town with Spaniards should see to it that it should have at least thirty neighbors, each one with his own house, ten cows, four oxen or two oxen and two young bulls and a mare, five pigs, six chickens, twenty sheep from Castille; ... and it should have a clergyman who can administer sacraments and provide the ornaments to the church ...

110

... a plan for the site is to be made, dividing it into squares, streets, and building lots, using cord and ruler, beginning with the main square from which streets are to run to the gates and principal roads and leaving sufficient open space so that even if the town grows, it can always spread in the same manner ...

111

... the town is to be ... in an elevated and healthy location; ... [have] fresh water ... ease of transport, access and exist; [and be] [open to the north wind; ... and if possible not near lagoons or marshes in which poisonous animals and polluted air and water breed.

112

the main plaza is to be the starting point for the town ... inland [locations] should be at the center of the town. The plaza should be square or rectangular, in which case it should have at least one and a half its width for length inasmuch as this shape is best for fiestas in which horses are used ...

113

The size of the plaza shall be proportioned to the number of inhabitants, taking into consideration the fact that in Indian towns, inasmuch as they are new, the intention is that they will increase, and thus the plaza should be decided upon taking into consideration the growth the town may experience. [The plaza] shall be not less than two hundred feet wide and three hundred feet long, nor larger than eight hundred feet long and five hundred and thirty-two feet wide. A good proportion is six hundred feet long and four hundred wide.

114

From the plaza shall begin four principal streets; One [shall be] from the middle of each side, and two streets from each corner of the plaza; the four corners of the plaza shall face the four principal winds, because in this manner the streets running from the plaza will not be exposed to the four principal winds, which would cause much inconvenience.

115

. . . around the plaza shall be portals, for these are of considerable convenience to the merchants . . .

116

In cold places the streets shall be wide and in hot places narrow; but for the purposes of defense in areas where there are horses, it would be better if they are wide.

118

Here and there in the town, smaller plazas of good proportion shall be laid out . . . such that everything may be distributed in a good proportion for the instruction of religion.

121

Next, a site and lot shall be assigned for the royal council and cabildo house and for the custom house and arsenal, near the temple, located in such a manner that in times of need the one may aid the other; the hospital for the poor and those sick of non-contagious diseases shall be built near the temple and its cloister; and the hospital for the sick with contagious diseases shall be built in such a way that no harmful wind blowing through it may cause harm to the rest of the town. If the latter be built in an elevated place, so much the better.

123

It shall be of considerable convenience if those towns that are laid out away from seaports, inland, be built if possible on the shore of a navigable river,

and attempts should be made to lace the town on the side from which the cold north wind blows and that buildings that cause filth be placed on the side of the river or sea below the town.

124

. . . The hospital for the poor who are not affected by contagious diseases shall be built near the temple and near its cloister, and the [hospital] for contagious diseases shall be built in an area where the cold north wind blows, but arranged in such a way that it may enjoy the south wind.

129

Within the town, a commons shall be delimited, large enough that although the population may experience a rapid expansion, there will always be sufficient space where the people may go to for recreation and take their cattle to pasture without them making any damage.

133

They shall arrange the building lots and edifices placed thereon in such a manner that when living in them they may enjoy the winds of the south and north as these are the best . . .

134

They shall try as far as possible to have the buildings all of one type for the sake of the beauty of the town.

148

The Spaniards, to whom Indians are entrusted [encomendados], should seek with great care that these Indians be settled into towns, and that, within these, churches be built so that the Indians can be instructed into Christian doctrine and live in good order . . .

SOURCE

Dora P. Crouch and Axel I. Mundigo, "The City Planning Ordinance of the Laws of the Indies Revisted," *Town Planning Review* 48 (3): 247-259.

CHAPTER 1 PART 3 H HILLSIDE DISTRICT

130 INTENT

The Hillside District is intended to provide for limited uses of hillside areas which are consistent with the City's General Plan. The mix of permitted uses, their intensity, and their distribution are to be based largely on natural environmental factors and accessibility to necessary facilities and services. The hillside areas must be kept in a natural state to the greatest extent feasible in order to protect the public health, safety and general welfare from the harms identified in the Natural Environment Section of the General Plan. Slope density regulations which correlate intensity of development to the steepness of terrain will be used to minimize grading, removal of vegetation, land instability and fire hazards. Clustering of residential units will be encouraged. Transfer of development credits will also be used as a means of limiting residential development to areas designated on the General Plan.

131 PERMITTED USES

A. The following uses and development shall be permitted in the H District:

    1. In areas shown as hillside housing clusters on the General Plan Diagram or in areas within 500 feet of Webb Canyon Road as designated on the General Plan Diagram where building sites and accessibility can be provided that meet the requirements of this Part, the following uses are permitted:

        a. Residential structures for use and occupancy by not more than one (1) dwelling unit per lot.

        b. Buildings accessory to and subordinate to residential structures.

        c. Home occupations, subject to approval pursuant to Chapter 5, Part 1.

        d. The growing of crops and fruits when accessory to and subordinate to a residential use.

        e. The keeping of animals as pets (not for commercial purposes), subject to Title 6 of the Claremont Municipal Code.

    2. Low intensity uses such as watershed, pasture, trails and scientific study requiring no more than minor structures or minor terrain modification.

    3. Public parks and open spaces.

B. The following uses and developments may be permitted in the H District with a Conditional Use Permit:

    1. Residential Unit Developments per Chapter 1, Part 7.

    2. Residential Unit Developments per Chapter 1, Part 7 utilizing transfer of development credits per Section 133.

    3. The keeping of large animals for commercial purposes and the keeping of large animals for non-commercial purposes in excess of that number permitted by Title 6 of the Claremont Municipal Code.

    4. The growing of crops and fruits.

    5. Organized equestrian riding, training and boarding.

    6. Limited commercial recreation uses suitable to open space areas.

    7. Other uses listed in Chapter 6, Part 2, as permitted in any district with a Conditional Use Permit subject to these uses being consistent with the intent of the Hillside District and the City's General Plan.

C. No building, structure or land shall be used, and no building or structure shall be erected, altered or enlarged except in accordance with the provisions of this Section.

132 REQUIREMENTS

The following requirements shall apply to all land and structures in the Hillside District:

A. Residential Density

    1. Maximum residential density for a specific parcel shall not exceed the density limits set out in paragraph 2 below. The Planning Commission may, for reasons related only

to the applicant's parcel, require a density less than the maximum otherwise permitted upon a finding that the reduced maximum is necessary to implement specific policies in the General Plan.

In the case of Residential Unit Developments or residential developments utilizing transfer of development credits, the overall maximum density in a cluster area shall be 0.5 acres per dwelling unit.

2. All Hillside District classifications are combined with a Slope-Density standard denoted as SD-l, SD-2, or SD-3. These several Slope-Density standards establish different densities based on accessibility and location within the City. The Slope-Density standards are set forth on Tables 1, 2 and 3 of this section.

    Column One, Gross Area per Dwelling Unit, shall be used for Residential Unit Developments, and Column Two, Minimum Lot Area per Dwelling Unit, shall be used in all other cases. Gross Residential Area is the total area devoted exclusively to the use of the residents plus all trail easements, road rights-of-way and any open spaces meeting the requirements of Section 133.D—Transfer of Development Credits. Net residential area is the total area devoted exclusively to the use of the residents. Where lands are in excess of 50% slope, such lands shall be assigned a slope of 50% for purposes of determining the average slope of the parcel.

3. Average slope shall be calculated by the following formula:

    $$S = \frac{IL\ (0.00229)}{A}$$

    where

    S = average natural ground slope of the total project area in percent

    I = the contour interval in feet. (For parcels 20 acres or larger, the maximum contour interval shall be 40 ft. For parcels of less than 20 acres, contours shall

meet the standards of Section 901-A.3 of this code, unless the Director of Community Development finds a larger contour interval will provide reasonable accuracy for purposes of determining the average slope of the parcel under consideration.)

L = the total length of all contour lines within the total project, in feet.

A = the gross area of the project, in acres.

0.00229 = a constant used to convert square feet into acres x 100%

or $\dfrac{1\ acre}{43{,}560\ sq.ft.}$ x 100%

The calculated average natural slope shall be rounded to the nearest whole number.

B. Property Development Standards

The following standards govern unless modified as part of a Residential Unit Development or Architectural Commission Review:

	SD-1	SD-2	SD-3
Minimum lot size	See Tables 1, 2, 3		
Minimum lot width	150 ft.	200 ft.	250 ft.
Minimum lot depth	150 ft.	200 ft.	250 ft.
Minimum front yard setback	20 ft.	20 ft.	20 ft.
Minimum rear yard setback	10 ft.	10 ft.	10 ft.
Minimum street side yard setback	20 ft.	20 ft.	20 ft.
Minimum interior side yard setback	10 ft.	10 ft.	10 ft.
Maximum height	25 ft.	25 ft.	25 ft.
Required parking	2 spaces per dwelling unit*		
*Parking need not be covered but must be screened from any public right-of-way.			

For exceptions and explanatory descriptions, for standards of fences, walls, and signs, for off-site improvements and dedication requirements, see Chapter 4, General Use and Development Standards.

Table 1. Slope Density Standards (SD-1*)

Slope Category in Percent	Gross Area Per Dwelling Unit in Acres (1)	Min. Lot Area Per Dwelling Unit in Acres (2)	Slope Category in Percent	Gross Area Per Dwelling Unit in Acres (1)	Min. Lot Area Per Dwelling Unit in Acres (2)
			(Density Range of 1 acre per dwelling unit to 20 acres per dwelling unit)		
0	1.00	.92			
1	1.02	.94	25	1.90	1.75
2	1.04	.95	26	1.98	1.82
3	1.06	.97	27	2.05	1.89
4	1.08	.99	28	2.14	1.97
5	1.10	1.02	29	2.23	2.05
6	1.13	1.04	30	2.33	2.15
7	1.15	1.06	31	2.43	2.24
8	1.18	1.08	32	2.55	2.35
9	1.21	1.11	33	2.68	2.48
10	1.23	1.13	34	2.82	2.61
11	1.26	1.16	35	2.99	2.75
12	1.30	1.19	36	3.16	2.93
13	1.33	1.22	37	3.37	3.12
14	1.36	1.25	38	3.60	3.33
15	1.40	1.29	39	3.86	3.58
16	1.44	1.32	40	4.17	3.87
17	1.48	1.36	41	4.52	4.20
18	1.52	1.40	42	4.95	4.61
19	1.56	1.44	43	5.46	5.09
20	1.61	1.48	44	6.10	5.70
21	1.67	1.53	45	6.90	6.46
22	1.72	1.58	46	7.94	7.46
23	1.78	1.64	47	9.35	8.83
24	1.84	1.69	48	11.36	10.81
			49	14.49	13.94
			50 & Over	20.00	19.61

* The values in this table are derived from the equations:

(1) Gross Area Per Dwelling Unit in Acres $\dfrac{1}{1.0 - 0.019S}$

(2) Minimum Lot Area per Dwelling Unit in Acres $\dfrac{1}{1.089 - 0.02076S}$

where S is the average natural ground slope in percent.

Table 2. Slope Density Standards (SD-2*)

Slope Category in Percent	Gross Area Per Dwelling Unit in Acres	Min. Lot Area Per Dwelling Unit in Acres	Slope Category in Percent	Gross Area Per Dwelling Unit in Acres	Min. Lot Area Per Dwelling Unit in Acres
(Density Range of 2 acres per dwelling unit to 20 acres per dwelling unit)					
	(1)	(2)		(1)	(2)
0	2.00	1.85			
1	2.04	1.89	25	3.64	3.38
2	2.07	1.92	26	3.76	3.50
3	2.11	1.96	27	3.89	3.62
4	2.16	2.00	28	4.03	3.76
5	2.20	2.04	29	4.18	3.90
6	2.24	2.08	30	4.35	4.06
7	2.29	2.12	31	4.52	4.22
8	2.34	2.17	32	4.72	4.40
9	2.39	2.21	33	4.92	4.60
10	2.44	2.26	34	5.15	4.82
11	2.49	2.31	35	5.41	5.06
12	2.55	2.37	36	5.68	5.32
13	2.61	2.42	37	5.99	5.61
14	2.67	2.48	38	6.33	5.94
15	2.74	2.54	39	6.71	6.31
16	2.81	2.61	40	7.14	6.72
17	2.88	2.68	41	7.63	7.19
18	2.96	2.75	42	8.20	7.74
19	3.04	2.82	43	8.85	8.37
20	3.13	2.90	44	9.62	9.12
21	3.22	2.99	45	10.53	10.01
22	3.31	3.08	46	11.63	11.10
23	3.41	3.17	47	12.99	12.45
24	3.52	3.28	48	14.71	14.17
			49	16.95	16.45
			50 & Over	20.00	19.61

* The values in this table are derived from the equations:

(1) Gross Area Per Dwelling Unit in Acres

$$\frac{1}{0.5 - 0.009S}$$

(2) Minimum Lot Area per Dwelling Unit in Acres

$$\frac{1}{0.54 - 0.00978S}$$

where S is the average natural ground slope in percent.

Table 3. Slope Density Standards (SD-3*)

Slope Category in Percent	Gross Area Per Dwelling Unit in Acres	Min. Lot Area Per Dwelling Unit in Acres	Slope Category in Percent	Gross Area Per Dwelling Unit in Acres	Min. Lot Area Per Dwelling Unit in Acres
	(Density Range of 5acres per dwelling unit to 20 acres per dwelling unit)				
	(1)	(2)		(1)	(2)
0	5.00	4.59			
1	5.08	4.66	25	8.00	7.43
2	5.15	4.73	26	8.20	7.62
3	5.24	4.81	27	8.40	7.82
4	5.32	4.89	28	8.62	8.03
5	5.41	4.97	29	8.85	8.25
6	5.49	5.05	30	9.09	8.49
7	5.59	5.14	31	9.35	8.74
8	5.68	5.23	32	9.62	9.00
9	5.78	5.32	33	9.90	9.28
10	5.88	5.42	34	10.20	9.57
11	5.99	5.52	35	10.53	9.89
12	6.10	5.62	36	10.87	10.23
13	6.21	5.73	37	11.23	10.59
14	6.33	5.84	38	11.63	10.98
15	6.45	5.96	39	12.05	11.40
16	6.58	6.08	40	12.50	11.84
17	6.71	6.20	41	12.99	12.33
18	6.85	6.33	42	13.51	12.87
19	6.99	6.47	43	14.08	13.44
20	7.14	6.61	44	14.71	14.08
21	7.30	6.76	45	15.34	14.77
22	7.46	6.92	46	16.13	15.54
23	7.63	7.08	47	16.95	16.39
24	7.81	7.25	48	17.46	17.34
			49	18.87	18.40
			50 & Over	20.00	19.61

* The values in this table are derived from the equations:

(1) Gross Area Per Dwelling Unit in Acres

$$\frac{1}{0.2 - 0.003S}$$

(2) Minimum Lot Area per Dwelling Unit in Acres

$$\frac{1}{0.218 - 0.00334S}$$

where S is the average natural ground slope in percent.

C.   New Developments

Any division of land into five (5) or more lots or any proposal which would allow the construction of five (5) or more dwelling units shall be permitted only in conjunction with a Residential Unit Development application per Chapter 1, Part 7 of the Land Use and Development Code.

D.   General Design Criteria

All new developments shall be required to be reviewed and approved by the Architectural Commission per Chapter 6, Part 1 of the Land Use and Development Code. Residential Unit Developments shall be required to be reviewed and approved by the Planning Commission and Architectural Commission per Chapter 1, Part 7. In addition to the review criteria denoted in Chapter 1, Part 7 and Chapter 6, Part 1, the Architectural Commission and Planning Commission shall use the following criteria during their review process:

1.   Plans for hillside developments shall conform to the provisions of the General Plan and any Specific Plans adopted for the hillside area.

2.   There shall be flexibility in the siting of dwelling units so as to best fit the natural terrain, minimize spoilage of the land and maintain the level of quality of the surrounding area.

3.   Outstanding natural features such as the highest crest of the hill range, canyons, natural rock outcroppings, particularly desirable vegetation, and natural water courses, and areas particularly abundant in wildlife shall be preserved.

4.   The introduction and conservation of plant material shall be required to protect slopes from slippage or soil erosion and to minimize the visual effects of any grading or construction on hillside areas, including the preservation of prominent trees.

5.   Buildings shall be designed to accommodate sloping sites and minimize the amount of grading required. The use of innovative building techniques to best blend buildings into the terrain is encouraged.

6.   Streets shall follow the natural contour lines wherever possible to minimize the amount of grading required, and street improvements and lighting shall harmonize with the natural character of the hillsides.

7.   Any view corridors or scenic vistas from adjacent development shall be preserved to the maximum extent possible.

8.   The proposed development shall not be in conflict with the goals and policies of the Los Angeles County Fire Department or the Los Angeles County Flood Control District unless there is a finding by the Planning Commission that said goals and policies are not consistent with other adopted goals and policies of the City of Claremont.

E.   Fire Protection Standards

For fire protection standards see the Fire Code and Building Code of the City of Claremont. Placement of buildings shall be such that required brush clearance may be performed within the limits of the development of which such buildings are a part. The entire foothills area shall be considered to be Fire Zone Four (4).

F.   Grading

The following standards shall apply to the grading of land and shall be in addition to the Grading Standards contained in the Building Code.

1.   No excavation or fill exceeding three (3) feet vertical height and no cut or fill slopes in excess of three (3) feet vertical height shall be created without the prior approval of the Director of Community, or the Planning Commission when such grading is in conjunction with a Residential Unit Development. The Director's decision may be appealed to the Planning Commission. The Director, and the Planning Commission on appeal or in reviewing grading plans for Residential Unit Developments, shall find the following criteria are met by the grading plans:

a.   The extent of grading indicated is necessary for the use of property to the extent of the uses permitted by the Zoning Ordinance.

b. The proposed grading will have no adverse environmental effect on surrounding property or the permitted use thereof.

c. The proposed grading plan, when compared to possible alternative plans which would serve the same function, will result in the most natural appearance and greatest preservation of natural terrain and water courses possible.

d. The landscape plans indicate sufficient permanent fire-resistant plantings, preferably native, with adequate root systems to protect slopes from erosion and slippage and to minimize the visual effects of grading and construction.

e. The irrigation plans indicate a full-coverage system, adequate to permanently sustain the slope plantings.

2. No cut or fill slopes shall be created which exceed thirty (30) feet vertical height, or four hundred (400) feet in horizontal length (except that slopes required for public streets may exceed 400 feet in length); except that the Planning Commission may permit slopes exceeding these dimensions where the slopes will be the result of earth contouring which the Commission finds will result in a natural appearance and will not create geological or erosion hazards.

3. All cut and fill slopes shall be contoured to present a natural appearance and shall be blended in with the natural grade, per a plan approved by the Director of Community Development or the Planning Commission when such grading is in conjunction with a Residential Unit Development.

G. Other Requirements

1. All applications for subdivisions of land or Residential Unit Developments shall be accompanied by sufficient information to demonstrate compliance with the provisions of the General Plan, especially the Natural Environment Section. The Natural Environment Section describes many safety, environmental and economic concerns in general terms, and it shall be incumbent on

applicants to perform additional studies as are deemed necessary by the City to measure the applicability of such concerns to the applicant's property and to provide an acceptable response to each such environmental concern.

2. Open space easements shall be dedicated to the City covering such lands shown as hillside open space as the City may require to implement the General Plan, said easements to be dedicated during final map recordation or during Architectural Commission review.

(Rev. Ord. 89-5, 2/28/89; Rev. Ord. 91-9, 12/10/91)

133 TRANSFER OF DEVELOPMENT CREDITS

A. Purpose

To provide a procedure whereby development credits may be transferred from parcels in the hillside district to other parcels in the hillside district with areas shown for housing clusters on the General Plan, and, furthermore, to stipulate conditions for ownership and use of hillside open space.

B. Definitions

1. Donor Parcel—Parcel from which development credits are transferred.

2. Receiver Parcel—Parcel to which development credits are transferred.

3. Development Credit—A development credit is a potential entitlement to construct one dwelling in a designated cluster area which can only be exercised when the development credit has been transferred pursuant to the provisions of this Part (Chapter 1, Part 3) from a donor to a receiver parcel and other requirements of law are fulfilled.

C. Applicability

The transfer of development credits may be authorized when the following conditions are met:

1. Donor and receiver parcels are:

a. designated "Hillside Development Conservation" in the General Plan,

b. in the same "sub-area" of the General Plan.

2. The Planning Commission finds the receiver parcel has sufficient area designated for housing cluster on the General Plan to accommodate development otherwise permitted under City regulations plus the development credits to be transferred, and that such total development meets all of the applicable requirements of the City's General Plan and regulations.

D. Procedure

The transfer of development credits shall be authorized as part of a Residential Unit Development pursuant to a conditional use permit. A conditional use permit application shall contain as the subject property both the donor and receiver parcels.

E. Provisions Governing Donor Parcel

1. When development credits are transferred, all such credits are thereafter extinguished with regard to the donor parcel. Excess development credits of that donor parcel which are not initially transferred to a receiver parcel may be subsequently transferred to another receiver parcel in accordance with the provisions of this section.

2. The number of development credits which may be transferred shall not exceed the number of dwelling units determined for the donor parcel through applying established slope-density standards.

3. The fee title to the donor parcel may, upon approval of the City, be retained by the owner of the donor parcel, be transferred to the receiver parcel, be transferred to a quasi-public agency or private institution or body, or be transferred to a public body. Approval

by the City must be based on findings that the option is consistent with the General Plan and provides for the long-term maintenance of the property as open space.

4. The donor parcel, after development credits have been extinguished, shall be kept essentially in a natural condition. However, the City may, pursuant to a conditional use permit, authorize the following uses if it deems they are compatible with maintaining the natural condition of the property and are consistent with the General Plan:

a. Watershed, pasture, trails, scientific study.

b. The growing of crops and fruits.

c. Low intensity recreation.

d. Other uses of similar nature.

e. Such accessory uses as are necessary to support uses a.–d. above.

5. Lands from which development credits have been transferred shall have such easements dedicated to the City or other agreements entered into running with the land which will ensure that such lands remain as open space in perpetuity.

6. A parcel from which development credits have been transferred shall not be considered as "common open space" pursuant to Chapter 1, Part 7 of this ordinance, unless such parcel is transferred in fee to the receiver parcel.

F. Provisions Governing Receiver Parcel

The maximum number of dwelling units permitted on a parcel receiving development credits shall not exceed the sum total determined by applying the established slope-density standard to the receiving parcel and adding the number of development credits transferred.

(Rev. Ord. 89-5, 2/28/89; Rev. Ord. 91-9, 12/10/91)

Index